CW00524452

© 2015 *David Moore*

Published in Australia by:
Einstein's Moon
330 St Georges Road
North Fitzroy, Victoria 3068
Australia
Tel: 61 3 9486 5900
Email: info@einsteinsmoon.com
Website: www.einsteinsmoon.com

First published in Australia 2015

Cover design, typesetting: Thurnheer Publications
All rights reserved. No part of this publication may be reproduced, stored in a retrieval system, or transmitted, in any form
or by any means without the prior written permission of the publisher, nor be otherwise circulated in any form of binding or
cover other than that in which it is published and without a similar condition being imposed on the subsequent purchaser.
Cover photography by: iofoto/Shutterstock
Layout and design by: Thurnheer Publications
Typeset in Minion Pro Regular 10pt on 14pt
Printed by: CreateSpace
All care has been taken in the preparation of the information herein, but no responsibility can be accepted by the publisher or
author for any damages resulting from the misinterpretation of this work. All contact details given in this book were current
at the time of publication, but are subject to change.

The advice given in this book is based on the experience of the individuals. Professionals should be consulted for individual
problems. The author and publisher shall not be responsible for any person with regard to any loss or damage caused directly
or indirectly by the information in this book.
ISBN: 9780994262516 (paperback)

YOGA
and the
ALEXANDER TECHNIQUE

Dedicated to Frederick Matthias Alexander, the founder of the Alexander Technique

CONTENTS

Acknowledgments ———————————————— VI

Foreword ————————————————————— VII

Introduction —————————————————— VIII

PART ONE: Background

Chapter   1   *My story* ——————————————————— 2

      2   *Yoga* ————————————————————— 6

      3   *Alexander Technique* —————————— 10

PART TWO: Principles of the Alexander Technique

      4   *The use of the self* ——————————— 14

      5   *The interrelationship between use, structure,* ——— 16
          and functioning

      6   *Psychophysical unity* ————————— 18

      7   *Diagnosis: Analysis of the conditions present* —— 20

      8   *The force of habit* ——————————— 22

      9   *Inhibition* ———————————————— 24

     10   *Direction* ————————————————— 26

     11   *Conditioning and reconditioning* ————— 32

     12   *The primary control* ————————— 34

     13   *Unreliable sensory appreciation* ————— 38

     14   *Incorrect conceptions* ———————— 42

     15   *End gaining and means whereby* ————— 44

     16   *The Alexander Technique as an indirect procedure* — 46

     17   *The priority of prevention over cure* ———— 48

     18   *What happens in an Alexander Technique lesson?* —— 52

CONTENTS

PART THREE: Considerations Regarding Yoga Practice

Chapter | 19 | *Variability* | 58
| 20 | *Flexibility* | 62
| 21 | *Injuries* | 68
| 22 | *Breathing* | 72
| 23 | *Autonomic nervous system* | 84
| 24 | *Tensegrity* | 88
| 25 | *Movement muscles, postural muscles, and energy flow* | 98
| 26 | *Core strength* | 102
| 27 | *Neuroplasticity* | 108
| 28 | *Pain* | 110
| 29 | *Mindfulness and meditation* | 114
| 30 | *Pregnancy* | 120
| 31 | *Constructive rest: semisupine position* | 124

PART FOUR: Yoga Poses/Asanas

| 32 | *Tadasana: Mountain Pose and Good Posture* | 134
| 33 | *Floor stretches* | 142
| 34 | *Monkey: poses based on the position of mechanical advantage (Utkatasana)* | 150
| 35 | *Squatting* | 156
| 36 | *Standing poses* | 162
| 37 | *Twists* | 172
| 38 | *Forward bends* | 180
| 39 | *Downward facing Dog Pose: Adho Mukha Svanasana* | 190
| 40 | *Back bends* | 194
| 41 | *Side bends* | 202
| 42 | *Poses from kneeling* | 206
| 43 | *More hip openers: moving toward cross-legged sitting* | 210
| 44 | *Inverted poses* | 212
| 45 | *Plank variations* | 218

Conclusion | 222
References | 226
Attributions for photos and illustrations | 230
Useful contacts | 232
Glossary of terms | 234
Index | 236

ACKNOWLEDGMENTS

Although a book is the work of a single author, there are numerous people without whose teaching, help, and support this book would never have been created. I wrote it over the course of about a year, but it was in gestation for decades prior to that. I would like firstly to record my appreciation for the teachers whom I have had over those many years. There are too many to list individually, but those who have had the greatest influence, from the yoga and the Eastern traditions. are Martin Jackson, T.K.V. Desikatchar, and Christopher Titmuss; and from the Alexander Technique, these are Marjorie Barstow, Nili Bassan, Cathy Madden, and Jean Clark. I also owe a great debt of gratitude to Jeremy Chance, who was instrumental in establishing the first Australian training school at which I trained.

In addition to those teachers with whom I have been able to work directly, I also owe a great debt of gratitude to the many teachers, ancient and modern, whom I have never met, but whose writings provided clarity and inspiration. They are too numerous to mention, but some (though by no means all) have been quoted in this book. I have dedicated the book to F. Matthias Alexander.

A number of people have been instrumental in helping me to complete this book. My content editor, Niema Lightseed, made intensive suggestions for clarifying my sometimes clumsy prose. Thomas Finnegan, my copyeditor, gave great attention to detail in the process of getting the final version of the book as error-free as possible. Fiona Bryant's intelligent and uncompromising feedback was invaluable in several of the chapters, and she furnished some of the text for the chapters on breathing and the semisupine. Jennifer Kellow offered invaluable feedback and advice for my chapter on breathing. I'd also like to thank these people for going through parts of the early drafts and for feedback on corrections or improvements: Jenny Thirtle, Wendy Smith, Alysha Bingham, Steve Poskitt, and Anne Mallen.

Many thanks go to Isobel Knowles, who took most of the photographs for the book, as well as those who acted as models for those photos: Alysha Bingham, Steve Poskitt, Rose Phelan, Yu-Ting (Justine) Chang, Teresa Meares, Dan Hoey, Lailani Burra, Fiona Bryant, Leonardo Canales, Jack Mintz and Jana Boronova. I also need to thank Michael Avery, who came through on very short notice to help me complete the last few photos for the book. I appreciated the generosity of Paul and Suzee Grilley in allowing me to reproduce some of the photos of bones from their website, and that of Jean Fischer in furnishing me with a copy of the photo from *Man's Supreme Inheritance* for the chapter on breathing.

And I'd like to thank Pedro de Alcantara. Because he is one of the most clear, intelligent, and talented writers on the Alexander Technique, I presented the book to him with some trepidation and was pleased and honored that he agreed to write the Foreword.

My heartfelt thanks go to the teachers at the School for F. M. Alexander Studies for their support over the years, including Ria Soemardjo, Julianne Eveleigh, Robert Schubert, Alysha Bingham, Michael Avery, and Matthew Wasley. I want especially to thank my assistant director at the school, Jenny Thirtle, who has been a constant, supportive, and intelligent presence at the school over the past ten years.
And finally, thanks go to my students, from whom I have learned and continue to learn so much.

FOREWORD

The history of ideas is the history of transformation and appropriation. From your teacher or from a friend you learn something useful: a concept, a technique, a procedure, a way of organizing your work methods, a way of moving. Perhaps the concept has been around for a long time, and thousands of people have learned before you. Or perhaps the concept is so fresh you're the first person in the world to receive it from your teacher. It doesn't matter how popular or ancient the concept may be: once you learn it, it becomes yours. Inevitably, the thing that is now yours—living in your body and mind, breathing with you, moving with you—isn't the exact same thing that used to be your teacher's.

F. M. Alexander bequeathed us some wonderful ideas regarding the unity of body and mind, the workings of sensory perception, and our capacity to make choices when faced with the endless stimulation of existence. Do I get upset, or do I laugh? Do I tense my neck, or do I keep it free? In life, am I a passenger or am I the driver? Alexander's whole philosophy makes sense only if you appropriate it for yourself. After all, Alexander can't free your neck for you. Either you'll free your own neck, or you'll stiffen it yourself.

Yoga, too, is a fountain of wisdom. But the wisdom of yoga will come to you only if you make your own decisions as regards yoga. Will I stand on my head? I don't have to. It may be a good idea, or not. I might try it, if the conditions are right. "My" yoga is wise, precisely because it's mine.

David Moore's book has many merits, including clarity of purpose and lightness of style. David's overview of yoga is concise and clear-headed; and therefore useful both to someone who has practiced yoga steadily and to someone coming to it for the first time. His introduction to the Alexander Technique is comprehensive without being overwhelming. As I see it, the book's greatest merit comes from the author's level of comfort with transformation and appropriation. David made yoga his own, and he also made the Alexander Technique his own; and he made the intertwining of yoga and Alexander Technique his own. It's quite a feat of initiative and creativity. And his book now invites you to undertake a similar feat—that is, to appropriate these ideas and transform them into what you find good (for you) and right (for you) and life-affirming (for you). To help you along, the book offers practical tools, interesting stories and anecdotes, enticing images, and—above all—the expertise and friendliness of an author who's "for you."

Here's wishing you a pleasant appropriation.

Pedro de Alcantara
PARIS, APRIL 2015

INTRODUCTION

I vividly remember doing an interview, very early in my career as an Alexander Technique teacher, on the local radio station. We were about four or five minutes into the interview when the interviewer, obviously a little confused by my explanation, asked me: "But what exactly is the Alexander Technique?" I'm not quite sure, but I would like to think that my revised approach to the interview gave him some sort of answer.

The Technique is notoriously difficult to describe to someone with no experience of it. It is simple but essentially formless, when not discussed in relation to some activity. Unlike modern postural yoga practice, it has no series of physical exercises. It deals with the "use of the self" and as such, it involves application of a trained awareness and of certain principles described in this book, to all the activities of life, whether that involves doing a yoga pose, brushing our teeth, walking, running, sitting in the office, eating, sleeping, or any other activity you can do during your day. And it involves development of attention and sensitivity to things that are normally outside of our consciousness. As George Bernard Shaw, who was helped greatly by Alexander, humorously remarked on the difficulty involved in explaining the Technique: "Alexander calls upon the world to witness a change so small and subtle, only he can see it."

If we are to describe the Technique, it is easier to focus on particular outcomes that people will get from applying the Alexander Technique, and explain the process by which those outcomes can be attained.

People come to the Technique for many reasons. Many come to find relief from physical pain, often in the mistaken belief that the Alexander teacher is some kind of therapist. And even though the work with a teacher often has a therapeutic effect, the effective teacher points the student back to what she is doing with herself. But people come for many other reasons as well. Alexander developed the Technique as a means of overcoming his vocal and breathing problems, and the Technique is widely used by actors as a means of developing their vocal performance and stage presence. The Technique's ability to ease breathing and bodily stress means that it is also an effective approach for those suffering from anxiety and depression. Neil Strauss, author of The Game: Penetrating the Secret Society of Pick Up Artists, recommends the Alexander Technique to aspiring Casanovas to improve their posture! Sportspeople find that the Technique helps them develop coordination and economy of movement as they refine their skills. And many who practice yoga find that the Technique gives them added self-awareness, which can assist their practice.

Unlike with the Alexander Technique, almost everybody has a picture of what they believe yoga to be. Normally this picture involves the practice of yoga poses or asanas. But this practice is just one corner of a vast edifice of psychophysical and spiritual practice, which like the Alexander Technique encompasses subtle and sophisticated approaches to moving out of the habitual ruts which restrict and limit us.

This book gives readers an in-depth discussion of the Alexander Technique and its application to yoga practice: a discussion both of the practice of yoga as well as that of yoga in its wider sense, as a psycho/physical/spiritual practice that supports us in our everyday living.

PART ONE
BACKGROUND

MY STORY

From a young age, I was always told to "stand up straight." Probably through genetic inheritance, stress, and natural shyness, I had developed significant curvature in my upper spine.

When I was nineteen, I experienced back pain for the first time. I suffered a severe lower back spasm, for which the doctor prescribed muscle relaxants. He diagnosed the back pain as being caused by my posture. However, he had no suggestions as to how to change my posture. After this first incident, from time to time I would find my back going into a spasm that would last from a few days to a couple of weeks. A visit to the osteopath or chiropractor would normally fix the problem until it recurred.

It was my back pain rather than any spiritual impetus that first took me to yoga classes. In the mid-1960s yoga was a fringe activity with a somewhat dubious reputation in mainstream society. In fact, in New Zealand many churches refused to rent their halls for yoga classes, as yoga was considered to be some kind of pagan practice. I did eventually find a class, and from that time on yoga practice became part of my life.

Practicing the yoga poses did not come easily to me. I have naturally tight musculature. Even today, after many years of practice of both yoga and the Alexander Technique, I am hardly a poster boy for many of the yoga poses that require flexibility! This doesn't mean I don't get tremendous benefits from these poses, but I modify them to suit my body, rather than trying to fit my body to a preconceived idea of how the pose should appear.

As the psychedelic sixties wore on, my "doors of perception" were opened and the more spiritual aspects of yoga came to the fore. I also developed a deep interest in Buddhism. In 1974 I traveled to Asia, where I was to spend the next seven years of my life. This time included two and a half years as a Buddhist monk in Thai meditation monasteries, undertaking an intensive practice of "insight" meditation. This approach stressed being in the present moment and developing a constant awareness of body, feelings, thoughts, perceptions, and whatever phenomena were arising in one's consciousness.

At that time, one of the American monks in the monastery received a parcel of books from his sister. One of them was The *Alexander Principle*, by Wilfred Barlow. I read it with a feeling of growing excitement. Here was an approach, I realized, that might offer a way of transforming my postural problem with a technique that resonated with Buddhist practice. I promised myself that as soon as I was near an Alexander teacher I would follow up on this possibility.

It was to be several years before I would be able to work with an Alexander Technique teacher. After my time in Thailand, I studied at the Krishnamacharya Yoga Mandaram in Madras for two years, with breaks in the winter months for Buddhist meditation retreats in Bodh Gaya. Although the legendary Krishnamacharya was still alive, he was not teaching foreign students. During my time there I had two private lessons a week with other teachers, which evolved into a daily asana and *pranayama* practice. There were also weekly classes in the Yoga Sutras of Patanjali. I even managed a few private lessons with Desikachar in the hot season when fewer students were there.

The practice of yoga poses at the Mandaram was more sophisticated than my previous yoga experiences. No group classes were taught there. Desikachar believed that the poses should be tailored for the individual student; therefore individual tuition was deemed the appropriate way to share the practice. Desikachar and his teachers, well aware of the dangers of unskillful yoga practice, ensured that their students were taught the poses and methods of practice that were safe and effective for them. There was great emphasis on coordinating the movements of the yoga poses with the breath and on *pranayama* (breathing exercises) in addition to the asana practice.

Finally, in 1981 I was able to undertake a series of thirty Alexander Technique lessons in England. My teacher requested that I suspend my yoga practice during this series. We did a lot of work at a chair, moving between standing and sitting, and "semisupine" work with me lying on a table. In between lessons I would lie in the semisupine position at least once a day for twenty minutes, and brought as much awareness as possible to my day-to-day activities.

At the end of this time I was amazed, when I returned to my yoga practice, to find that my upper back was considerably more mobile and flexible. But how could this be, considering I had done no exercises apart from getting into and out of a chair and lying on a table or the floor?

I moved to Sydney in late 1981 and continued to have Alexander lessons. In 1983 the first teacher training course in Australia opened, and I began my three-year training as an Alexander Technique teacher. The year before this I had started taking Iyengar Yoga classes with Martin Jackson, which I continued to attend until 1984, when I undertook an Iyengar teacher training course with Martin. I enjoyed the strength and precision of the Iyengar practice, but by the end of my second year of Alexander training I had begun to feel an unbridgeable disconnection between the two practices, so I discontinued yoga practice for the final year of my Alexander training.

It was about two years before I returned to yoga practice, and eventually I did return to studying the teaching of yoga. I was inspired by working with Karyn Chapman, a yoga teacher who had trained as an Alexander teacher and was teaching the application of the technique to yoga.

Really it was just a matter of putting the Alexander principles into practice in this activity, as in any other. Because of the physical nature of Hatha Yoga practice, a deeper study of anatomy was also helpful, and to this day I continue to read and study in this area. It is amazing how much depth there is in this field, and the degree of subtlety we can develop in our practical and theoretical knowledge of anatomy.

Teaching both yoga and the Alexander Technique brings me a great deal of joy, because I am privileged to see people opening to the possibilities inherent in these traditions and developing within them. From personal experience, I find that practicing yoga poses with my naturally tight body as well as bringing mindfulness to everyday activities, are essential components of my well-being.

This book is the outcome of many years of experience and practice, and I hope that it will raise new questions for you, as well as help to inspire, instruct, and assist you in your own journey to wholeness.

The rich

will make temples for Shiva.

What shall I,

a poor man,

do?

My legs are pillars,

the body the shrine,

the head a cupola

of gold.

Listen, O lord of the meeting rivers,

things standing shall fall,

but the moving ever shall stay.

— ***Basavanna*** —

The essence of the religious

outlook is that religion should

not be kept in a compartment

by itself, but that it should

be the ever-present guiding

principle underlying the "daily

round," the "common task."

So also it is possible to apply

this principle of life in the

daily round of one's activities

without involving a loss of

attention in these activities.

— ***F. M. Alexander*** —

The ceaseless moment-to-moment arising and passing away of all phenomena is encapsulated in this aspect of Shiva, who dances everything into both creation and destruction.

Figure 1.1. Shiva, the God of Yogis, in His Manifestation as Nataraja, the Lord of the Dance

YOGA

Yoga is one of the main spiritual traditions of India. The word yoga comes from the Sanskrit yuj, meaning "to yoke or bind," and is normally interpreted as "union" with the divine. The broad term yoga covers numerous approaches and schools of thought, the ultimate aim of which, in the Indian tradition and worldview, is to attain this union and thus step out of the endless cycle of birth and death.

Yoga includes various philosophical schools with much depth and subtlety that do not necessarily agree with each other. Its practices include: participating in devotional activities such as chanting; attending religious events and praying to a whole range of deities who, by the more sophisticated, are regarded as emanations of a single unified divinity; developing psychic and other powers; practicing a number of meditation traditions; engaging in breathing exercises, known as *pranayama*; and moving the body through the physical practices, which is what people normally think of when yoga is discussed in the West.

Over the past two and a half millennia of written records there are an astounding number of yoga texts presenting the wisdom of diverse schools. Various aspects of traditional yogic knowledge and technique are found in Buddhism, Jainism, and Hinduism. Although philosophically there are many divergences between these traditions, one thing these approaches have in common is that they all provide practical paths for self-development. A good survey of yoga's history, literature, philosophy, and practice can be found in Georg Feuerstein's book *The Yoga Tradition*.[1]

Two traditions that have been enthusiastically embraced in the West are the meditative and insight-focused Buddhist practices, and the physically oriented practices of Hatha Yoga. Buddhist insight meditation and Hatha Yoga have spread well beyond their original cultural confines to become embedded in the lives and practices of many people outside of Asia. They have also been incorporated in therapeutic settings, which is unsurprising since both traditions aim to overcome suffering. The question of whether these adapted modern iterations of ancient traditions are "really" Buddhist or yogic is of little concern to the many people who are benefiting from these practices here and now.

Hatha Yoga

Although Hatha Yoga occupies only a tiny corner of traditional yoga practice, it is this psychophysical snippet that has been adopted with the greatest enthusiasm in the West over the past few decades. The most famous aspect of Hatha Yoga is the practice of *asanas* or yoga poses.

Yogic literature interprets the word *hatha* in two ways. *Ha* means "sun" and *tha* means "moon." This is a reference to the practice of balancing and uniting the opposites within us. In some theories of the energetic underpinnings of life, humans and all living systems have two primary and complementary types of energy. These polar opposites are called masculine and feminine, solar and lunar, active and receptive, or yang and yin. One of the principal goals of yoga practice is the balancing and uniting of these two opposing forces. *Hatha* has also been translated as "forceful," since, unlike any other form of yoga, Hatha Yoga is based on a set of physical exercises designed to open up the free flow of energy through the *nadis* or energy channels of the body. Special emphasis is paid to the main energy channel, which follows the path of the spine from the perineum to the top of the head and transcends the duality of the oppositional polarities of *ha* and *tha*. Opening this central channel is a way of finding the unity that is at the heart of yoga. Hatha Yoga is a practice that focuses on developing strength, flexibility, balance, and physical health as the basis for meditative practices.

It is said that in the sound HA the sun is contained, in the sound SA the moon. Hatha-Yoga means uniting the sun and the moon.

— *Yoga Shikha Upanishad* —

The History of Hatha Yoga and Its Development in the West

The earliest Hatha Yoga texts—the *Hatha Yoga Pradipika*, the *Shiva Samitha*, and the *Gerhida Samitha*—outline classical Hatha Yoga practice, but these texts are rarely referenced today. Some of the more extravagant claims made about the ability to develop psychic powers strain credulity, and the sexual practices described in these texts were scandalous to both the Victorian English and the orthodox Hindus. In the late nineteenth century, on the cusp of the development of the modern practice of Hatha Yoga, practitioners of the traditional methods mentioned in the ancient texts were considered suspect and unsavory by much of Indian society.

Then in the late nineteenth and early twentieth centuries, teachers such as Krishnamacharya and Swami Kuvalayananda developed a modern form of Hatha yoga, adding practices taken from British physical education to the restricted number of poses listed in the classic Hatha Yoga texts. For example, the flow sequences *(vinyasa)* do not appear in the classic Hatha Yoga texts, nor do many of the individual poses in those sequences. Swami Kuvalayananda also began to study the effects of yoga practice from a Western scientific perspective.

In addition, rather than the traditional Hatha Yoga texts, the *Yoga Sutras of Patanjali* was chosen as the philosophical and practical underpinning for this new form of Hatha Yoga This choice was made despite the fact that the word *asana*, which means "pose" or "seat," is mentioned only once in the text Furthermore, this was almost certainly a reference, to posture in general, or sitting meditation poses in particular, rather than to the poses of Hatha Yoga practice.

Choosing the *Yoga Sutras* as the central text of modern Hatha Yoga established it within a framework of practice resting on a firm ethical foundation, which underpinned the practical advice it gave on a range of meditative practices. These practices start off with simple breath control *(pranayama)* and lead to the highest state of enlightenment *(samadhi)*. The individual sutras are so concise that varying and conflicting interpretations can be, and have been, extrapolated from them. Like Buddhism, Patanjali's teaching is based on an attitude of extreme detachment from the world, which is deeply foreign to our contemporary sensibilities. Many modern yoga practitioners have only minimal understanding of, or interest in, the various philosophical and meditative traditions underlying their practices. The tangible benefits of practice, such as health, well-being, and stress reduction, are obvious to them and provide sufficient motivation.

The Hatha Yoga tradition is not static, but rather a dynamic, ever-changing, and developing process. The practice of Hatha Yoga has undergone enormous changes, and in the past half century there have been numerous permutations as it becomes ubiquitous in the West.

Western practices from psychophysical and somatic systems continue to be incorporated into Hatha Yoga in recent years. This book is an engagement in the ongoing development of this amalgamation, using the sophisticated psychophysical insights of the Alexander Technique to help illuminate and deepen yoga practice. I hope that it will play a part in helping to develop and uplift the standard of current yoga practice and teaching. Ultimately, of course, this development can take place only within the individual being of each practitioner. One of the foundational philosophical frames of yoga is the eight limbs *(astanga)*, listed below as a base to understand one of the roots of modern yoga practice.

If you are interested in more detail on the development of modern Hatha Yoga, you can see how this subject has been traced out in detail by Mark Singleton [2] and Norman E. Sjoman.[3]

The Eight Limbs of Yoga from Patanjali's Yoga Sutras

1. Yama (Universal Morality)

Nonviolence (ahimsa), truthfulness (satya), nonstealing (asteya), celibacy or sexual fidelity (brahmacharya), releasing attachment to possessions (aparigraha)

2. Niyama (Personal Observances)

Cleanliness and purity (saucha), contentment (santosa), asceticism (tapas), self-study (svadhyaya), devotion (isvarapranidhana)

3. Asana

Posture: developing ease of posture and movement and refining the body for meditation practices

4. Pranayama

Control of the vital energy of the body (prana) through breathing practices

Fig 2.1 Patanjali

5. Pratyahara

Sense withdrawal: moving the attention inwards; the basis of the higher stages of meditation

6. Dharana

Concentration: focus of the mind on a single point

7. Dhyana

Contemplation: a deeper and subtler level of meditation

8. Samadhi

Bringing together or merging; there are different types and levels of Samadhi, the highest of which involves total absorption in the Transcendent

NOTES 1. FEUERSTEIN (2001). SEE THE REFERENCES AT THE BACK OF THIS BOOK FOR FULL INFORMATION ON CITED SOURCES. 2. SINGLETON (2010). 3. SJOMAN (2009).

CHAPTER 3

ALEXANDER TECHNIQUE

The Alexander Technique gives us a means of refining the coordination patterns that underlie all of our activities. It is not about imposing a particular external form onto those activities, but rather setting up the conditions for more effective functioning.

In Alexander lessons, a teacher may work with a student in an unlimited range of activities such as: simply sitting, standing, or walking; playing a musical instrument or singing; practicing tai chi or yoga; working at a computer; running or jumping; meditating; and so on. Although the activities may be "physical," the focus is on the students' mental and psychological approach to these activities, their established habit patterns, and the ideas and beliefs they have about these activities.

Alexander teacher Patrick Macdonald outlined what he felt were the five essential components of the Alexander Technique, which taken in combination made it different from any other practices:

1. Recognition of the force of habit
2. Inhibition and nondoing
3. Recognition of faulty sensory perception
4. Sending directions
5. The primary control [1]

All these terms will be explained in the following pages.

A Brief History of the Technique

The Alexander Technique was developed by Frederick Matthias Alexander (1869–1955), an Australian actor who lost his voice on the stage. Through careful observation he discovered that the loss was due to an overall pattern of contraction, which he described as a misuse of himself. Through a long process of experimentation, he worked out a way to regain healthy functioning of his voice by changing this overall pattern of misuse. He then began to teach his work to others, first to those seeking a voice teacher, but increasingly to people with diverse medical problems. It became clear that altering overall patterns of discoordination had a profound effect on many pathological conditions.

The winner of the Nobel Prize in Physiology and Medicine, Nikolass Tinbergen, devoted half of his Nobel oration to Alexander's discoveries, saying, "This story of perceptiveness, of intelligence and of persistence, shown by a man without medical training, is one of the true epics of medical research and practice."[2]

Alexander moved to London in 1904 and developed a busy practice working with many leading actors, doctors, intellectuals, and politicians of his day. One of his major supporters was the influential philosopher and educationalist John Dewey, in whose own works the influence of Alexander can be clearly discerned. Dewey's influence can also be seen in Alexander's books, three of which contain an introduction written by Dewey.

Alexander set up a school for teachers of the Technique in London in 1931, running a three-year full-time training. After his death, more such schools were set up in the UK and in many other countries throughout the world, including the School for F. M. Alexander Studies in Melbourne that I established in 1998.

Alexander was a man well ahead of his time. In the early twentieth century he not only had a clear understanding of the plasticity of the brain, a term coined by the psychologist William James in the late 1800s, but also developed an immensely sophisticated system. Alexander's system was based on this understanding of brain plasticity, and our ability to alter ingrained dysfunctional patterns through intentional movement. Indeed, he described his work thus:

> My technique is based on inhibition, the inhibition of undesirable, unwanted responses
> to stimuli, and hence it is primarily a technique for the development of the control of
> human reaction.[3]

Although this definition may be rather opaque for those coming across this work for the first time, those familiar with the *Yoga Sutras of Patanjali* or the Pali Buddhist suttas will be able to see in this description a link to the practices outlined in those disciplines, which I shall explore later in the book.

The chapters in Part Two of this book contain fuller descriptions of the Alexander Technique. They cover the key principles and ideas to which Alexander refers repeatedly in his writings. If you are unfamiliar with the Alexander Technique, it will be useful to read these first, as it will give you a better understanding when I use the terms later on. I will also briefly relate some of these ideas to the practice and philosophy of yoga.

NOTES 1. MACDONALD (2006), 86. **2.** TINBERGEN (1973). **3.** ALEXANDER (1947), 93.

PART TWO
PRINCIPLES OF THE ALEXANDER TECHNIQUE
❋❋

CHAPTER 4

F. Matthias Alexander as a young man

THE USE OF THE SELF

Use is the technical term in the Alexander Technique to denote an overall pattern of moving that includes posture, muscular tone, thought processes, and the manner in which we act and respond in our day-to-day lives. Use refers to neither mind nor body exclusively; an act as simple as moving an arm depends on thought, intention, and motivation as much as on the muscles that actually carry out the movement. The term refers to a global pattern of movement and reaction.

In the list below, none of the elements in isolation describes the meaning of use, but if we combine all these elements in the observation of an individual, we will have a broad picture of how she is using herself.

- Posture
- Movement
- Reactions to external and internal stimuli
- Breathing
- Emotional state
- Cognitive functioning

All the variables listed tend to form a reasonably constant underlying psychophysical state, which may vary in intensity but not in overall quality. This constant state can be altered, but only through a gradual process of reeducation using the Alexander Technique. This alteration can happen only in the entire physical and mental system: none of the individual elements can be adequately understood, much less dealt with, in isolation from the others.

CHAPTER 5

THE INTERRELATIONSHIP BETWEEN USE, STRUCTURE, AND FUNCTIONING

The Alexander Technique is based on the premise that how we use ourselves affects how we function. Change our use of ourselves, and we alter our functioning.

Any effective intervention to stop pain will turn what has become a vicious cycle into a virtuous cycle, in relation to these three variables.

The various treatments for musculoskeletal pain all focus on one point in this cycle. Surgery, orthotics, and certain forms of manipulative therapy focus on structure. Acupuncture, massage therapy, and medication focus on functioning. The Alexander Technique is a process of education rather than treatment that focuses directly on the use of ourselves.

From the Alexander point of view, many forms of remedial exercise tend to focus too narrowly on the structural aspects of movement and pain intervention, neglecting the wider aspects of the issues they are attempting to address.

Overemphasis on the role of individual muscles or muscle groups as movers of particular body parts causes one to lose sight of the overall process of coordination in which these muscles operate.

When you make a movement, any movement, you use:
- Primary movers, the muscles that contract to create the movement
- Antagonists, the opposing muscles that need to release in order for the movement to happen
- Muscles stabilizing the part of the body that is moving
- Muscles responsible for maintaining the balance of the whole body in the changing situation created by the movement
- Muscles responsible for maintaining the shape of the body and the integrity of the structure

You also need to inhibit conscious or unconscious muscular activity that would interfere with the movement you are making.[1]

NOTE 1. ADAPTED FROM LANGFORD (1999).

THE WAY YOU USE YOURSELF [AFFECTS] **THE WAY YOU FUNCTION**

Anything used in a way for which it was not intended...

...will, in time, cease to function properly.

The mis-use of a thing will create a malfunction.

The way you use yourself affects the way you function.

Have you ever stopped to consider whether you are mis-using yourself or not?

ARE YOU "FUNCTIONING" EFFICIENTLY OR ARE YOU MALFUNCTIONING?

Figure 5.1

USE

STRUCTURE ⟷ FUNCTIONING

Figure 5.2

In Figures 5.1 and 5.2 we see how use affects and is affected by both structure and functioning.

CHAPTER 6

PSYCHOPHYSICAL UNITY

Our most sacred convictions are judgments of our muscles.

—— *Friedrich Nietzsche* ——

An understanding of the *psychophysical unity* of the human being is absolutely basic to practice of the Alexander Technique. Talking of his own process of recovering his voice, Alexander explains that he initially thought he had a "physical" problem with his voice, and that he took for granted the commonly accepted view of the separation of the "body" and "mind." However, by the end of his investigations he had come to the conclusion that it was impossible to separate "physical" and "mental" aspects in any activity.

This realization of Alexander's would not be a new one to yoga practitioners. The very practice of yoga poses, (which are traditionally combined with breathing and meditation), has always provided them with a very concrete experience of the essential interrelationship between their physicality and their mental and emotional states. Indeed, the fact that altering bodily process can affect mental and emotional states, and vice versa, is the reason Hatha Yoga and meditation practices are so effective at creating shifts in the body, the emotions, and the mind.

Although the concept of psychophysical unity is much more commonplace today than it was in Alexander's time, in most areas of contemporary life concerning education or health, the real implications of this unity are very rarely fully appreciated and put into practice.

Figure 6.1

*"The Thinker" by Rodin demonstrates
the intrinsic interrelationship between
mental, emotional, and muscular activity.*

CHAPTER 7

DIAGNOSIS: ANALYSIS OF THE CONDITIONS PRESENT

"This story of perceptiveness, of intelligence and of persistence, shown by a man without medical training, is one of the true epics of medical research and practice."

— Nikolaas Tinbergen, Nobel Oration 1973 [1] —

Both the Alexander Technique and yoga are based on the principles of preventing unnecessary pain or suffering, and of relieving present pain, suffering, or dysfunction. The first step in this process is always a proper *analysis of the conditions present.*

For all of us, the journey of transformation begins with a desire to change something. In Alexander's case, the desire was to continue his career as an actor by overcoming his voice problem. And this led him to ask the question, "What am I doing with myself to cause this problem?"

After the failure of a range of treatments he had undertaken, Alexander began to wonder whether the problem might be something he was doing to himself while using his voice. He put that question to his doctor, who thought this was very likely the case, although he was unable to diagnose the exact nature of the "misuse." So Alexander decided to find out for himself.

Using mirrors, he examined his posture and actions when attempting to project his voice. He noticed that as soon as he went to project his voice, he pulled his head back, depressed his larynx and audibly gasped for air through his mouth. With further exploration, Alexander discovered that if he eliminated these actions, his voice worked much better.

Thus he was able to *diagnose* the root cause of his vocal troubles and then, from a clear understanding of his use of himself, he was able to experiment further and gradually develop a process by which he could consistently use his voice on the stage without hoarseness.

What Does This Mean for Yoga Practice?

When I observe people doing a particular exercise or yoga pose, I often ask them about the purpose or intention underlying it. The most common answers are that these movements have been given to them by a therapist or yoga teacher; or that they have read about them or seen them in a video and believe the movements will be good for their overall health; or to address a particular problem. It is quite rare for anyone to have any understanding of how that particular exercise or pose works for his or her unique body, and thus, to understand how to do the pose in a way that provides the most benefit.

Our yoga practices must be based on a clear understanding of our own psychophysical states and individuality. Just as Alexander studied his own unique pattern of use to overcome his own problems, the more accurate our self-diagnoses, the more intelligently we will be able to use our yoga practice for our own improvement.

Some questions you need to explore for optimal practice:
- What is my overall flexibility: tight, medium, flexible, or hypermobile?
- Within my overall flexibility, do I have areas that are overflexible or very tight?
- What are my overall habits in the use of myself—mental, emotional, and physical?
- How exactly do I habitually interfere with my coordination?
- What do I want out of my yoga practice?

Answers to some of these questions may be clear; some can be clarified with the help of a skilled teacher. Our approaches to yoga should be informed by the answers. As Parker Palmer reflects, regarding teaching in general, "The way we diagnose our students' condition will determine the kind of remedy we offer."[2]

NOTES **1.** TINBERGEN (1973) **2.** PARKER (2007), 42.

CHAPTER 8

THE FORCE OF HABIT

All our life so far as it has definite form, is but a mass of habits — practical, emotional and intellectual — systematically organized, for our weal or woe, and bearing us irresistibly toward our destiny whatever the latter may be.
— **William James** [1] —

A flexible, sensitive habit grows more varied, more adaptable by practice and use.
— **John Dewey** [2] —

An unawakened existence, in which we drift unaware on a surge of habitual impulses, is both ignoble and undignified.
— **Stephen Batchelor** [3] —

W e mostly associate the term *habit* with the adjective "bad." But habits in themselves are not the problem. Every activity we engage in is based on learning and repetition, which develop neural pathways for their execution. We couldn't tie a shoelace, read a book, or drive a car if we had not laid down neural pathways to allow us to do these activities. The problem arises when the habits we have developed are dysfunctional, like Alexander's original method for projecting his voice. "What makes a habit bad," says Dewey, "is enslavement to old ruts"

> *"The real opposition is not between reason and habit but between routine unintelligent habit and intelligent habit or art."*
>
> — *Dewey* —

We tend to group habits into types: *psychological*, such as a tendency to react to particular situations with feelings of depression, anger, or calmness; *mental*, like obsessive thinking, the ability to speak another language, mathematical ability, and so on; and *physical*, as with good or bad posture in standing, sitting, or moving and the ability to manipulate objects in sporting or work activities.

In actual fact, there is no activity that excludes any of these three areas. The famous neurologist Sir Charles Sherrington emphasized the relationship between all brain activity and the muscular system:

> I may seem to stress the preoccupation of the brain with muscle. Can we stress too much that preoccupation when any path we trace in the brain leads directly or indirectly to muscle? The brain seems a thoroughfare for nerve action passing on its way to the motor animal.[5]

As Alexander saw it, the totality of a person's habits is determined by her underlying use and functioning. Unified feeling, thinking, and motor activity are essential components of every action in which we engage. Any approach to changing habit must include the total use of ourselves, including the overall postural and bodily "set" that underlies our movements, feelings, and beliefs.

In the case of Alexander's voice problem, his task was to replace this old dysfunctional habit with a new and more intelligent response to the stimulus of projecting his voice. Such habits can't be directly undone or changed simply by application of will power. The first part of Alexander's process of overcoming his voice problem, was to identify what was causing him to lose his voice. Once this was identified, he needed to prevent the habitual reaction. Then he needed to train himself to direct his head forward and up in such a way that the pressure was taken off his larynx and whole body. Finally, he needed to continue with his *directions* in the act of vocalizing, so that instead of gasping for breath and pulling his head back and down with the concomitant whole body contraction, he would continue to allow his head to release forward and up and his whole body to follow that release.

It was exactly at this final point that Alexander found himself stumped. The habit of tightening in response to the very idea of projecting his voice was overwhelming, and the very thing he needed to do to free his voice felt "wrong", while the old habitual way felt right.

As we have no option but to base our actions and activities on habit, the question is how to raise our awareness of those habits and change unhelpful habits into ones that support our well-being and development. Alexander referred to this conscious process as *reconditioning* ourselves, and a key aspect of this process was choosing to intervene in order to stop the old *habit* and thus allow something new to arise—a process that he called *inhibition*.

NOTES **1.** JAMES (1925), 580. **2.** DEWEY (1922), 72. **3.** BATCHELOR (1998), 6. **4.** DEWEY (1922), 66. **5.** SHERRINGTON (1933), QUOTED IN ALEXANDER (1947), 90.

CHAPTER 9

INHIBITION

The technique is based upon the inhibition of the habitual wrong use.
— *F. M. Alexander* —

Often to refrain from an act is no less an act than to commit one,
because inhibition is co-equally with excitation a nervous activity.
— **Sir Charles Sherrington** —

Alexander discovered that the very intention to project his voice resulted in his gasping for breath, tightening his whole body, and pulling his head backward. This put pressure and constriction on his vocal folds, causing vocal strain. Before he could do anything different, he had to stop *(inhibit)* this reaction.

Alexander uses the term *inhibition* in its positive neurological sense rather than the negative psychological meaning that is commonly associated with this term. He defines *inhibition* as "refusing to give consent," and therefore not sending the messages that would normally result in the habitual reaction we wish to change.

A unique aspect of the Alexander Technique is that the very first step involves preventing the wrong or unwanted action or response, before a change for the better can be made. In other words, if we attempt to do something differently, without stopping the old habit, the new way of doing things will be superimposed on a preexisting faulty manner of use. Inhibition is essential to allowing the natural postural reflexes that support us in movement to reestablish themselves. The choice to *"inhibit"* preexisting faulty habits is essential, if we wish to allow our natural postural reflexes free reign to reestablish optimum 'movement'.

This process works on a simple stimulus-response model. As such, the emphasis on breaking the link between the stimulus and the response is central and crucial to Alexander work. The process involves increasing awareness of the impulses that take us into activity. These impulses are activated by stimuli, which may be internal (I want to get out of my chair because I am thirsty and want a drink) or external (I want to get out of my chair because the door bell has just rung). In either case, we will activate habitual motor patterns in order to get out of our chair.

If I decide to change how I get out of the chair, or how I react in a difficult social situation, I first need to catch the initial muscular set that is activated prior to the habitual reaction, which would set me up to go into that activity in the habitual way. As we develop the sensitivity to catch these impulses, we have the possibility of inhibiting, of refusing to give consent to them. Only once this initial muscular set is absent, do I have the possibility of activating a different pattern of movement and response, a pattern which will be based on freeing the overall coordination of the head, neck, and torso. The resonances of this process (of inhibition for the sake of liberation) with Buddhist mindfulness practice will be discussed further in Chapter 29.

For Alexander, discovering how we interfere with our coordination (primary control) and then intervening in order to inhibit that interference was of primary importance. But this was not enough. The next step was to send messages for another manner of using oneself—a process initiated by sending *directions*.

DIRECTION

Alexander described the term "directing" as indicating "the process involved in projecting messages from the brain to the mechanisms and in conducting the energy necessary to the use of these mechanisms." [1]

This unique aspect of the Alexander Technique involves sending energy and intention by using conscious directions to ease the body out of habitual contractive patterns. Instead of repeating dysfunctional physical habits, the directions give us an alternative way of acting or reacting. In Alexander lessons these directions are given verbally, along with gentle manual guidance. This combination of verbal and manual instruction provides the student with both a mental and sensory experience, which enables a deeper embodiment of these more supportive patterns. As the students' sensory awareness begins to improve they are asked to apply the directions in their daily activities.

As mentioned previously, while undertaking his detailed study to discover why he was losing his voice, Alexander noticed the presence of subconscious contractions, which interfered with the freedom of his voice. He saw that these physical patterns were caused by messages from his brain to his muscles, via his nervous system. From this awareness, he reasoned that he must inhibit those interfering messages and replace them with ones that would support proper functioning of his vocal mechanism.

The primary problem was not isolated in the muscles directly concerned with vocal production, but rather caused by a whole body contraction. Indeed, it was not particularly important to understand the precise details of the workings of his vocal mechanisms, because if he could change the overall pattern in his entire body, the vocal mechanisms would indirectly be freed.

The subconscious "instructions" were causing Alexander to discoordinate himself and lose his voice, so he developed a set of conscious subvocal directions to override the constricting impulse. He later taught these instructions to his students as an essential part of the process of reeducation.

Initially the words would be repeated without any attempt to "do" the actions, as Alexander physically guided the students to give them the kinesthetic experiences and motor pathways that were the counterpart to those verbal directions.

The verbal directions for opening the voice were:
1. To let the neck be free.
2. To let the head go forward and up.
3. To let the back lengthen and widen.

But be warned that these words only hint at the essence of the directions! Alexander did not feel that these words adequately represented what he was trying to convey. They were the best he could come up with, even after considerable discussion with his large network of literary, medical, and scientific friends who had personally experienced his work. He frankly admitted that he found the verbal directions inadequate, unless a teacher could physically demonstrate them to a student by means of manual guidance. Regarding the words "head forward and up" he adds that this "is a dangerous instruction to give any pupil, unless the teacher first demonstrates his meaning, by means of manipulation, the exact experiences involved."[2]

These directions need to be given in this exact order: "one after the other all at the same time." They activate the central coordination of the whole body immediately prior to activating the "secondary directions" required for a specific activity.

For example, the directions for the muscular coordination required in my fingers to type this sentence were initially consciously developed but now have become quite habitual and subconscious. Sometimes, in this process of skill development people ingrain faulty habits that may need to be relearned. In my case, however, while maintaining my central coordination I can allow the subconscious skill in my fingers to operate without any need for self-conscious focus on the precise details of their movements.

Mastering the ability to inhibit old patterns and send directions for improved functioning, requires consciously and consistently sending these directions, without getting sidetracked into habitual grooves. Cultivating this degree of focus requires steady application; it takes some time to develop, and a lifetime to master. It is a skill that, although not identical, is akin to the energetic practices of qigong and tai chi, as well as some of the meditative focusing practices in yogic and Buddhist traditions.

Patrick Macdonald, one of the first-generation Alexander teachers, identifies four types of direction:
1. Negative (i.e., "Don't stiffen your neck")
2. Positive ("If you've stiffened it, release it")
3. Those to make a physical movement ("Move your hand")
4. Those for energy: "Sending a flow of force to alter the condition of a part or parts. In this case the movement is so small as to be practically no movement at all. It can be regarded as similar to a flow or electricity along a wire or of sound along a metal bar."

He adds: "Direction number 4, forward, in Forward and Up is an unlocking device . . . the direction of Up should produce a tiny elongation of the spinal column and it should be curved forward so as to bring about a widening of the back."[3] This "unlocking" refers to the release of tension at that atlanto-occipital joint where the head sits on top of the spine. We will discuss this further in Chapter 12 on the primary control.

Macdonald also elucidates important distinctions between position, muscle movement, and direction. "Position" is placing the whole body or a body part in a particular place, often thought of as the "correct posture." "Muscle movement" is a movement achieved by muscular contraction and may be large or small. "Directing" involves projecting a subtle flow of force or energy though the body, which creates a change in the quality of the musculature. He points out that in most people, these directions are largely unconscious and tend to be centripetal and contractive. The conscious directions developed by Alexander are aimed at replacing these centripetal, contractive directions with centrifugal, expansive directions, leading toward openness and unfolding.

These are important distinctions to make. Beginning students of the Alexander Technique often think that they have to be in the "correct position" and make exaggerated movements to try to put themselves into it. Then, once they feel they are there they stiffen themselves, making it impossible to access the subtle flow of the directions that would create freedom and aliveness within the system. Likewise in yoga poses, a narrow focus on correct alignment may achieve only stiffness rather than energetic expansion and opening.

Macdonald suggests an exercise to give a practical example of the meaning of these terms.
1. Hold one forefinger in front of you. This is "your spine." And it is now in a "position."
2. Move that forefinger around. This is "muscle movement."
3. Take hold of the top of that forefinger with the opposite hand. This is "your head."
4. Now gently stretch that finger with the opposite hand. This is giving a lengthening "direction" to your finger.
5. Let go of your finger and continue to sense the flow of that "direction" through your fingers.[4]

Walter Carrington, also a first-generation Alexander teacher, outlines another dimension to directing, in which the inhibitory or nondoing aspect of the directions is emphasized. He explains that the postural reflexes that have been suppressed by poor use, are waiting to be activated once we remove what has been restricting them. Talking to teacher trainees, Carrington said:

> The basic thing is, the up is built in. You as a teacher don't do it any more than your pupil does it. You both encourage it to happen. . . . But the main encouragement is the desire and the wish. And over and above the desire and the wish, take measure to prevent the wrong thing from happening.[5]

He continues by using the metaphor of a gardener who gently channels the flow of water toward the plants, blocking the flow here and there and channeling it to where the gardener wants it to flow. But he observes that the actual flow is what the water does and what the setup does, not what you do.[6]

Marjorie Barstow, another of Alexander's students, simplified the directions to just a few words: "The head moves and the whole body follows." Her emphasis was on the movement, but movement out of our normal habit: "It is the delicacy of movement that gives you your release."[7]

Yoga, Meditation, and the Directions

Talking of the directions and of directing in the Alexander Technique obviously raises questions about the relationship to the yoga concepts of *prana*, life energy; the *nadis*, energy channels of which there are said to be seventy-two thousand in the body; the chakras, energy centers in the body; and *kundalini*, the energy stored at the base of the spine, which is raised and channeled through Hatha Yoga practice along the central channel to the *chakra* at the top of the head. As this book is primarily aimed at practical matters, I won't go deeply into this topic, but simply make some observations of similarities and relationships.

First, the key focus in the Alexander Technique is on establishing a clear connection through the center—the head, neck, and torso—as the basis for health and proper coordination. This connection improves the primary control, which is described in Chapter 12. The experience of activating this connection freely and without any excess muscle tension can subjectively be experienced as a very easy and free flow of energy, which effortlessly supports the body.

Second, in the Alexander Technique we don't talk of *prana* or life energy, simply because it is not a concept that is required for practice of the technique. When Alexander refers to "conducting the energy" in the quote at the top of this section, this could be interpreted in contemporary terms as sending the instructions via the nervous system, or in traditional yogic terms as activating a *pranic* force. In its practical application, the precise framework used for explaining this is not important.

Third, regarding the *nadis* or energy channels, the subjective experience of learning and applying the technique gives the feeling of an energetic opening and expanding. Again, it doesn't matter whether this is activation of the nervous system and its interaction with the muscular system, or the flow of *prana* and the opening of the *nadis*. It is probable that these are identical phenomena, but this can be left to scientists and metaphysicians to work out.

Chinese medicine is also founded on working with the flow of the life energy, which it calls *qi* or *chi*. Many illnesses are said to be caused by blockages of the flow of qi through the meridians of the body, and the practice of needling in acupuncture is to stimulate or regulate those flows. Discoordination and muscular contraction, which Alexander calls interference with the primary control, affect the flow of *qi*. Without undoing this underlying contraction, the effect of the acupuncture needles is counteracted by the underlying pattern of use. In fact, the Chinese have developed a practice of qigong, which when done correctly consists of moving the body in a coordinated fashion through a number of movements.

In 2012 I attended the Neuromatics and the Neuromatrix Conference in Adelaide, Australia, where they had an Illusions Room. In one of the illusions you could put your hand under a glass screen and point one finger. The experimenter then took hold of the end of your finger and with a computer created the visual illusion that as the finger was being pulled it physically lengthened, and when it was pushed it was physically shortened.

Regarding the therapeutic uses of this illusion, the authors of a report on this process observed:

> Overall, illusory manipulation was extremely beneficial for patients with arthritic pain in their fingers, on average halving the reported pain in 85% of participants. Some reported greater reduction in pain for stretching, some for shrinking and some for both."[8]

Reporting improvement when a shortening sensation was felt, may seem counterintuitive, but one of the techniques that advanced Alexander teachers use to access the directions is to send an opposite force through the spine. If this opposite force is very precisely directed, it activates an upward and expansive energy, much like pressing down on a spring. This can be seen in the very few films that were taken of Alexander, in which he is working with his hand on top of his pupil's head; the pupil springs up toward his hand as Alexander delicately balances the head and sends a very precise force through the whole body. We also see the same phenomenon in women in Third World countries who carry water vessels and other loads on the top of their head as pictured in Figures 24.14 on page 96 and 32.3 on page 138. This phenomenon is explored further in Chapters 24 and 32.

NOTES 1. ALEXANDER (1932, 1955), 13. By the term "mechanisms" Alexander is referring to the individual parts of the whole of the body as it moves into activity. (see glossary) 2. ALEXANDER (1923, 1955), 109. 3. MACDONALD (2006), 67. 4. IBID., 64. 5. CARRINGTON (1994), 36. 6. IBID., 36. 7. BARSTOW (N.D.). 8. PRESTON AND NEWPORT (2011).

CHAPTER 11

CONDITIONING AND RECONDITIONING

Avital aspect of yoga and meditation practice in the Hindu and Buddhist traditions is development of practices for overcoming the conditioning that chains us to mindless repetition of unskillful or harmful actions. The other side of this cultivation is development of habits that result in skillful or positive actions, which bring the practitioner into a state of harmony and balance. As we saw in Chapter 8 on the power of habit, these unskillful actions are underlaid by unconscious ingrained patterns, or *samskaras*, which are reinforced and deepened every time they are activated.

Alexander identified these habits as being deeply rooted in our very physicality. We are deeply but often unconsciously sensitive to the thoughts and emotions of other people in their posture, demeanor, and movement. The neuromuscular system provides an expression of our whole personality and character.

As Alexander saw it, our reaction to the stimulus to carry out the simplest action reflects our underlying predispositions. The inability to inhibit the stimulus to interfere with the relationship of the head, neck, and torso, the primary control, in such a simple activity as getting out of a chair, mirrors an inability to inhibit responses to a whole range of stimuli in our everyday lives. Surely, he claims, if people are not able to alter their habits in a matter as simple as getting out of a chair, what chance do they have of succeeding in making the grand spiritual or psychological improvements to which they may aspire?

John Dewey, in discussing Pavlovian conditioning, describes Alexander's approach to changing conditioning thus:

> There are certain basic, central organic habits and attitudes which condition every act we perform, every use we make of ourselves. Hence a conditioned reflex is not just a matter of an arbitrarily established connection, such as that between the sound of a bell and the eating-reaction in a dog, but goes back to central conditions within the organism itself. . . . The discovery of a central control which conditions all other reactions brings the conditioning factor under conscious direction and enables the individual through his own co-ordinated activities to take possession of his own potentialities. It converts the fact of conditioned reflexes from a principle of external enslavement into a means of vital freedom.[1]

The "central control" to which Dewey refers in this quote is what Alexander calls the primary control.

NOTE 1. DEWEY (1955), XXI.

THE PRIMARY CONTROL

Healthy coordination can take place only if the various parts of the body are in proper relationship to each other, starting from the balance of the head on top of the spine. Alexander referred to "a certain use of the head in relation to the neck, and of the head and neck in relation to the torso and the other parts of the organism," as constituting a primary control over the coordination of the whole body. This central coordination provides the essential support to any type of movement. Sometimes in discussions on the technique, the term 'primary control' is used to refer to a good and efficient relationship of head, neck, and back. However, the term simply refers to this relationship, and not to whether it is good or bad. In Alexander's terms, it can be employed "correctly" or "incorrectly," and therefore it will either beneficially or harmfully affect the functioning of the whole person. As Alexander saw it, the great majority of people were constantly interfering with their primary control, with negative effects on their health and well-being.

In Chapter 32, on *Tadasana*, the Mountain Pose, we will look in detail at the question of finding a fine balance of our upright posture. This balance of the head on top of the spine starts at the atlanto-occipital joint. You can locate this joint by putting your fingers directly under your earlobes (Fig. 12.1). As we discover when we "nod off," the head's center of gravity is in front of this joint. Therefore, to facilitate the fine and dynamic balance of the head and keep it upright, the muscles of the back of the neck have to work constantly. Ideally, there is a subtle, ever-changing activation of the stretch reflexes in these muscles to maintain the balance of the head, instead of these muscles being overcontracted to forcibly hold the head in place.

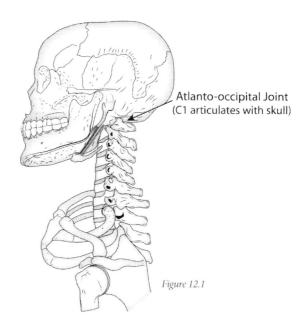

Atlanto-occipital Joint
(C1 articulates with skull)

Figure 12.1

Figure 12.2

Figure 12.3

Babies, in the process of coming onto their feet, need to freely and easily balance their head on top of the spine in order to maintain their initially precarious balance (Figs. 12.2 and 12.3). However, once that initial balance is attained, we can begin to do all sorts of rather nasty things to ourselves and still stay upright. A common pattern that develops once we lose this fine balance of the head on the spine is that these muscles overwork and begin to fix the head back and down. This contraction of the neck muscles and the misplacement of the head are not isolated actions. The muscular overcontraction continues throughout all the extensors of the back, and the misplacement of the head on the spine throws out the relationship of all the vertebrae through the spine, the position of the pelvis, the knee joints, and the ankle joints. We will look at this relationship in more detail in Chapter 24, on tensegrity.

Even the feet are affected by a misplacement of the head, leading to conditions such as bunions and flat feet as the weight is badly distributed through the feet in walking and running. It is easy to see how this relationship of the head to the torso, when interfered with, can affect our freedom of movement through the simple experiment of comparing raising your arms in the air while deliberately "scrunching" your neck to doing the same when your neck is "unscrunched."

This overcontraction of the muscles leads to a deadening of our kinesthetic sensitivity and begins to put pressure on all the internal organs. This may lead to a variety of symptoms that are rarely recognized as being associated with our postural imbalance. Interference with the primary control also affects our breathing. We will look at this in more detail in Chapter 22 on breathing.

If we look at Figure 12.4 we can see a severely collapsed posture, which not only restricts the breathing but also puts pressure on the heart. The heart is enclosed in the sac of the pericardium, which is attached to the diaphragm, (Fig. 12.5) and the movement of the diaphragm is constantly moving the internal organs of the abdominal cavity. Little wonder, then, that Alexander put so much emphasis on reeducation in relation to our primary control, as it has such a profound effect on all our vital organs.

At the same time Alexander was working on the postural mechanisms of human beings, scientists such as neurologists Sir Charles Sherrington and Rudolf Magnus, and the biologist George Coghill, were working on the postural reflexes of lower animals. These experiments helped them discover that in the case of cats or newts, as Magnus wrote, "The entire body follows the direction assumed by the head."[1]

Both Sherrington and Coghill acknowledged the relationship between Alexander's discoveries and their own work. Coghill wrote to Alexander, "I am . . . amazed to see how you, years ago, discovered in human physiology and psychology the same principle which I worked out in the behavior of lower vertebrates."[2] It is likely that Alexander developed the term *primary control* from Magnus's term *central mechanism*.

When we first get onto our feet, we have to position the head very precisely on top of the spine to achieve balance. For the first few years after we begin walking, we send the head and whole body slightly forward as we walk, which means we use gravity to walk in the most efficient way possible.

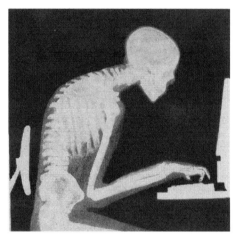

Figure 12.4

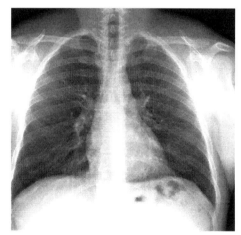

Figure 12.5

As pictured in Figure 12.6, many adults tend to lean backward as they walk, which means they are working against gravity. Wearing high heels may further exacerbate this tendency (Fig. 12.7). As the whole body is tilted forward by the heels, the most common impulse is to lean back even further to maintain balance. This pattern of leaning back is often seen in yoga classes with people attempting to "stand straight" or "lengthen the spine."

The process of *inhibiting* old habitual reactions and activating the *directions* for a new manner of *use* of ourselves are vital steps in the reestablishment of healthy primary control. The words of Magnus about his study with cats relate equally to human beings:

Figure 12.6

> The attitudinal reflexes form a group of tonic reactions, by which the whole body musculature is integrated for a combined and highly adapted function. The entire body follows the direction assumed by the head, this being very often moved in a certain direction under the influence of the telereceptive higher sense-organs. This provides one of the ways in which the relation of the body to its environment is regulated. It need only briefly be mentioned that the different attitudes, with their different distribution of tone and tension in the numerous muscles of the body, are associated with different distributions of reflex irritability over the central nervous system. Therefore one and the same stimulus may cause quite different reflex reactions according to the different attitudes of the animal at the moment the stimulus is applied.[1]

NOTES 1. MAGNUS (1926), 6.   2. COGHILL (1947), 120.

Figure 12.7

UNRELIABLE SENSORY APPRECIATION

The basis of correct knowledge is correct perception, correct deduction and correct evidence.
— **Yoga Sutras of Patanjali 1:7** —

❁

Everyone wants to be right, but no one stops to consider if their idea of right is right.
— *F. M. Alexander* —

The Lost Sixth Sense

Our culture's deep unawareness of the existence of the kinesthetic sense is underlined by its omission from the traditional listing of the five senses: sight, taste, touch, smell, and hearing. This list leaves out the most fundamental and basic of our senses: our kinesthetic/ proprioceptive sense. Our kinesthetic sense[1] is awareness of the position and movement of the parts of the body, by the sensory organs, known as proprioceptors, in muscles, organs and joints, in conjunction with information from the vestibular system of the inner ear.[2]

The brain interprets information from the proprioceptors and the vestibular system to give us an overall idea of the position of the body in space, muscle tension, and the relative relationship between parts of our bodies, as well as movement and acceleration. In other words, kinesthetic feedback subconsciously informs all our motor activities from moment to moment. Were we to lose our kinesthetic sense, we would lose our ability to stand, walk, or move.

Indeed we have a description of this in the case of Mr. Waterman, described in *Pride and a Daily Marathon*.[3] Waterman lost his kinesthetic capabilities and most cutaneous sensations, with the exception of pain and temperature, from his lower neck down. He retained the sensations of muscle effort, cramping, tiredness, and tension. Immediately after the loss, he was unable to walk or stand upright. He could move his limbs but had no precise control over them. He couldn't gauge the properties of objects, such as shape or texture, by handling them, and thus could not use force-feedback information about the environment to control his body or perceive the world. In the process of relearning mobility, he had to monitor every movement by sight to know the location of his limbs. After the loss, it took him two months to relearn how to sit up, more than a year and a half to stand, and several months longer to walk. He could only walk slowly and still needed his vision to assist him in walking. Among the very few recorded cases of this condition, Waterman is the only one who regained the ability to walk.[4]

As we see in the case of Mr. Waterman, vision also plays an important role in balance and coordination. Just as our vision can be tricked by visual illusions, our kinesthesia can play tricks on us. Airline pilots know that their sense of where they are in space, is not to be relied on when they are deprived of visual clues by cloud or darkness. If there is a discrepancy between their kinesthetic sense and what their instruments are telling them, they must rely on their instruments. Not doing so can have fatal consequences. In 2009, Air France Flight 447 from Rio de Janeiro to Paris plowed into the Caribbean Sea. French investigators found that the autopilot disconnected and the pilots, missing the visual information and computer data on which they relied, steered the aircraft very sharply upward, causing it to lose speed and stall.

People's sense of their overall body relationship in space and their sense of what they are doing as they move, is frequently inaccurate. Unlike airline pilots, however, we have no external instruments to correct our misperceptions. Also, unlike the case of visual illusions, which are normally transitory, these errors become ingrained and permanent. Like a ship with a compass that is inaccurate by a few degrees, we gradually steer ourselves off course. In Alexander's case he used his vision, with the help of mirrors, to correct his mistaken kinesthetic perceptions.

Alexander's discovery that he was unable to accurately sense his movements and spatial relationships was both alarming and perplexing, because if his kinesthetic sensing was unreliable, how could he tell he was doing what he thought he was doing? As he began to observe other people, he found that this inaccuracy was an almost universal condition.

This is a terrifically difficult idea to get across to people who have not had Alexander Technique lessons. We all have the same "common sense" assumption that Alexander initially had: that we are doing what we feel we are doing. In many cases, nothing could be further from the truth. And like Alexander in his own process of change and discovery, even after we realize the discrepancy between perception and reality, our intellectual understanding of this phenomenon does not necessarily translate into immediate practical action.

The Alexander Technique offers us a process by which we can restore reliability to our proprioceptive and kinesthetic senses, so that we can do what we intend to do rather than something different. This creates more ease of movement because the subconscious direction provided by our kinesthesia to our motor system becomes much more precise.

In Alexander's vivid description of the process of overcoming his voice problem, he returns again and again to his bewilderment at the predicament of how to change what he was doing, when the new direction felt "wrong" and the habitual action felt "right." He explains how, repeatedly, at the critical moment when he put his intention into action he instinctively returned to the feeling of "rightness," which constantly made him perform the "wrong" action.

What would have been a very discouraging discovery for most of us had the opposite effect on Alexander, who realized that this opened up a new field of inquiry, namely, the possibility of discovering a way of making the kinesthetic sense reliable. Indeed, he describes how he became "obsessed" with the desire to explore this possibility.

So how did Alexander finally overcome this stumbling block and make his own sensory appreciation reliable? He explains that he saw that in order to direct his use he must cease relying on his feelings, and employ his reasoning processes, in order:

- To analyze the conditions of use present;
- To select (reason out) the means whereby a more satisfactory use could be brought about;
- To project consciously the directions required for putting these means into effect.[5]

He goes on to explain that even at this point, in the examination of how he used himself when speaking, the stimulus to speak was so powerful that, against his conscious will, he frequently reverted to his old habit. At this point many would have given up, but he continued working with and strengthening his ability to direct. It became clear to him that he had to inhibit the initial reaction to this stimulus to project his voice through every part of the action, and that "my trust in my reasoning processes to bring me safely to my 'end' must be a genuine trust, not a half-trust needing the assurance of feeling right as well."[6]

This whole process is outlined in detail in the first chapter of *Use of the Self*, which is essential reading for anyone really interested in the Alexander Technique.

The attempt to change ingrained patterns of movement, often thwarted by this problem of unreliable sensory perception, may also be compounded by and associated with faulty ideas about how the body should be coordinated, misperception about the actual structure of the body, and misunderstanding of the location of joints and their range of possible movements, which Alexander referred to as "incorrect conceptions." This is discussed in the next chapter.

Professor G. R. de Beer published a fascinating article entitled "How Animals Hold Their Heads." He explains that mammals and birds tend to hold their heads so that the horizontal semicircular canals are actually horizontal whenever the animal is in a state of alertness; they orient their heads to relate to the space around them.

On the basis of his measurements of just ten human subjects who were working or studying in his department, he says that instead of aligning with true horizontal, humans carry their head so that their horizontal semicircular canal is tilted back about 10–15 degrees. Although ten subjects is a very small sample, I think it is probably representative, as the experience of Alexander teachers is that almost all their students pull the head backward when they attempt to assume an upright position. He comments, "The problem now arises, if mammals generally hold their heads in such a position that their lateral semicircular canals are horizontal, what advantage does it confer on them, and why does man differ and forgo such an advantage?"[7]

Responding to this research, T. D. M. Roberts wrote:

> However, if account is taken of the normal carriage of the head and of the consequent inclination of the reference plane, it has been found that, for some 30 species of mammals and for 20 species of birds, each animal characteristically carries the plane of its "horizontal" canal very nearly parallel to the horizon. We may apply the argument in reverse to decide what should count as the "normal" position of the head in man. When the horizontal semi-circular canal is parallel to the horizon, the head is in the position characteristic of

a boxer on the alert to defend his equilibrium.[8]

In many humans, once the head has been mispositioned for many years the semicircular canals send the information that the head is being held upright. We can easily imagine a carpenter with a spirit level that gives a reading 10–15 percent off horizontal as being level, and the types of structures he would build as a result of this error!

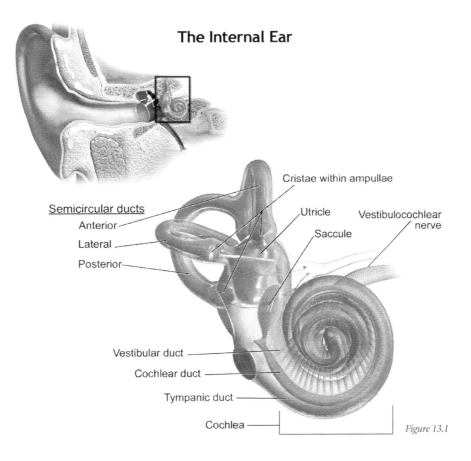

The Internal Ear

Cristae within ampullae

Semicircular ducts
Anterior
Lateral
Posterior

Utricle

Saccule

Vestibulocochlear nerve

Vestibular duct
Cochlear duct
Tympanic duct
Cochlea

Figure 13.1

NOTE 1. The term *kinesthesia* (or *kinesthetic*) is often used interchangeably with the term *proprioception* (or *proprioceptive*). **2.** The vestibular system located in the inner ear consists of three semicircular canals, oriented at right angles to one another, in the three planes of space (Fig. 13.1) This system provides vital information about movement and balance. Put very simply, it is the sensory system in our inner ear that detects movement of the head and helps control balance. It works rather like the spirit level tool of a carpenter, except that the semicircular canals of the ear measure the balance on three planes. As we can see from this description, the balance of the head on top of the spine directly affects the semicircular canals. **3.** Cole (1995). **4.** The effects of the loss of kinesthesia include: • Inability to sense limb movement and position • Major impairment in skilled performance • Abnormal movements and the inability to walk; relearning to walk takes a huge effort, and the walking is always slow • Major difficulty in executing tasks requiring fine motor skills • Loss of the unconscious ability to communicate through body language (a limited repertoire of gestures can be relearned) **5.** Alexander (1932, 1955), 17. **6.** Ibid., 22. **7.** de Beer (1947),138. **8.** Roberts (1967), 203.

CHAPTER 14

INCORRECT CONCEPTIONS

One of the major impediments Alexander mentioned in relation to people finding balance and coordination was the fact that they held "incorrect conceptions," which adversely affected their manner of use.

The combination of these mistaken ideas with our faulty sensory perception compounds their miscoordination, so it is essential to reeducate ourselves conceptually as well as kinesthetically. Some of these incorrect conceptions relate to the position of various parts of the body, some to the relative relationship of various parts of the body to each other, some to the movement possibilities of various joints of the whole body, and some to the amount and type of effort we need to employ in order to execute certain movements.

In relation to the coordination of the body, here are some of the most common errors:

- What it means to "stand up straight."
- The amount of effort required to undertake the activities of life. Mostly we bring far too much effort to the simplest of activities. Just observe how much effort you bring to unscrewing the lid off a jar, opening a door, or cutting into a loaf of bread.
- The positioning of the shoulder girdle. Many people attempt to use the muscles of the arms and shoulder girdle as postural muscles in an attempt to sit or stand up straight. In the process they interfere with free positioning of the shoulder girdle, with all the consequent tension that most people experience around this area.
- The position of the top joint of the spine—the point at which the skull joins the top vertebra of the spine. Many people do not think of their neck as being part of their spine, but actually it is the apex of it.
- The position of the hip joint.
- The position of the knee joint.
- The position of the ankle.
- The healthy and possible range of motion of the spine and of other joints of the body.
- The position and action of the diaphragm in breathing.
- The position of the lungs.
- The shape of the abdominal cavity and its movement in healthy breathing.
- Numerous other errors relating to the act of breathing.

Specific errors in body mapping, (our understanding of the structure of the body and its possibilities for movement) are covered extensively throughout this book. In addition, we look at some of the factors involved in chronic pain.

CHAPTER 15

END GAINING AND MEANS WHEREBY

The man who is devoted and not attached to the fruit of his actions obtains tranquility; while he who through desire has attachment for the fruit of action is bound down by it.

— *Bhagavad Gita 5:12* —

The term *end gaining* was coined by Alexander to describe the state of mind when a person's focus is totally on the end to be gained, without any consideration of how the process of gaining occurs. He contrasted this with an approach to action in which the focus is taken off the intended result and placed instead on the means whereby that result can be achieved. Shifting our attention away from the end, and toward applying improved *means whereby* the end could be achieved, will necessarily involve a change in our manner of use.

Observing our own yoga practices, we are likely to find end gaining as fully entrenched here as in any other activity. People frequently have a mental image of the end point of a particular pose, derived from the demonstration of a teacher, a picture in a yoga book, or the example of a more flexible person in the class doing the pose. This mental picture is likely to be an impetus for us to strive to practice in a way that is beyond our physical capacity.

In other words we tend to go, as Alexander put it, "directly for an end," trying to put our head on our legs in a seated forward bend, our hand on the floor in a triangle pose, etc. We may even manage to do this, but most often at the cost of collapse, compression, and even injury.

We do, however, have another option. We can mindfully use our yoga practice as an opportunity to develop the ability to inhibit our initial reactions and use the directions to coordinate ourselves. We can then open and expand within the pose. So instead of end gaining, we can develop new and improved means whereby we can make the pose work for us, rather than against us.

The phrase "bringing the ego into the practice" is often used in yoga to describe this end-gaining mind-state. And of course, in the *Yoga Sutras of Patanjali* (II:46) it is mentioned that in all activities our body needs to be both steady and easeful, *sthira-sukham-asanam*. This can be attained only if attention is paid to the means whereby, in both our yoga practice and the activities of our everyday lives.

CHAPTER 16

THE ALEXANDER TECHNIQUE AS AN INDIRECT PROCEDURE

This is an indirect procedure, and, as has already been shown, it involves the inhibition of familiar messages responsible for habitual familiar activity, and the substituting for these of unfamiliar messages responsible for new and unfamiliar activity.

— *F. M. Alexander* —

A basic aspect of Alexander work is reorientation of a person's attention away from a presenting problem, in order to focus on the wider picture of which the presenting problem is a part. This is one of the things that differentiates the Alexander Technique from treatment modalities that focus directly on a specific problem. Instead, the focus in the Alexander Technique is firmly on the overall pattern of *use*.

The human being is a unified whole, and this means a change in any one part, inevitably creates a change in the whole; and a change will often result in unintended consequences. Therefore, the focus of the work is always on changing and improving the overall use of the self, and allowing specific problems to resolve themselves within the context of that overall change.

An Italian friend who would later become an Alexander teacher herself tells an amusing tale of being confused in her first Alexander lesson. She explained her knee problem to her Australian teacher and then had to assume that her English was really bad, because the teacher began to work with the balance of her head on top of her spine, paying very little attention to her knees.

For centuries, yoga books have extolled the virtues of particular poses for particular organs, or as remedies for particular illnesses. The earliest Hatha Yoga texts are full of such claims. For example, the *Hatha Yoga Pradipika* outlines the benefits of *Mayurasana*, the Peacock Pose, thus: "This asana soon destroys all diseases and removes abdominal disorders and also those arising from irregularities of phlegm, bile and wind; digests unwholesome food taken in excess; increases appetite; and destroys the most deadly poison."[1] More recent books have lists of *asanas* relating them to particular glands, organs, and diseases on which they are reputed to have a beneficial effect.

Although some of these claims may be questionable, I have no doubt there are specific yoga poses that may have benefits for associated conditions. But to be beneficial, they need to be based on a proper *analysis of conditions present* and practiced in a way that takes into account the coordination of the primary control.

NOTE   1. YOGI SUATMARAMA (ND), 32.

THE PRIORITY OF PREVENTION OVER CURE

The suffering which has not yet arisen should be avoided.
— **Yoga Sutras of Patanjali II:16** —

❖

An ounce of prevention is worth a pound of cure.
— **Proverb** —

❖

It is the recognition in practice of the principle of prevention which makes possible man's advancement to higher and higher stages of evolution and opens up the greatest possibilities for human activities and accomplishment.
— **F. M. Alexander** —

Figure 17.1

H ere is the Buddhist parable regarding the Four Horses:
The first horse runs before he sees the shadow of the whip; the second will run just before the whip hits his skin; the third will run only when he feels the pain of the whip striking his skin; and the fourth will only run when the pain penetrates to the marrow of his bones!

It is the nature of the human condition that we all have to live with some level of physical, mental, psychological, and emotional distress: the First Noble Truth in the Buddhist tradition.

Almost everybody has some system or area of the body that is particularly susceptible to imbalance, especially when we find ourselves overstressed physically or emotionally. For many of us, this is not an overwhelming problem most of the time; if we have at least some degree of self-awareness, we can develop strategies of diet, exercise, and general lifestyle to moderate the stressors that might irritate our vulnerabilities. In addition to physical problems, we often tend toward experiencing thoughts, emotions, and behaviors that cause us and others distress. Prevention is greatly preferred over cure, and both yoga and the Alexander Technique offer excellent prevention strategies for an exceptionally wide range of ills to which human beings are prone. Both systems also provide means of curing diseases and conditions that have arisen as a result of ignoring the basic laws of healthful living. And both of these aim at bringing the whole person into a state of greater balance and ease.

If we look at it from a purely physical level, consistently using ourselves in a dysfunctional way means that over the years and decades, irritating pressure is constantly being placed not only on our muscles, tendons, and joints but also on our internal organs. This misuse eventually manifests as organic and functional dis-ease. It would be a mistake to look at it simply as a physical process. Physical contraction and restriction feeds into, and is fed by, our mental and emotional processes. The most we can say, if we try to separate the psychological from the physical, is that one side may be more predominant than the other in particular circumstances. For example, if I break my leg in an accident, the resultant physical restriction will affect my mental and emotional state: if I am in a constant state of anger or irritation this will be reflected in my breathing, muscles, joints, everyday movement, blood pressure, digestion, and indeed every physiological process of my body.

The Alexander Technique's focus on the very visible and concrete processes of posture, movement, and breathing should not blind us to the fact that all these processes are a reflection of the whole person. Indeed, we cannot change these processes by working with them directly, but only by dealing with what underlies them.

Thus the path of both Patanjali yoga and the Alexander Technique is cultivating focused and intelligent awareness in order to identify the underlying causes of our problems, and in developing the strategies of direction and inhibition in order to alter the underlying habitual "grooves." In yoga these grooves are known as *samskaras* or *vasanas*,[1] and they deprive us of the ability to pursue more wholesome action.

Over the past twenty-five years I have come across all four types of "horses" in my teaching practice. Most of my students have been in the second or third category. For those who wait until the pain penetrates to the marrow of their bones, there is often a considerable level of tissue damage. In some cases, these people have undergone surgical intervention that may or may not have been necessary.

The role of the Alexander Technique is not to treat that damage but to change the manner of the person's use of herself, in order to take the constant pressure off and permit the natural healing process to work.

Alexander frequently described his work as "a technique for prevention," by which he meant that it promotes conditions of well-being that would make development of pain or disease much less likely.

Yoga was not envisaged primarily as a curative or remedial practice, but rather as one aiming toward the higher functioning of the human being, encompassing all aspects of our social, physical, psychological, and spiritual dimensions.

NOTE 1. *Samskara* is a Sanskrit term used in the *Yoga Sutras of Patanjali* that refers to habit patterns. *Samskaras* are impressions derived from past experiences that form desires and fears that influence future responses and behavior. They are predispositions accumulating from actions and choices that in the yoga tradition are looked at as accruing over many lifetimes, and the more we repeat the particular action or behavior the more we reinforce the samskara. Effectively, we are manipulated by unconscious and unseen forces. The aim of yoga is to undo the consequences of the samskaras. The term *samskara* is used almost interchangeably with the term vasana, which could be translated as "trait" or tendency.

WHAT HAPPENS IN AN ALEXANDER TECHNIQUE LESSON?

You come to learn to inhibit and to direct your activity. You learn, first, to inhibit the habitual reaction to certain classes of stimuli, and second, to direct yourself consciously in such a way as to affect certain muscular pulls, which processes bring about a new reaction to these stimuli. Boiled down, it all comes to inhibiting a particular reaction to a given stimulus. But no one will see it that way. They will all see it as getting in and out of the chair the right way. It is nothing of the kind. It is that a pupil decides what he will or will not consent to do. They may teach you anatomy and physiology till they are black in the face: you will still have this to face: sticking to a decision against your habit of life.

— *F. M. Alexander* —

Although approaches to teaching the Technique may vary from teacher to teacher, all genuine training in the Alexander Technique involves "inhibiting a particular reaction to a given stimulus" and sending directions as a means of improving the primary control in some activity. Teachers will use differing means to achieve this, but most Alexander lessons will include the processes described here.

Assessment/Diagnosis

We have already discussed the central importance of skillful diagnosis and assessment; this was the basis for Alexander's being able to correct his own faulty manner of use, regain the use of his voice and massively improve his health.

In an amusing passage, Alexander describes his assessment process to a lady, who was initially somewhat affronted when told she was the worst case of misuse of self that he had seen in his fifty-six years of teaching! "I diagnosed you at a glance. . . . A wrinkle speaks volumes. The expression of the eyes can tell the whole story. Posture is a complete giveaway. But don't be downhearted. You'll be throwing that horrible stick away one of these days."[1] And indeed she did.

While observing the totality of students' use of themselves, Alexander teachers are trained in particular to observe interferences with the primary control, the the incorrect ideas their students may have about how to coordinate themselves, their level of reactivity, and the underlying emotional states.

Alexander frequently described the method behind his teaching process, which always included diagnosis as the first step. This diagnosis was given to the student along with a "means whereby" proposal for remedying the underlying problems. In addition to this initial diagnosis and assessment during Alexander Technique lessons students receive immediate, moment to moment feedback regarding their use of themselves.

Chair Work

Alexander worked mostly with his students' coordination by having them sit on and rise from a chair. These are movements we perform many times a day, but when we closely examine our actions we see that we are often using a good deal of excess muscular work in these movements. Observing a person rising from a chair, we frequently see the neck contract as the head is pulled back. In addition, the shoulders are pulled up and the lumbar area pulled in, which pushes out the abdominal wall. This tightens the torso, forcing the legs to work more than is necessary to lift the body out of the chair. Less commonly, the head drops forward, the shoulders rise and tense, and the whole spine rounds, forcing the legs to lift the dead weight of a heavy, collapsed torso.

Moving into sitting, we frequently see people drop heavily into the chair. The misuse begins with the head being contracted backwards, which initiates a tightening of the extensor muscles of the back and a shortening of the spine.

Firstly students are taught to inhibit their initial reactions to the impulse to sit, and subsequently, send the directions that will create coordination rather than contraction. This then, allows their head to lead the movement and their whole torso to both lengthen and widen permitting them to bend both hips and knees as they move into the chair. There is no "correct" angle of the torso in relation to the legs. What is "correct" in this movement is to maintain the directions and coordination throughout the movement, and to support the movement from the feet, rather than using excess gripping and tensing elsewhere in order to stabilize and support the body. Rising from the chair reverses this process. In lessons, students are often instructed to keep their feet level with one another. But in everyday life Alexander suggests placing one foot slightly back from the other when rising from a chair, which is easier.[2]

Again, it is a matter of inhibiting the initial response, sending the directions for the coordination of the whole body and maintaining these directions throughout the movement.

Alexander would only see students who would commit to five lessons a week for a minimum of three weeks, and this process of getting into and out of a chair was invariably a major part of their lessons. In Chapter 27 on neuroplasticity, the wisdom of this approach will become apparent, as well as demonstrating why it is necessary to repeat and develop a new habit pattern for a considerable amount of time before it replaces an old one. The neurological patterning that underlies sitting and standing and the movements from the one to the other, are the foundation of many other movements, and the new mental process that becomes ingrained in this procedure of sitting and rising can be applied to all life activities.

Figure 18.1

Monkey/Lunge

Related to chair work, Alexander teachers also work with two basic positions and movements required for bending forward or lowering our center of gravity (Figs. 18.2, 18.3, and 34.1). As we shall see later, working with these movements also develops both the strength and the elasticity of our muscular support.

Skilled movement requires that we maintain the central coordination of the head, neck, and torso (the primary control), and that we not compromise this coordination as we bend forward, move toward the ground, or lower our body in space. Think of the surfer, the aikido master, the skier, or the tennis player waiting to respond to a serve. What we see in all of these skilled practitioners is a releasing forward of the knees, a lowering of the center of gravity, an open and expansive body, and an alert relationship to the environment without the slightest fixing. It is fixing the body that interferes with our ability to move and respond immediately and appropriately.

Figure 18.2 The lunge in action

Figure 18.3 *The monkey in action*

— *Table Work* —

Table work involves the student lying on her back on a table with knees bent while the teacher works on her. In this process the teacher can assist the student to gain more expansion and release than would normally be available. Repatterning movement both in upright and in functional activities is essential during a lesson, and this is complemented by work in this semisupine position in which deep contractions that the teacher and student can't easily undo whilst upright can begin to be released. Once a student comes off the table into upright, he often finds that overall coordination is much easier.

— *Application Work* —

Application work refers to employing the Alexander Technique in the whole range of activities. Although the learning and thinking process gained from chair work can inform other activities, particular activities may require specific attention. How, for example, is a musician to organize himself or herself in response to the demands of an instrument; the office worker in response to the demands of working at a computer; or the yoga practitioner in response to the demands of a particular yoga pose?

NOTES 1. MORGAN (1998), 51. 2. ALEXANDER (1910, 1946), 170–71.

PART THREE

CONSIDERATIONS REGARDING YOGA PRACTICE

❋ ❋ ❋

VARIABILITY

It is clear that textbook writers and teachers over the centuries, even until today, fail to understand or to transmit to their students the crucial concept that anatomical and physiological diversity and variation is a canon of living organisms. This failure leads to the belief that textbooks are conveying immutable facts with only few anomalous exceptions.

— Illustrated Encyclopedia of Human Anatomical Variability —

We are all unique. Except for identical twins, no two humans are alike. This ranges from our mental, psychological, and emotional makeup, to the physicality of our bodies. For thousands of years, yogis have worked to develop and refine their whole psychophysical being. This was always carried out in the context of a one-on-one relationship between the teacher, or *guru*, and the student, or *chela*.

In the 1970s, when I studied at the Krishnamacharya Yoga Mandaram in Madras, all Hatha Yoga lessons were taught one-on-one. Only the yoga sutras were taught to a group. Nowadays, however, Hatha Yoga is normally taught in group classes, where all students go through a similar sequence of poses during the class. Some classes are so large that teachers have no chance to observe how an individual is doing within the class. They can't see if the poses are supporting or harming each student, let alone offer a modified or alternative pose if the one being done by the rest of the class is unsuitable for a particular student.

When we examine anatomy books, we tend to believe the images shown there demonstrate immutable facts about the structure of all human beings. Within the realm of "normal structure," however, there is great variability. Many of the basic anatomical "facts" repeated in every anatomy text don't hold true for everybody. For example, about one in every twelve thousand people has the heart on the right side of the chest, not the left! Indeed, variability is the rule rather than the exception. Every aspect of "normal" human anatomical structure is subject to variation. The routes of blood vessels and nerves, the precise positioning of organs, the exact points of origin and insertion of muscles, the shape of bones, and the orientation of joints are only a few of the many variable components of the human body.

These variations predispose us toward a whole range of advantages and disadvantages. For example, successful sprinters have unusually long heel bones (calcanei), which give their calf muscles superior leverage. Successful long distance runners have a much higher ratio of red muscle fibers to white muscle fibers than the "average" person. Neural, vascular, tendinous, and muscular variations around the carpal tunnel, can create a predisposition toward nerve impingement in the hand, known as carpal tunnel syndrome. Variations in the shape and orientation of the head of the femur and the acetabulum can affect a person's ability to squat easily, and some variations will predispose him toward hip problems.[1]

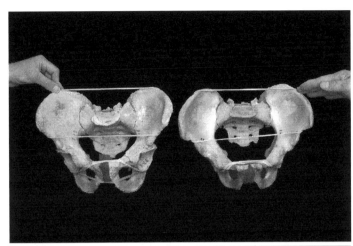

Figure 19.1A

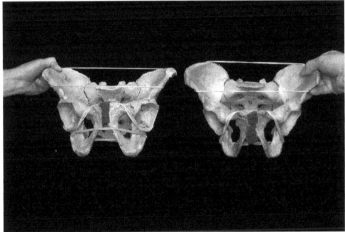

Figure 19.1B

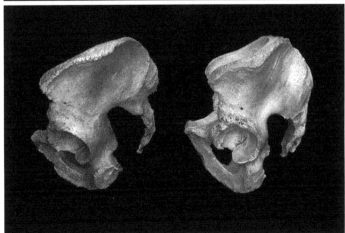

Figure 19.1C

It is fascinating, in working as an Alexander/yoga teacher, to see how misuse can impact on individuals is such diverse ways. For some people, the outcome of prolonged poor use may be headaches; or neck, back, hip, knee, or foot pain; or problems with breathing or the vocal apparatus. In some cases, those with terrible use suffer from very little pain or dysfunction, while others who appear to use themselves much better may be in considerable pain. We will consider this conundrum further in Chapter 28.

When we approach a practice like Hatha Yoga, we tend to think that if only we can practice hard enough and long enough, we will reach the end range for the poses, as pictured in yoga books or as demonstrated by our flexible yoga teachers. However, we need to be in touch with the true capacity of our body. For example, after many hours and years of quite intense yoga practice, in which I attempted to stretch my hamstrings in poses like *Paschimottanasana* (seated forward bend), it became clear that I was overstretching ligaments around my knees, and accentuating my kyphosis. This was causing knee pain and putting stress on my already over-rounded upper back. This is not to say that the pose won't work for me, but just that I need to approach it intelligently to receive its benefit.

Gains in flexibility are highly variable among people doing a similar practice, as are gains in muscle size or strength. A large study assessing the variability in gains in muscle size and strength after unilateral resistance training concluded that, "men and women exhibit wide ranges of response to resistance training, with some subjects showing little to no gain, and others showing profound changes, such as an increase in size of over 10 cm and as well as doubling their strength."[2]

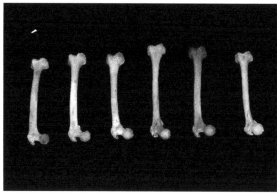 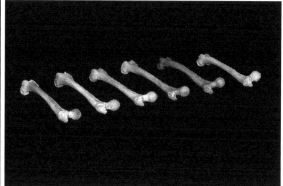

Figure 19.2A   *Figure 19.2B*

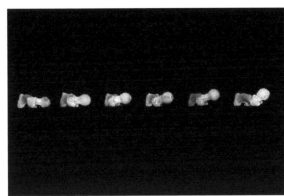

Figure 19.2C

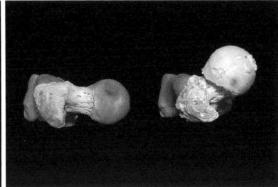

Figure 19.2D

Of course the other aspect of variability we are all familiar with is the difference in people's personality and character, as demonstrated in their approach to life in general, as well as to their yoga practice. The gung-ho will have a very different approach to their practice from the more laid-back or lazy person. An understanding of our temperament and how it affects our yoga practice is important in modifying our approach to that yoga practice. The gung-ho person will be a firm "end-gainer," impatient to strain himself in the effort to do whatever pose he is aiming for. The lazier person, by contrast, may fail to work with sufficient energy to gain the full benefit from her practice. Teachers may have to encourage or discourage effort, in the same pose for different students in a yoga class.

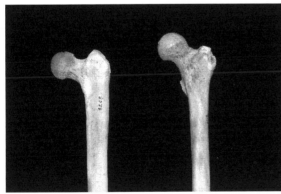

Figure 19.2E

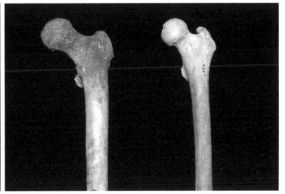

Figure 19.2F

Notes 1. This chapter presents a number of bone photos from the Yin Yoga teaching website of Paul and Suzee Grilley. They show a remarkable range of variation in the angle and positioning of the acetabulum (the socket of the ball and socket hip joint): Figs 19.1 A – C and variations in the torsion through the femur, and the size, angle, and orientation of the head of the femur (the ball of the hip joint): Figs 19.2 A – F. **2.** Habaletal (2005).

FLEXIBILITY

Flexibility relates to the range of motion of a joint or joints. It is the degree to which our joints move freely, in their various directions and planes. Each one of us is genetically predisposed to some overall level of muscle tightness or flexibility. In addition, each of us has variable flexibility in different areas of the body. For example, some people can do forward bends much more easily than back bends, while for others the opposite is true.

In Alexander yoga practice our first priority is always on coordination rather than flexibility. Those who are not dancers or gymnasts require only a modest degree of flexibility to comfortably engage in daily life activities, but the ability to coordinate appropriately is highly beneficial for our comfort, well-being, and health. Practicing the range of yoga poses gives people an opportunity to be mindful of how they are moving, so that they can catch and refuse to respond to constricting habitual impulses (inhibit) and coordinate themselves more appropriately (direct) within those poses. This work is beneficial for self-awareness and proper use, whatever a person's level of flexibility.

There appear to be two major factors governing our flexibility. First, there is the physiological state of our muscles and connective tissue. And second, there is our neurological make-up, which determines a "set point" for our muscles, a point at which the stretch reflex kicks in and initiates contraction against a stretch. The relationship of neurology to flexibility is unequivocally demonstrated by the fact that, under anesthesia all muscle tone is lost and the tightest body can be manipulated into a whole range of extreme contortions.

People coming to yoga classes have a greatly varying flexibility, from hypermobile to very tight. People can, and do, increase their mobility and range of motion by practicing yoga. But for many who have very tight musculature and ligaments there is a limit, and sometimes quite a modest one, to the increased range of motion they can attain. These are the sort of people who say "I've tried yoga but I can't do it," meaning there is no way they can get anywhere near the poses demonstrated in the yoga class they attend. Those who have been put off from attending yoga classes are in fact, the ones who would benefit highly from gaining more flexibility. But they need to be introduced to modified poses that they can manage in a coordinated way.

Without going deeply into the topics of muscle and connective tissue physiology and the workings of the nervous system, the issue of flexibility is still an interesting one. The reason stretching works is not that the muscle or fascia is permanently lengthened, (at least not over the course of only a few weeks), but that our sensation of the stretch is modified so that we are able to tolerate further stretch. We can notice this effect ourselves: if we stay in a stretch for a length of time, or if we repeat a stretch a number of times, we will tend to go further into it, even though there obviously hasn't been time to alter the length of the muscle or the connective tissue. There have been no studies longer than eight weeks on the effectiveness of stretching regimes and yoga for changing muscle and connective tissue. But an alteration in our nervous system is the major factor in our ability to gain more flexibility.

Those who are naturally tight may never end up on the front cover of *Yoga Journal* or gain the ability to bring their head to their legs in a forward bend, or experience the end point of many poses. However, gradually easing the body out of overcontraction with intelligent practice will bring more ease and comfort to everyday movement and release built-up tension. Indeed, those who are stiff (or reasonably stiff) can take comfort from the fact that having tighter muscles and ligaments prevents their joints from moving into the harmful extremes of their range of motion. People with limited flexibility have less reason to envy those who can maneuver their body like a pretzel in the yoga class, than they might at first believe.

At the other end of the scale are those who are hypermobile, which means having a level of connective tissue laxity that allows them to move their joints through excessive ranges of motion. Hypermobility can be more problematic than extreme tightness, because if joints are held in extreme positions, either as part of everyday posture and movement, or as a result of intense stretching, then joints and ligaments can be damaged. Those with hypermobility that causes pain and other symptoms may be diagnosed with "hypermobility syndrome." But joint hypermobility also gives dancers and gymnasts the means to excel in these activities.[1]

A good medical overview of joint hypermobility syndrome (JHS) notes, "Research has identified that posture, proprioception, education, strength and motor control are important components in achieving enhanced joint stability, as is physical activity and general fitness." This looks like a pretty good description of what is involved in both the Alexander Technique and yoga! The article gives an estimate that one in five musculoskeletal pain referrals are associated with JHS.[2]

Many hypermobile people are attracted to yoga because, unlike those who are less flexible, they can do the poses easily. But for safety, their emphasis needs to be on achieving overall coordination and strengthening, rather than increasing their range of movement. Usually in hypermobile people, there are areas that are being held very tightly to compensate for lack of support in the rest of the body. They may need to work on increasing flexibility in those particular areas, as the coordination and stability of their postural support improves.

Some things to keep in mind in yoga practice for those with hypermobility:
- In a case where some joints are more mobile than others, be mindful of the safety of the less-mobile joints.
- Extreme stretches may be easy to achieve though without awareness of how much the joints are being stressed. It is important to develop a level of sensory awareness that enables you to identify these sensations of overstretch.
- Hypermobile people have feelings of muscle stiffness just as much as, if not more than, other people.

- Hypermobile people frequently hold some joints, especially the knees, in permanent hyperextension. Therefore, strengthening the surrounding muscles to support joints is often recommended. This is best achieved by working with good coordination in strengthening yoga poses, in addition to well-coordinated everyday activities to increase joint stability. The problem is actually less one of strength and more one of faulty kinesthetic awareness.
- Balance can be a challenge with hypermobile ankles, knees, and feet. Poses that challenge balance can be highly useful for such people, because they develop reflex coordination, which helps support these joints.

In the end, whether we are very tight, hypermobile, or somewhere between, we need to make sure that we practice yoga in accordance with the conditions present rather, than trying to impose some outside idea of perfection.

Reducing Unwanted Flexibility

Even those who are not hypermobile may have particular joints that are habitually flexed or extended well beyond their healthy range. Here are a couple of examples.

Spine

Thirty years ago I could bend forward and almost place my head on my knees. I am very happy to say that I can no longer do that. The movement was achieved by bending through my thoracic spine, which flexed and worsened an already severe kyphosis. After many years of doing forward bends by flexing from the hips instead of the back, and practicing the Monkey position to use the hip joint for bending in everyday activities, there is no way I could take my spine into that extreme position today. Or maybe I should say, from what we now know about flexibility, my nervous system would refuse to accommodate the muscles and ligaments in this area being stretched to that extreme.

Over those years I have also worked at gaining flexibility in the opposite direction; working with the Alexander directions to maintain length through the spine in everyday activities, practicing the semisupine position to gain more softening and release, and exploring twists and some back bends to gain more flexibility in extension.

Knees

Another area in which many people are habitually hypermobile is in the knees. Knee hypermobility manifests as a locking of the knee joints by hyperextension and inward rotation, causing long-term consequences such as knee problems, and very often foot and lower back problems.

Once knee lockers release their knees, their quadriceps have to turn on and take over the work that was formerly being done passively by the bones and ligaments of the joint. And they find that these muscles tire amazingly quickly. But exercises to strengthen the quadriceps are not nearly as effective as making sure that these muscles are being used functionally, in day-to-day upright activities.

How Do We Become More Flexible?

As discussed above, increase in muscle extensibility observed after stretching was traditionally ascribed to a mechanical increase in muscle length. A growing body of research refutes these mechanical theories. Furthermore in studies of single sessions or three-to-eight-week stretching regimes, increases in flexibility appear to be due predominantly to modification in subjects' sensation.[3] This makes sense when we consider that at the end of a single yoga session we find that we have the ability to move further into stretches, yet we couldn't possibly have done enough to change the underlying structure within the hour or two of that session.

And How Do We Become Stiffer?

If we can train the nervous system to allow muscles to stretch, we can also train the nervous system to allow muscles to develop more tone. Particular strengthening exercises clearly do develop muscle strength and stiffness. This is what we want for the particular muscles or groups of muscles that are failing to adequately stabilize joints or give us sufficient support in our upright poses. Our aim then should not be just flexibility, but rather a proper balance between flexibility and strength, which we can develop through proper coordination.

Flexibility and Stretching as Part of Warm-ups for Sports Activities

Stretching and the importance of flexibility are some of the most contested subjects among sports experts, coaches, and athletes. Some claim the widespread belief, that stretching before exercising or playing sports will "warm up" the body and reduce injuries, is wrong, and that stretching prior to engaging in speed or power sports actually decreases athletic performance by temporarily reducing muscle strength! Others claim that stretching should be part of any warmup routine.

There is no consensus on this point and whether stretching prior to athletic performance is useful or harmful, probably depends on individual variability. The Australian Institute of Sport, which has obviously followed this discussion very carefully, has these guidelines:

> Stretching activities can be included in the warm-up and cool down. There is now less emphasis on static-stretching during the warm-up, so stretches should move the muscle groups through the full range of movement required in the activity being performed (active stretching). Static stretching is still appropriate during the cool down and can be used to improve flexibility.

Some rules when stretching:
- Warm-up the body prior to stretching.
- Stretch before and after exercise (active stretching during the warm-up, static stretching during the cool down).
- Stretch all muscle groups that will be involved in the activity.
- Stretch gently and slowly.
- Never bounce or stretch rapidly.
- Stretch gently to the point of mild discomfort, never pain.
- Do not hold your breath when stretching; breathing should be slow and easy.
- Do not make stretches competitive.[4]

NOTES **1.** Hypermobility may also be associated with relatively rare disorders in which the collagen is overelastic, such as Ehlers Danlos Syndrome and Marfans Syndrome, which may sometimes be undiagnosed. **2.** Hickmott (2013). **3.** Weppler and Magnusson (2010).   **4.** Australian Institute of Sport (2010).

INJURIES

In 2012, the writer William J. Broad started a lively debate when he alerted the general wellness community about the issue of injuries resulting from yoga practice in his book *The Science of Yoga* and his articles in the *New York Times*.

Of course yoga is not the only activity that may result in injuries. One of the most dangerous activities, with a very high risk of morbidity and mortality, is sitting for prolonged periods of time. An influential longitudinal study examining the links between time spent sitting and mortality, in a sample of more than seventeen thousand Canadians, demonstrated very clear links between spending long periods of time sitting, and both all-cause mortality, and cardiovascular disease (but not cancer).[1] Of course, most people whose work involves long hours of sitting are familiar with the various aches, pains, and outright injuries involved in doing this activity for a long time.

There is inevitably a risk of injuries associated with any activity. The risk of injuries in our activities is in direct proportion to how well or badly we use ourselves while doing them, and the extent to which we listen to messages from the body indicating pain or strain. I have worked with people with really debilitating injuries caused by using a computer mouse and keyboard, jogging, gardening, weight lifting, singing, playing a musical instrument, dancing, aerobics, driving a car, playing golf, skiing, painting, swimming, or any of a host of other activities. The common factor in all those injuries was a consistent pattern of misuse, combined with inattention to clear messages from the body that injury was taking place. In reading Broad's chapter on yoga injuries, it is clear that misuse of and inattention to the body underlie the injuries that he mentions. It is also clear that there are particular yoga poses that are much more likely to result in injury than others, as I shall outline below.

I expect that anyone who has practiced yoga has at one time or another had some sort of strain or injury. But for those practicing with attention, working with proper coordination, and listening to the messages of their body, yoga is more likely to release patterns of tightness that predispose one toward injuries than to cause them. Indeed, the practice of Alexander yoga is about developing these very qualities.

However, this is frequently not how yoga is practiced. Many yoga classes are taught with insufficient care. Indeed, Broad states that many of the "star" yoga teachers suffer from serious injuries. It is well known that a number have had serious hip issues leading to a hip replacement operation. The instruction to "work through the pain" was very common twenty years ago, but fortunately it seems to be less so now. Yoga practices that resemble a gym or aerobic workout will result in more injuries than the traditional more inwardly focused and contemplative practices.

Among the examples of serious injuries that Broad lists in his book, is a man who suffered from a stroke after shoulder stand practice. In this case, doctors noted that there were bruises over his lower neck vertebrae, caused by repeated impact on the hard floor surface while doing shoulder stands. Another example is, a woman who suffered from serious and permanent nerve damage after falling asleep in *Paschimottanasana*, the seated forward bend. Yet another is, a man who suffered serious nerve damage after sitting for hours a day in *Vajrasana*, the Thunderbolt Pose, another obvious case of failing to listen to clear signals from the body.

One rare but extremely serious potential injury from yoga practice, of which I was unaware until I read this book, is the occurrence of strokes in vulnerable individuals, as a result of the blockage of the vertebral arteries while practicing headstands, shoulder stands, or extreme back bends. For many years I have removed the full shoulder stand and headstand from my yoga classes and personal practice, not because I was aware of the risk of strokes, but because the extreme pressure these poses put on the delicate vertebrae of the neck, was quite obvious to me. It seems that awareness of the potential harm of the headstand has become more widespread in recent years. The medical editor for the Yoga Journal suggests that the headstand is "too dangerous for general classes"[2] and cites this pose as the probable cause of the thoracic outlet syndrome from which he himself suffered. I will cover this further in the chapter on inversions.

These are questions to which we need to return again and again in our yoga practice. And in a class, these are questions that the teacher needs to constantly put to the students:

- "What am I noticing?"
- "Is the sensation I am feeling in this posture one of opening and expansion? or compression? or pulling?"
- "Is this sensation a 'good' one or a 'bad' one?"
- "After doing this pose in this way, do I feel more openness and expansion, or do I feel more closed, compressed, or even sore?"
- "If I feel worse after doing this posture, is the problem my coordination within the pose? Or is this pose detrimental to my body? And what do I need to do differently to gain more openness and ease?"

Working with this type of awareness greatly reduces the risk of injuries.

In the chapters on the poses, we will explore aspects of them to which we need to pay particular attention, if we are to avoid injury and experience the maximum benefit.

NOTES 1. KATZMARZYK ET AL. (2009). 2. MCCALL (2007), 449–500.

An unfortunate report from a yoga student.

"I actually originally thought I had a sports related injury so I tried doing yoga, thinking that would help, and then after a couple of weeks I was walking around and was suddenly in some of the worst pain I'd ever felt! I stopped doing it and have now been told by my physical therapist never to do yoga.

That said, I am not entirely convinced that yoga would be a bad thing, given the right circumstances. As many people have said, the main problem is that often the class is huge and the instructors don't really understand your issues. The place I went to had these cheerleader types for instructors and they were constantly saying to 'Push the stretch more! Yeah! Wow, you're doing great! And after only two weeks?!?' Now I realize what was going on and why it wasn't good. But anyway, I did feel like the core strengthening was great for me, and someday I may try again (but not at the same place, obviously!)" (From a discussion on Hypermobility Syndromes Association Forum)

BREATHING

That's not breathing. That's lifting your chest and collapsing it.
— F. M. Alexander —

✦

Anything that makes for good may be rendered harmful in its effect by injudicious application or improper use, and many authorities have referred to this fact in connection with breathing exercises.
— F. M. Alexander —

The nature and quality of the breath is recognized in both yoga and the Alexander Technique, as a key indicator of overall well-being. Breathing is a reflex activity governed primarily by the autonomic nervous system, but greatly affected by our manner of use. Conscious attempts to change our breathing pattern by such things as *pranayama,* voice training, or learning to play a wind instrument can, over time, alter the normal reflex pattern of our breathing for good, but also for ill. Just as we need to approach any overt attempt to change our breathing with a good deal of caution and a great deal of knowledge, we also need to recognize that we have already previously developed subconscious ways of voluntarily altering our breathing in the processes of eating, drinking, and speaking. In Alexander's case, it was the process of speaking that first brought his attention to his dysfunctional breathing pattern.

Breathing is affected when the sympathetic nervous system is overaroused, that is, in a state of stress, which for many people is a chronic state. When we are stressed, our bodies operate in the fight-or-flight response mode to whatever is scaring us. In an emergency, this is exactly the sort of breathing we need to be doing, but outside of a situation of real danger, it starts to take a toll on our mental, physical, and emotional well-being. In this state, people typically take short and frequent breaths, longer inhalations than exhalations, and shallow breaths into the upper chest only. The ribcage may be fixed in a frozen startle response.

For millennia it has been understood that altering the breathing can alter one's whole psychophysical state. As we shall see in Chapter 29 on mindfulness and meditation, calming one's mind by paying attention to the breath is a basic tool in Buddhist meditation, and Hatha Yoga has developed a whole field of breathing awareness and exercises called *pranayama.*

Our manner of breathing is a key aspect of the use of ourselves. When the accessory muscles are overused for breathing, typically by raising and lowering the rib cage on inhalation and exhalation, or working the abdominal muscles in the mistaken belief that this is diaphragmatic breathing, then the whole body is thrown out of balance. As Alexander describes it, once the breathing becomes disordered then "the symmetry of the body, the graceful curves of the whole frame suffer alteration and change."[1] Once this happens, the attempt to alter faulty breathing patterns without attending to our overall coordination, will be less than successful.

Physiology of Breathing

A faulty breathing pattern, however, does more than alter the overall symmetry of the body: it also deregulates our body chemistry, affecting the health of all the organs. Respiratory acidosis is a condition in which the lungs can't remove sufficient CO_2; this causes the blood to become too acidic. Much more commonplace, however, is hypocapnia, a condition in which a carbon dioxide deficiency caused by rapid shallow breathing, makes the blood overly alkaline.

Carbon dioxide is a smooth-muscle relaxant. If we have too little of it in our bodies, the smooth muscles, including those around the bronchioles in the lungs, the arterial blood vessels, and the gut, may constrict. This constriction may cause the chest tightness of asthma; contribute to high blood pressure, because the heart has to pump harder to get the blood through the constricted blood vessels; aggravate digestive disorders; and cause irritable bowel syndrome. An optimal level of carbon dioxide in the red blood cells is required for the most efficient release of oxygen to the cells. If you breathe poorly for a long time, you become accustomed to inhaling as a response to a lower level of CO_2, and the blood and interstitial fluid become chronically over-alkaline as a result. Cognitive functioning may also be impaired by this habitual hyperventilation. It is well known that restoring the CO_2 level by breathing in and out of a paper bag, will assist people who are hyperventilating and therefore suffering from a panic attack.

The Buteyko breathing method, best known as an approach for dealing with asthma, is based on raising the carbon dioxide level in the blood, by preventing overbreathing and mouth breathing. A part of this technique includes prolonged pausing after exhalation, in order to build up the CO_2 level in the body. The Alexander Technique uses the "whispered ah" technique, discussed below, as a method of training both mechanical and physiological aspects of breathing.

Ujjayi Breathing

Ujjayi breathing, a *pranayama* practice taught in some forms of Hatha Yoga, is maintaining a steady, rhythmic breath in coordination with the yoga pose being practiced. A slight, whispered "hhhaaa" sound on exhalation and inhalation is produced by a slight constriction through the throat, with the mouth remaining closed. Working in this way, avoids panting and overbreathing in the poses, and it calms the mind.

I don't use it in my practice or classes, because I prefer to ensure that both breath and body are not being strained. The first priority of the Alexander Technique is to prevent faulty patterns of use, including breathing, therefore it is essential to ensure that any breathing technique not be overlaid onto an existing faulty breathing pattern. It particularly concerns me when the *Ujjayi* breath is taught with emphasis on filling the lungs on inhalation, as this is likely to lead to over-oxygenation. In any conscious alteration of breathing, the emphasis should always be on exhalation as the precursor to an inhalation that is caused by a healthy reflex.

Pranayama

There are many *pranayama* exercises in yoga that involve combinations of: inhalation, exhalation, and *Kumbakha*, the suspension or holding of the breath, after either an inhalation or an exhalation. This suspension of the breath replicates what happens spontaneously in deep meditation states, and aims at inspiring those states.

This practice raises the CO_2 level in the blood, thereby producing physiological effects such as: reducing the heart rate, lowering blood pressure, and balancing the autonomic nervous system. You can easily perceive this change in the heart rate by checking your pulse before and after a session of *pranayama*.

Alexander's whispered "ah" technique also has the effect of increasing a low CO_2 level, and it develops reflexive inhalation rather than forced inhalation. The emphasis when practicing the whispered "ah" exercise should always be on ensuring that the entire body is fully coordinated, and therefore is free to move with the wave of the inhalation and exhalation.

Alexander's Breathing

Alexander was born pre-term and was not expected to live. The major problem with pre-term babies is that their respiratory system is not fully developed, so they have difficulty breathing. Nowadays in neonatal intensive care units babies are given respiratory assistance, but in 1869 Alexander's mother carried him around strapped to her until he had passed the critical stage.

Premature babies have to work hard just to breathe. They grunt on exhalation to keep their airway (alveoli) open. If more and more alveoli collapse with every subsequent exhalation, CO_2 increases in the blood. If they cannot compensate for that increase in CO_2 by expelling it through other chemical means, such as combining the CO_2 with bicarbonate to excrete it, then they die.

Jennifer Kellow points out, that what Alexander was doing when he experienced the loss of his voice onstage, was almost certainly a survival mechanism he had developed as a premature baby. Pulling his head back as he narrowed his back and gasped for breath, was an ingrained habit that had kept him alive as a newborn, but it was destroying his health as an adult. As Alexander describes in *Use of the Self*, once he managed to radically change his own use of himself in the process of recovering his voice, he overcame the ill health that had plagued him since childhood, including constant throat, nasal, and respiratory illnesses. Kellow writes:

> Preterm infants develop a breathing pattern based on their struggle to breathe in the first 72 hours of life. They do not breathe normally when their lungs mature because they already have a breathing pattern that previously supported their survival. Their adaptive pattern works: they breathe, they live. Successful habits survive. This pattern becomes "normal" for them. To experience truly normal breathing they would first have to stop breathing the way they are already breathing.[2]

Nowadays, as more and more pre-term infants survive from ever-younger ages, we can expect to see an increasing cohort of people suffering from difficulties similar to Alexander's. And indeed, though not all those children will end up with asthma, we have seen an astounding rise in the incidence of asthma in first-world countries over the past few decades. In the United States from 1980 to 1994 the self-reported rate of asthma rose 75 percent. From 1975 to 1995 the estimated annual number of office visits for asthma more than doubled, from 4.6 million to 10.4 million.[3] And the rate since then has continued to climb, with 8.2 percent of the population having asthma in 2009 compared to 7.3 percent in 2001.[4] Similar rises have been seen in other countries.

Breathing Exercises

When talking of babies, Kellow clearly enunciates the problem faced by anyone who breathes poorly and wishes to breathe healthfully: "To experience truly normal breathing they would first have to stop breathing the way they are already breathing."[5]

Therein lies the problem with breathing exercises: How do we stop breathing the way we are already breathing? How can we do a breathing exercise without simply empowering a faulty habit even further?

Obviously babies cannot be given an instruction to breathe differently. Once the struggle for life is over, Kellow communicates through her hands to help them release the overall contraction that accompanies their breathing. They learn they do not need that overcontraction of musculature to breathe. With this gentle guidance, once they gain the experience of breathing in the new way, the healthier pattern can then take over.

Apparently, up to two years of age the constricting breathing pattern may be easily reversed. Unfortunately, adults don't have the same degree of nervous system plasticity as newborn babies, and are unable to alter faulty breathing in such a short period of time. The Alexander Technique does give us a means of transforming unhealthy breathing patterns, albeit over a longer time period.

Breathing is not an isolated function. It is intimately connected to the overall use of the self, and trying to alter our breathing directly, is counterproductive. The first thing that requires our attention is our overall coordination. To do *pranayama* or breathing exercises, while at the same time maintaining our habitual coordination, is simply going to emphasize the faulty habit.

The Mechanics of Breathing

The movement of breathing occurs throughout the whole torso in an organized, wavelike manner. On inhalation there is interplay between the intercostal muscles, which expand the ribs up and outward, and the diaphragm, which moves downward and is pulled by the central tendon as the ribs expand. The descent of the diaphragm pushes on the abdominal and pelvic contents, which moves the abdominal wall outwards in all directions and the pelvic floor downwards. This movement of the diaphragm and rib cage then creates a vacuum in the lungs, enabling the influx of air.

On exhalation, the ribs move downwards and inwards and the diaphragm ascends, during which the pelvic floor and abdominal wall spring back. The whole spine lengthens slightly on the exhalation, provided we don't interfere with our use. Unless we are involved in an action that requires extra muscular force (such as aerobic exercise, shouting, or singing), exhalation is largely a result of the breathing muscles releasing, in conjunction with the upward pressure from the viscera, as the diaphragm releases.

The diaphragm (Figs. 22.1 and 22.2) is a dome-shaped muscle that rises up inside the ribs and divides the torso into the abdominal cavity (lower) and the thoracic cavity (upper). It is asymmetrical, with the left side slightly lower, to accommodate the heart.

The diaphragm is described as having three origins:
1. Sternal origin, from the xiphoid process of the sternum
2. Costal origin, from the interior surfaces of ribs 7 through 12 along the costal arch
3. Vertebral origin, on the front aspect of lumbar spine L1–L3 on the right, and the front aspect of L1–L2 on the left

The diaphragm also has three openings, for:
1. The esophagus, to allow the passage of food and liquids
2. The inferior vena cava, to enable blood flow to the heart
3. The aorta, to enable blood flow from the heart

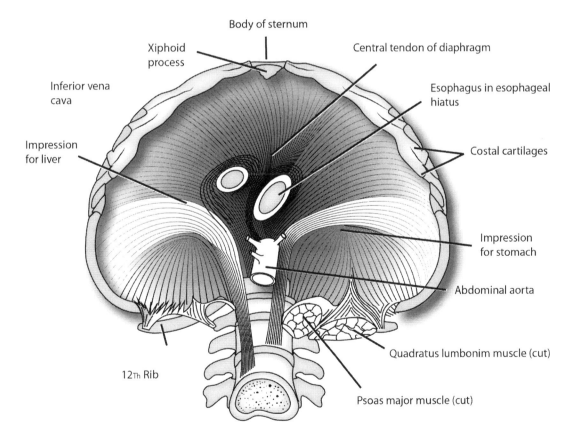

Figure 22.1

Rib movement goes hand in hand with good breathing. When the diaphragm moves, so do the ribs. However, the diaphragm is not the only muscle acting on the ribs. The external and internal intercostal muscles occupy the spaces between adjacent ribs, and are arranged atop each other in two thin layers. Neither intercostal muscle fibers nor ribs are horizontal. For this reason, if we think of moving our ribs straight in and out sideways when breathing we will only create tension.

When the diaphragm moves downward, the lower ribs move upward and outward along a curve, expanding the rib cage sideways like bucket handles being lifted. As it descends, the diaphragm pushes on the internal abdominal and pelvic contents, moving them outward against the abdominal wall in all directions: to the front, sides, and back, and downward against the pelvic floor.

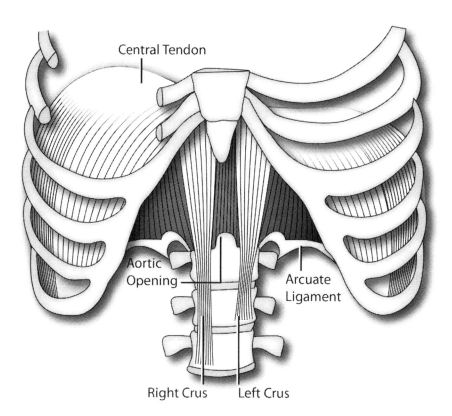

Figure 22.2

Tension in the abdominal wall dramatically limits the movement of the ribs and diaphragm, as does tension in the pelvic floor and lower back. This tension tends to be accompanied by fixing the pelvis, which occurs in conjunction with muscular holding in the buttocks and legs and locking of the knees. And indeed, all of these are part of an overall tightening and contraction through the whole body.

An opposite issue is, that the muscles of the abdomen may be overused in the act of breathing, often in the belief that this is abdominal breathing. Alexander comments on the "matronly appearance" that he observed in young girls who had been trained to breathe this way by their singing teachers. In fact, this pattern of breathing actually restricts the full movement of the diaphragm by contacting the lower back.

Common Misconceptions and Errors

In my *pranayama* practice I was instructed to draw the breath into the lower, middle, and upper parts of the torso consecutively. Although this wasn't stated, the way that I interpreted this instruction was, that breathing involved an expansion through the front of the body: the abdomen and chest. The result was, that I significantly overstretched and weakened my abdominal muscles, because of holding and overcontracting my back muscles, thus preventing the full expansion of the diaphragm.

When people tell me they are breathing "diaphragmatically" and I then ask them the location of their diaphragm, the most common response is a finger pointed at some vague spot somewhere in the front of the abdomen. Their understanding of the orientation of the diaphragm is often incorrect. Many people think it is on a vertical rather than horizontal plane within the torso. Likewise, people's conception of the location of their lungs is often below their actual location, or they sense that the lungs are located only in the front part of their chest cavity and not the upper back. Many are unaware that the very top of the lungs is higher than the clavicles (collar bones; Fig. 12.5). The subject of breathing is replete with misconceptions. Identifying these misconceptions is very important, as they affect our breathing and our ability to control or change it.

Common Misconceptions and Errors

In the process of "taking a deep breath," most people try to pull the breath in through the nose in a sort of sniffing or gasping action, and then lift their chest up and push the abdomen out. Of course, air is not inhaled by pulling it through the nose, but rather by attaining the proper expansion of the torso, which creates a vacuum, allowing the lungs to be instantly filled.

In his *New Method of Respiratory Vocal Re-education*,[5] Alexander said that when people activate this harmful breathing pattern these six things happen:

1. The larynx is depressed. If this happens on inhalation while preparing to vocalize, the natural movement of the tongue and freedom of the vocal folds are constricted, thus interfering with vocal production.
2. The upper chest is raised unduly.
3. The abdomen is protruded and the pressure through the abdominal area is not properly distributed.
4. In inhalation, the front of the body including the chest and abdomen is overexpanded and the back and lumbar area, (which need to be expanded for full excursion of the diaphragm to occur), are overcontracted.
5. In exhalation the chest collapses.
6. The neck is tightened and the head is thrown back. This pattern is often accentuated when the breath is inhaled through the mouth.

To this list Alexander added his opinion on the effect that these errors have on general health, and particularly the heart and abdominal viscera. In Figure 12.5 on page 36 we can see the intimate connection between the heart and diaphragm. The pericardium, the sack of connective tissue that encloses and protects the heart, is attached to the diaphragm. As the downward movement of the diaphragm moves all the abdominal organs, we can imagine what may happen if that movement is constantly at odds with the healthy arrangement of those organs.

In Alexander's day the mantra in physical education was to expand the chest, just as today it is to strengthen the core musculature. Here is a photo from Alexander's book *Man's Supreme Inheritance*,[6] of an unfortunate school boy who had mastered the art of "deep breathing and chest expansion" (Fig. 22.3). In Alexander's view, such exercises simply produced deformity, and looking at this picture we'll find it difficult to argue with his assessment.

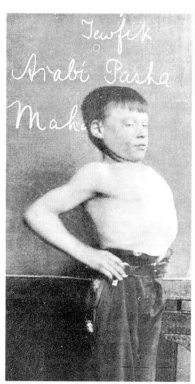

Figure 22.3

Breathing in Yoga Practice

We need to keep in mind that:

- Breathing is primarily a subconscious activity, which can be interfered with when we bring consciousness to it.
- If we interfere with it consciously for a sufficiently long period of time, we will change the underlying subconscious activity. Therefore, we need to be very careful that any change we make is beneficial rather than harmful.
- The ability of the body to move fully in breathing is affected by the underlying posture. In most people, because of collapse or overcontraction through the back, full and open breathing is not possible. Therefore, before any attempt is made to work on the breathing a process of postural and movement reeducation must be undertaken. Restoration of the breathing apparatus' ability to operate efficiently must be restored before breathing patterns can be beneficially altered.
- It is the creation of a vacuum by the expansion of the thorax, along with the downward movement of the diaphragm, that operates to bring in the breath. Trying to pull in the breath through the nose or mouth simply dis-coordinates both body and breath.
- Although we can expand and compress the upper torso through movement and posture, and thus reduce or increase the volume of the lungs and rib cage, the cavities below the diaphragm can change in shape but not in volume. The path of least resistance for this area, especially if a faulty habit of use has developed, tends to be to push the abdomen forward. But we need to develop the ability to expand both sideways and backward. Look closely at the area below the diaphragm of the abdominal and pelvic cavities and you may be surprised by the overall shape (Fig. 22.4).

- Most people are tight and contracted through the lower back, and thus limiting the potential expansion of the floating ribs and full movement of the diaphragm. Alexander's direction to lengthen and widen the back, accompanied by freeing the neck and releasing the head forward and upward, further optimizes this mobility.
- Emphasis should always be on exhalation and avoiding any overinhalation by letting inhalation simply be a reflex one.

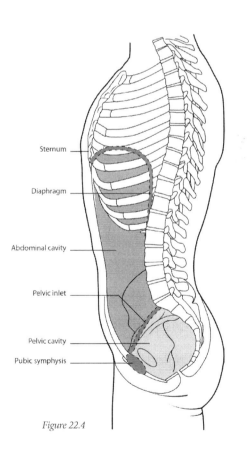

Sternum

Diaphragm

Abdominal cavity

Pelvic inlet

Pelvic cavity

Pubic symphysis

Figure 22.4

The "Whispered Ah"

Although Alexander spoke of respiratory reeducation, it may be best to simply call it "education" as some people, including Alexander, may never have experienced healthy breathing. Alexander recognized that faulty breathing was part of an overall pattern of stress and dis-coordination. It was clear to him that the first step in restoring adequate breathing is to achieve a basic level of ease and coordination, which establishes the conditions for healthy breathing. But he also recognized that this may not be enough in itself, so he developed a procedure known as the "whispered ah," which, among other things, consciously provides the autonomic nervous system with the information it needs to reset a faulty breathing pattern.

When we practice the "whispered ah," it is essential that the whole body be in a state of ease and coordination. Therefore, it is not recommended to practice it until reasonably good use of the self has been established. I often teach it to new students whilst they are in the semisupine position. (See Chapter 31 for a description of this position.)

This is both a vocal and a breathing exercise, in which one can work with the freedom of the jaw and tongue and the flexibility of the soft palate. Once the ability to coordinate the primary control is established, then one can begin to focus on properly coordinating the tongue, jaw, soft palate, and face, within the overall coordination. This coordination supports maintaining a precise balance of tension and relaxation through the vocal folds, so that the whispered sound has no roughness in it whatsoever. Any tension in these areas, or any excessive pushing from the diaphragm, will be reflected in a certain tension in the sound of the "ah."

In stressed breathing, inhalations are longer than exhalations. In the whispered "ah," this is reversed. The emphasis is on lengthening the out-breath, but only to a point where there is no strain. In the beginning, it is often difficult for people to lengthen the exhalation without straining, but as they continue to work carefully and attentively, a free-and-easy, lengthened out-breath gradually becomes available. On the exhalation one whispers an "ah." It is vital that at the end of the "ah" the next inhalation be a reflex, not a habitual gasping for air. Gasping for breath leads not only to muscular tightening, but also to over-oxygenation of the blood, and all the concomitant problems that this creates. People who have a strong tendency to gasp for breath are encouraged to pause before inhaling, to ensure that the next inhalation happens completely by reflex.

This is a procedure that cannot be adequately expressed in writing, as the appropriate instructions will be related to exactly what is happening in the moment. If you want to experiment with this, note that it should be done as an experiment rather than through mindless repetition. The quality of the sound yields good feedback about the procedure's efficacy. You need to catch any tendency toward overcontraction as you exhale, and always wait for the inhalation to occur as a natural reflex. Many people with asthma find that after as little as two or three rounds of inhalation and exhalation, they are forced to top up their breath with a quick gasp. People with severe asthma may need weeks or months to gradually extend the number of breaths they can do easily, and in the process the asthma is likely to improve.

NOTES 1. ALEXANDER (1910, 1946), 190. 2. KELLOW (2008), 254. 3. MANNINO (1998). 4. CENTERS FOR DISEASE CONTROL AND PREVENTION (2011). 5. ALEXANDER (1906, 2001), 60–61. 6. ALEXANDER (1910, 1946), 89.

AUTONOMIC NERVOUS SYSTEM

The management of anger and fear (which belong to the limbic system) is . . . crucial.
There is no yogic type system that does not seek to intervene in the prevention of these
two demonstrably destructive emotions.

— *Georg Feuerstein* —

Your hand opens and closes, opens and closes. If it were always a fist or always stretched open, you
would be paralyzed. Your deepest presence is in every small contracting and expanding, the two as
beautifully balanced and coordinated as birds' wings.

— *Rumi* —

The enormous popularity of yoga is undoubtedly due to its capacity to calm the nervous system. Those of us who practice yoga don't need research to tell us that, as we have experienced it directly.

The autonomic nervous system (ANS) controls the activities of organs, glands, and various involuntary muscles, such as cardiac and smooth muscles. The autonomic nervous system consists of:

- The sympathetic nervous system (Fig. 23.1), which stimulates activities that prepare the body for action and trigger the fight, flight, or freeze reactions. Designed to prepare us to defend ourselves or retreat from danger, this system activates many preparatory responses such as increasing the heart rate and releasing sugar from the liver into the blood.
- The parasympathetic nervous system (Fig. 23.2), which activates functions that occur when the system is more at rest and in a state of safety, including stimulation of saliva and digestive enzyme secretion and sexual arousal.

Both aspects of the ANS are obviously vital for our survival, but in our culture the sympathetic nervous system is in overdrive for many people. In this overactive state people feel themselves to be in a state of "chronic stress." Patanjali, in yoga sutra I:31, accurately outlines the symptoms of the autonomic nervous system in sympathetic overload: "physical and mental pain, negative mental states, bodily restlessness and instability, disordered breathing, and distraction." In his writings, Alexander uses the term "unduly excited fear reflexes" to refer to this overstimulation of the sympathetic nervous system, and he identified this state as a significant hindrance to people's ability to learn how to change their fixed habit patterns in an Alexander lesson.

Sympathetic System

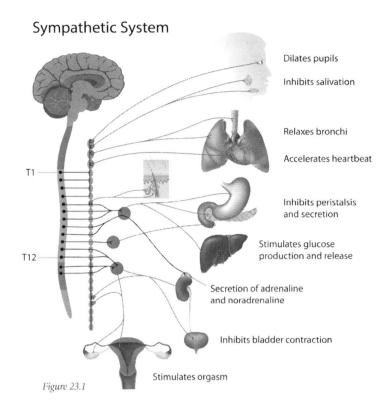

Dilates pupils

Inhibits salivation

Relaxes bronchi

Accelerates heartbeat

Inhibits peristalsis
and secretion

Stimulates glucose
production and release

Secretion of adrenaline
and noradrenaline

Inhibits bladder contraction

Stimulates orgasm

T1

T12

Figure 23.1

Both yoga and the Alexander Technique work on balancing the autonomic nervous system, but because the autonomic nervous system is involved in visceral, hormonal, glandular, and involuntary muscular functions that are outside our conscious control, we can affect these functions only indirectly. Indeed, Alexander referred to his technique as constituting an "indirect procedure" that would remove not only our interference with the normal reflexes underlying posture and movement, but also interference with the healthy functioning of the breathing mechanism and all the organs and glands of the body.

Parasympathetic System

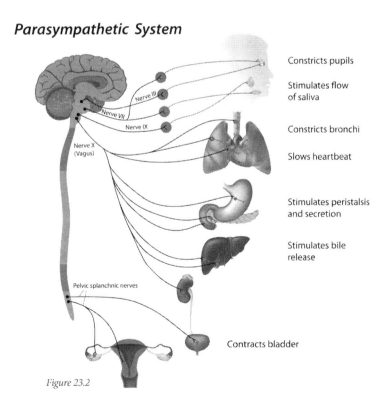

Constricts pupils

Stimulates flow
of saliva

Constricts bronchi

Slows heartbeat

Stimulates peristalsis
and secretion

Stimulates bile
release

Contracts bladder

Nerve III

Nerve VII

Nerve IX

Nerve X
(Vagus)

Pelvic splanchnic nerves

Figure 23.2

— *Yoga* —

One way in which the ANS is affected by yoga practice is as a result of stretching muscles. Although it is easily experienced by practitioners, the precise processes by which this works scientifically, are not well studied or understood. A study on the effects of stretching on heart rate variability found that "the parasympathetic activity rapidly increased after stretching, whereas the sympathetic activity increased during exercise and had a slower post-exercise reduction. Stretching sessions, including multiple exercises and sets, acutely changed the sympathovagal balance in subjects with low flexibility, especially enhancing the post-exercise vagal modulation."[1] In layperson's language, stretching is good for the heart. Here are some other ways in which yoga practice can calm the ANS:

- *Savasana*, or Corpse Pose. This pose, which can induce a deep state of relaxation, is a staple in all forms of Hatha Yoga.
- Consciously working with the breathing can calm the nervous system. The emphasis in yoga is on breathing smoothly while practicing yoga asanas, and Hatha Yoga has a complex array of breathing exercises collectively known as *pranayama*.
- Meditation is another means by which the ANS can be balanced. There are many meditation practices, but any act of focusing the attention can have a marked calming effect. This is covered further in the chapter on meditation.
- The quality of our interactions with the world: our interpersonal relationships, how we earn our livelihood, and our orientation toward living our lives, which are referred to in the first two limbs of Patanjali's yoga and the first five steps of the Buddha's eightfold path, form an essential foundation for gaining any sort of balance or serenity.

— *Alexander Technique* —

On a muscular level, the Alexander Technique works by inhibiting dysfunctional muscular contractions and bringing the body into a state of dynamic alignment in which only the appropriate muscles are working to maintain our upright stance. There are number of ways in which the Alexander Technique can balance the ANS:

- Inhibiting the faulty breathing patterns that accompany and perpetuate sympathetic nervous system overdrive brings the sympathetic nervous system into balance.
- Alexander's whispered "ah" has the effect of increasing a low CO_2 level, and it develops reflexive inhalation rather than forced inhalation. The emphasis when practicing the whispered "ah" exercise is always on making sure that the entire body is fully coordinated, and therefore free to move with the wave of the inhalation and exhalation.

- Sympathetic nervous system overdrive is accompanied by collapse or muscular holding and contraction. The process of bringing the body to a state of equilibrium in both stillness and movement is a powerful factor in balancing the sympathetic and parasympathetic systems.
- On the mental and emotional levels, bringing attention to habitual patterns of thought and reaction, (which cause both bodily and emotional discoordination), is the beginning of cultivating the ability to change these patterns. As Alexander describes it, the technique is primarily about changing our reaction patterns, and not about directly trying to relax.

The Problem with Relaxation

In the Alexander Technique, we tend to avoid the term *relaxation* because students usually interpret this as an overall lessening of muscle tone, which can lead to discoordination and collapse. Alexander gives a definition of relaxation that differs from what is frequently meant by the term:

> Relaxation really means a due tension of the parts of the muscular system intended by nature to be constantly more or less tensed, together with a relaxation of those parts intended by nature to be more or less relaxed, a condition which is readily secured in practice by adopting . . . the position of mechanical advantage.[2]

> Alexander uses the term "position of mechanical advantage" to refer to a position like the monkey pose which allows for optimal openness and expansion throughout the body.

Relaxation in his sense of the term is inseparable from proper and efficient coordination of the whole body, and consistent with a proper balance of the sympathetic and parasympathetic nervous systems. When we say that a runner has a relaxed style of running or a singer a relaxed way of singing, what we are observing is economy of movement and functioning. This efficiency results in an impression of ease, despite the large amount of muscular work involved in those activities.

So in bringing the Alexander Technique to our yoga practice, both to the more active practice of yoga poses and to the still work of *pranayama* and meditation, we want to develop this quality of ease and proper coordination. This refines our ability to observe and undo any excess that we are bringing into our practice, and into our daily life. The type of relaxation that involves letting go of everything, with its overemphasis on the parasympathetic nervous system, is not one that can be incorporated into daily life.

NOTES 1. FARINATTI ET AL. (2011), 1579. 2. ALEXANDER (1910, 1946), 14.

TENSEGRITY

The term *tensegrity*, coined by Buckminster Fuller, is a combination of two words, tension and integrity. Civil engineer Landolf Rhode-Barbarigos describes the term as "systems in stable self-equilibrated states comprising a discontinuous set of compressed components inside a continuum of tensioned components."[1]

If this description is somewhat opaque, look at Figure 24.1. What we have here is a structure composed of solid struts, none of which are connected to each other but all of which are held in dynamic relationship by tensioned cords. If I pick this model up and squeeze it, I will deform the existing shape, but once the pressure is taken off, the tensioned cords will restore its original shape. Without the sticks, the network of strings would have no shape, and without the strings the sticks would collapse to the ground.

Figure 24.1

The opposite of tensegrity structures are compression structures. These are the architectural structures with which we are very familiar: columns, walls, temples, houses, etc. In compression structures, support is created through direct weight-bearing, one object on top of another. Unlike with the tensegrity structure, where the tensile members distribute the strain evenly throughout the structure, the lower elements of compression structures bear all the force of those above them. Tensegrity structures are lightweight and can easily support the solid components of a structure without the need for stacking. As we can see from the column of blocks in Figure 24.2, we would need to displace only one of the blocks very slightly and the whole structure would fall to the ground.

Figure 24.2

Biotensegrity

Figure 24.3

Figure 24.4

The idea of the body as a tensegrity structure is part of a relatively new and emerging paradigm. Details are still being worked out, and acceptance of the concept among those who know of it is far from universal. But even if we don't accept the body as being a pure tensegrity structure, it is undoubtedly a "tension dependent" structure. And the insights from this model of looking at the structure and functioning of the body are certainly fruitful and furnish better explanations for numerous phenomena than the traditional biomechanical model.

Stephen Levin worked for many years as an orthopedic surgeon and became dissatisfied with the anatomical model he had been taught. Levin reports that the "Needle Tower" (Fig. 24.3), a sculpture by Kenneth Snelson, inspired his study of biotensegrity. He had been studying dinosaur skeletons and attempting to comprehend how their great size could be organized according to current theories of animal structure and movement. As Levin explained, the Tower enabled him to realize that its articulation of floating islands of compression in a comprehensive tension net was a more elegant explanation than the classic lever and fulcrum. He contacted Snelson and began his long career of research and publication on the subject.[2]

Tom Flemons of Intension Designs has been creating tensegrity models for decades and has recently focused on developing designs based on human anatomical structures (Fig. 24.4).

The work of Thomas W. Myers has popularized the idea of myofascial "meridians," or vertical and spiral lines of mechanical tension through the body that need to be in a dynamic balanced relationship with each other for the body to be ideally balanced. Myers does not, however, accept that the body is a "pure" tensegrity structure.[3]

As we have discussed in the chapter on flexibility, much of our muscle elasticity is a function of our nervous systems, and is for the most part present only when we are conscious. When a person is anesthetized, virtually all muscle tone is lost, and the body can be moved into positions not attainable while the person is conscious. Nonetheless, the tensegrity model offers very fruitful insights into the body's structure and movement.

Reeducation

Alexander referred to his teaching as being a "reeducation" of coordination: a return to a preexisting state that we have lost. There appears to be an underlying genetic template for coordination, which is achieved by all normal children in the process of attaining upright posture and movement. The initial process of balancing on two feet is so unsteady at first that everything needs to be accurately aligned for optimal balance. Once we have attained balance and are able to maintain an upright posture, we can interfere with this balance without falling over. Unfortunately, for most of us it takes only a few short years before we experience serious interference in this balance (Fig. 24.5).

If you look at the little girl in Figure 24.2, you can see a somewhat unsteady balance in which all parts of the body are in dynamic alignment. From a tensegrity perspective the balance of the head on top of the spine organizes the bones of the skeleton in just the right way to promote an optimal level of stretch through the musculature. In addition, from a biomechanical perspective we can see that in this position all the structures are stacked on top of each other in the most efficient way to maintain the upright posture, in relation to gravity. In Figure 24.5 we can see a typical situation in which this interference with dynamic alignment begins. There is a shortening through the front of the torso to compensate for the backward movement of the torso. This is accompanied by a rounding of the back and a tightening through the legs. These conditions, when repeated over a long enough period of time, will begin to habituate the nervous system, muscles, ligaments, and connective tissue to a much less functional pattern. This suboptimal pattern will include overstretch in some muscles and lines of connection, and overcontraction in others.

Figure 24.5

Maintaining Elasticity

A major focus of the Alexander Technique is restoring elasticity and tone to the musculature and connective tissue. It is impossible to immediately regain optimal posture if certain groups of muscles and connective tissue are being held in chronic contraction while other groups are overstretched.

The stretch reflex plays an important role in allowing or preventing muscle movement. The stretch reflex also plays a critical role in maintaining muscle tone, as well as, responsiveness to unexpected external mechanical force.

Put very simply, our muscles contain muscle spindles, receptors that are sensitive to stretch. When a muscle is stretched, a message is sent to the spinal cord, which responds by sending a message back to the muscle commanding it to contract. The most common example of this is the response that occurs when a doctor hits the patellar ligament with a reflex hammer (Fig. 24.6). This stretches the muscle spindles in the quadriceps femoris, which send a message directly to the spinal cord at the level of L4. Then, without the intervention of any higher nervous system centers, this message is processed and an impulse to contract the muscle is sent from the spinal cord, resulting in the "knee–jerk" reaction.

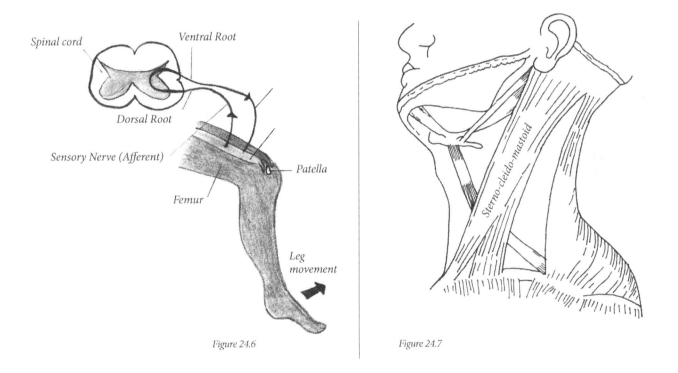

Figure 24.6

Figure 24.7

We have two types of muscle spindles. One type produces the strong knee-jerk reaction and is sensitive to both muscle stretch and velocity. The other type responds to muscle length changes, but with less sensitivity to velocity. The constant activity of this reflex arc maintains muscle tone and holds the various body parts in their proper relationship to each other.

For example, the head is positioned on the top of the spine with the weight of the skull sitting forward of the atlanto-occipital joint (Fig. 12.1). This creates a constant forward pull of gravity on the head, which we notice when we "nod off." When we are upright the head is constantly supported by the muscles at the back of the neck, with the aid of the nuchal ligament. But rather than the neck forcibly contracting in response to a stretch, as the quadratis femoris does with the knee-jerk reaction, there is a very delicate process whereby the muscles maintain their length while just a few groups of muscle fibers are recruited for short periods of time. Before these muscles tire, other groups of muscle fibers take over to support the head in turn. This process of "asynchronous stimulation" is operating in all the postural muscles when we are upright.

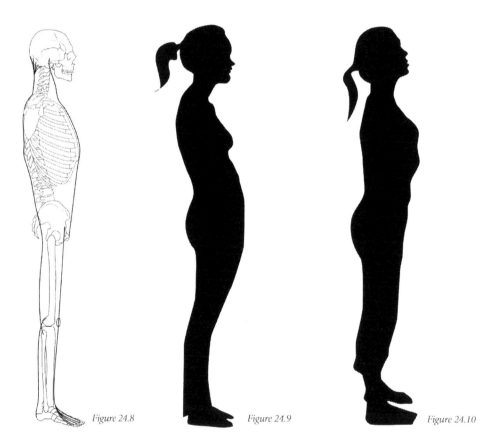

Figure 24.8   *Figure 24.9*   *Figure 24.10*

In an ideal situation, the head releases forward and upward within this delicate interplay of gravity and the tonic action of the muscles. As the head releases forward and upward, the weight of the head causes a stretch through the sternocleidomastoid (SCM) muscles (Fig. 24.7) and the back of the torso. The SCM attaches to the muscular and fascial connection through the front of the body, which Myers refers to as the "superficial front line." According to Myers, the postural balance between the front and back of the body is primarily determined by the relationship, either easy or tense, between this superficial front line and the superficial back line.[4] Figure 24.8 demonstrates the position of the front and back lines in upright posture. If we lose this stretch through the torso by, for example, pulling the head back and down, then there is a collapse through both the front and back lines (Fig. 24.9). We lose the "antagonistic pulls" that in a properly coordinated body would activate stretches through both the flexors and extensors for balance. These stretches are optimally accompanied by a spiral expansion through the torso as the back simultaneously lengthens and widens. There are many permutations of ways we can interfere with the optimal antagonistic pulls. In Figure 24.10 we see another very common pattern, called "standing up straight," where the backline is shortened and compressed and the frontline is overstretched. Figure 24.11 gives us a look at more possibilities for distorting ourselves.

In addition to the activity of the stretch reflex, the physical properties of muscles and ligaments lend us support. In Chapter 38 we look in some detail at the mechanical support supplied to the spine by the ligaments, as well as the process by which these ligaments lose their elasticity through long-term misuse. According to Masi and colleagues, there is also a passive tonus of skeletal muscle with intrinsic viscoelastic properties independent of the stretch reflex: "Normal passive muscle tone helps to maintain relaxed standing body posture with minimally increased energy costs (circa 7 percent over supine), and often for prolonged durations without fatigue."[5]

Figure 24.11

The difference between the mathematical precision of an inanimate tensegrity structure such as Figure 24.1 and the shapes that human beings manifest, is striking. If Masi is correct, the normal passive tone of various muscles and muscle groups has the possibility of creating grotesquely deformed structures. The caricatures in Figure 24.11 are immediately recognizable from our everyday experience. If we use the tensegrity model as a metaphor for how our bodies are designed and structured, we have to recognize that our everyday use of ourselves imposes severe strains on that design and structure, often to the point of major deformation. There was originally a much more balanced relationship of the body parts, such as that normally seen in small children, before these deformities set in (Fig. 24.2). If we can alter this overall misalignment, beginning with the balance of the head on top of the spine and continuing through to the balance of the torso, pelvis, and legs over the feet, we can begin to restore elasticity and aliveness in the muscles and therefore the whole person.

Humans move with the spine vertical to the ground; four-footed animals such as horses have their spine horizontal to the ground. The concept of the head leading the movement is therefore much clearer in these animals. The head of a four-footed animal is even more strongly under the pull of gravity because of the forward positioning.

Looking at horse anatomy and movement is instructive, and it is perhaps not surprising that Alexander was a keen and skillful horseman. Horses need to be trained to carry a rider, because the weight might otherwise collapse their lumbar area and seriously interfere with their primary control, or what dressage riders refer to as "correct outline." Whereas humans have a relatively small nuchal ligament, horses have a large one, which furnishes powerful support for the head. When the horse's head is "forward and down," there is a powerful stretch through the nuchal and supraspinous ligaments, which creates a strong elastic connection between the head and pelvis. This raises the spinal processes of the withers (the highest point of the thoracic spine, between the shoulder blades) and this stretch raises and widens the back. As in well-coordinated humans, this forward-acting force is opposed by a backward elastic force from the pelvis, creating an opposing pull through these lines of expansion. There is a connected stretch through the front line of the horse: when the neck flexor muscles are used correctly there is a corresponding elastic pull through the horse's abdominal muscles, which tilts the pelvis forward and allows the hind legs to step more under the body and help lift the back.

In badly coordinated human beings, as in badly trained horses, the head does not offer tensile support for the muscles and tendons through the neck and torso. Instead, its position causes this pull to be lost. Frequently, the muscles of the neck are contracted and the head is pulled back and down. The suboccipital muscles (Fig. 24.12) are the deep muscle layer that connects the head to the first two vertebrae of the neck. They have the highest density of muscle spindles in the body, which means they are designed to optimally monitor and regulate the balance of the head on top of the spine. However, when the head gets pulled back and down, this action of the larger muscles of the neck interferes with the proprioceptive and feedback functions of these smaller deep muscles, and they become shortened, inelastic, and insensitive to stretch.

This process of discoordination and interference continues throughout the musculature of the whole body. We can see the process happening right down to the legs and feet, with the common pattern of the pelvis tilted forward, knees locked, weight thrown back on the ankle joints, or forward onto the front of the foot, and the feet collapsed. Instead of the muscles having the quality of elasticity required to maintain the integrity of a tensegrity system, some tighten and contract, others become slack, and the whole system is thrown out of balance.

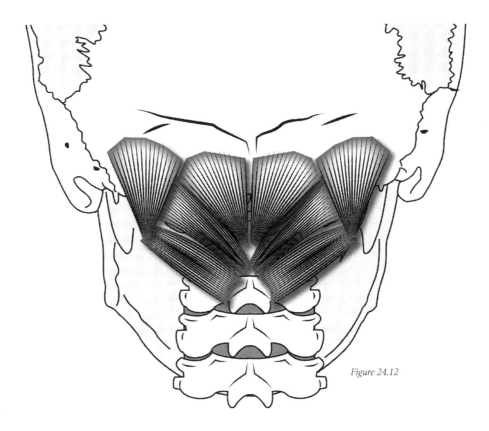

Figure 24.12

Joints

Tensegrity structures are ones in which the struts (the bones) do not support each other but rather are supported in a tensile web (muscles and connective tissue). According to Levin and Flemons, however, the connecting bones are not primarily separated by intervening discs, menisci cartilage, etc., but are actively held separate by the compressive wrapping of the fascia: "In vertebrates the skeleton would be compression elements within a highly organized soft tissue construct rather than the frame supporting an amorphous soft tissue mass."[6] This is a structure with a lot of potential spring and expansion.

The geometry of this is pretty complex. It is difficult to see how this process can work for a joint like the knee joint. In fact Myers could find no evidence of how this could possibly work in the knee joint. However, during Levin's arthroscopic surgery on his own knee, once the synovial fluid had been drained he put direct loading on the knee and a gap still remained between the bone surfaces.[7] As he points out, the menisci (cartilages of the knee) could not possibly survive the repeated impact forces of running a single marathon if they were compressively loaded. In regard to the spine, Flemons explains:

> The thoracolumbar fascia wraps the vertebral bodies in diagonal and lateral strands like a woven sleeve with multiple attachments to the vertebrae. Pre-stress maintains the integrity of the spine and slight contractions laterally or even diagonally can extend it, ameliorating compressive loading, separating the vertebrae and sparing the discs. The geometry of the vertebral bodies themselves in the thoracic and lumbar spine bears resemblance to a Fuller tensegrity mast.[8] (Figs. 24.3 and 24.4)

In Figure 24.13 Flemons's design illustrates the suspension of the discs and vertebral bodies in a fascial wrapping.

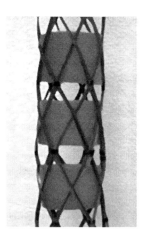

Figure 24.13   *Figure 24.14*

Humans can carry very large weights on the head, which sends compression directly through the vertebral column, and we can potentially do so with a good deal of grace and ease if the body is properly aligned (Fig. 24.14). Indeed, if the head is moving forward and up and the whole body is following this movement, the response to carrying something on the head is like a spring being loaded with weight. There is counterforce rising up to meet that weight.

However, if we pull the head out of alignment, the whole spine is immediately compressed. Instead of pressing down on a vertically aligned spring, it is as though we have bent the spring in the middle and all resistance has gone out of it.

Elasticity

Much of the work in the Alexander Technique is aimed at restoring elasticity and tone to the body: a training in re-establishing dynamic and balanced opposing stretches in the body. As Levin says, "tendons and bone can store large amounts of energy and return it like a spring in leaps and bounds."[9] Processes like the Monkey Pose, when done correctly, activate "antagonistic muscular actions."[10] These involve mutual lengthening of the flexors and extensors, which avoids the domination of one over the other, as well as activation along spiraling lines of expansion. My approach to the yoga poses is based on this principle of working with and restoring this dynamic balance.

All tensegrity structures have stored energy; they are prestressed. The image of the body as a spring mechanism is a useful one to hold in mind. We are sprung right from the contact of our feet with the ground (Fig. 24.15). The arch of the well-formed foot is like a bow, with the plantar fascia as a bow string that stretches from the tuberosity of the calcaneus (heel) to the head of the metatarsal bones. When the weight of the body is centered over the talus bone, and thus spread through the foot, a powerful upward force is generated. In addition, we get a powerful upward stretch from the weight of the head moving forward and up and the resultant expansion of the torso. Refining the primary control is all about getting all the body parts to function in relation to each other, in a manner that fosters both the optimal stretch and springiness of the muscles, as well as the connective tissue, allowing us to move with ease and grace.

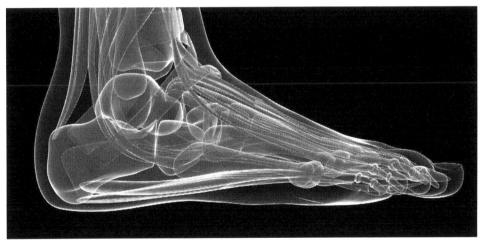

Figure 24.15

NOTES **1**. RHODE-BARBARIGOS (2011) **2**. LEVIN, *TENSEGRITY, WIKISPACES* (N.D.). **3**. MYERS (2012). **4**. IBID., 93. **5**. MASI ET AL. (2008). **6**. LEVIN, *TENSEGRITY: THE NEW BIOMECHANICS* (N.D.). **7**. LEVIN (2006). **8**. FLEMONS (2012). **9**. LEVIN, *TENSEGRITY: THE NEW BIOMECHANICS* (N.D.). **10**. ALEXANDER (1910, 1946), 125.

MOVEMENT MUSCLES, POSTURAL MUSCLES, AND ENERGY FLOW

Some forms of "modern yoga," as developed in India and the West in the past hundred years or so, have a strong anatomical emphasis. By contrast, in traditional Hatha Yoga practices the emphasis is on activating and directing energy flows through the body. In Alexander yoga we bring awareness to how these poses open up these energy flows through the body.

It is important to know that we have two types of voluntary musculature, which ideally carry out two different functions. First, there are what we may call the "movement muscles." These have a greater concentration of fast-twitch white muscle fibers, which can work rapidly and strongly but fatigue quickly. Then there are the "postural muscles," which have a predominance of slow-twitch red muscle fibers. These muscle fibers do not contract as quickly and strongly as the fast-twitch muscles, but they can continue contracting over long periods of time without fatiguing.

Ideally, we want to use the slow-twitch muscles for support and the fast-twitch muscles for movement. Learning how to turn off unnecessary activation of the movement muscles and allowing the postural muscles to activate immediately establishes a sense of springiness, lightness, and energy flow through the body. These slow-twitch fibers, along with the ligaments, create elastic support for our posture. When people use the movement muscles to try to hold themselves up, they both appear and feel stiff. This is regardless of how "correct" the pose may seem to be, from a biomechanical point of view.

For example, when you respond to the instruction to "pull your shoulders back" or "pull your shoulder blades back and down," you engage superficial muscles of the upper arms, neck, and shoulder girdle as if they were postural muscles. In response to this engagement, the nervous system sends messages to the rest of the body to do whatever is necessary to sustain upright posture, despite the interference you have imposed on your natural coordination. This inevitably creates a whole pattern of compensatory tightening.

Many people walk out of their first Alexander Technique lesson with a light, even floating, sensation. This is a result of the Alexander teacher working with the student to begin turning off the excess tension and overactivation of the movement muscles, and turning on the connection throughout the whole body in a way that enhances access to its natural springiness. This gives us the sensation of a free flow of energy throughout the body.

The Alexander Technique teaches us to recognize unnecessary and inappropriate muscular work, so that the movement muscles are not activated unless they are required for a particular task, and the deep postural muscles are recruited for their proper task of central coordination and support. These postural muscles include the very deepest layer of muscles around the spinal column, which cannot be activated directly. We can access them only indirectly, by:

- Learning to turn off any unnecessary work being done by the movement muscles.
- Then establishing a delicate rebalancing of the head on top of the spine, and sending conscious direction for length and expansion without trying to "do" this.

This attention to a proper balance of the head on top of the spine has a most positive global effect on the whole body, which is understandable when we consider its weight of 4.5 to 5 kg (10 to 11 lbs.). If our head is misaligned, everything below will have to compensate for this misalignment.

Also involved in upright posture are the larger, more superficial extensor muscles of the back. The thoracic portion of these muscles contains 75 percent red muscle fibers, while the lumbar portion contains 50 percent red and 50 percent white muscle fibers. According to Stuart McGill, who has done a significant amount of research in this area: "The thoracic components of the longissimus and iliocostalis follow a line of action parallel to the compressive axis of the spine and just underneath the skin. This provides the greatest amount of extensor movement with a minimum of compressive penalty to the spine." These muscles extend both the thoracic and lumbar spine, because their long tendons run parallel to the spine, to the posterior surface of the sacrum, and the medial border of the iliac crests. He adds that the great weightlifters "have visible bulk in the extensors of the thoracic area."[1] Figure 40.2 on page 195 illustrates the location of the longissimus and iliocostalis muscle groups.

However, what we tend to see is that the majority of people overuse their lumbar extensors in an attempt to sit or stand upright. This overextension of the lumbar spine is part of a pattern that includes:

- Pulling the head back and down, often in the mistaken belief that the head is being lifted up;
- Lifting the sternum and ribcage forward, often in the mistaken belief that this is what is needed to "stand straight";
- Overcontraction of the lumbar curve;
- Backward displacement of the head by overcontracting the cervical spine; and,
- Forward fixation of the sternum and rib cage.

Chronic contraction of the lumbar extensors when standing, combined with the habit of overflexion of the lumbar area when bending and sitting, contributes powerfully to lower back pain and dysfunction.

It is unfortunate that we frequently see this exact pattern in yoga classes, for example while standing in *Tadasana*, or the Mountain Pose, which is discussed in Chapter 32.

Improving Posture

Once we have interfered with our coordination, and the underlying reflexes, and connective tissue springiness supporting that coordination, attainment of poised upright posture becomes a much more complex task than is normally conceived. How then, can we develop better upright posture as a support for all our movements?

First, we need to have a clear understanding of common misconceptions about what it means to be upright. In particular we need to focus on those resulting in recruiting the movement muscles, and the subsequent excess tension that is commonly created by doing this. By undoing this excess tension, we will tend to move toward a quality of ease, as well as better overall alignment. This is dealt with in more detail in Chapter 32 on the Mountain Pose *(Tadasana)*.

Second, we need to understand that the well-coordinated body is a system that has its own intrinsic springiness, right from the soles of the feet through to the head on top of the spine, and this easy upright pose is about accessing this system of "springs", rather than using muscles to place it into the "correct" position.

Third, by using mirrors (ideally two, one in the front and one at the side so that the one mirror reflects you in profile into the other mirror) you can begin to explore your own sensory awareness and to work out whether this sensory awareness of what you are doing, is accurate or not. Indeed, this was how Alexander discovered that his processing of the kinesthetic and proprioceptive information he was receiving was, in fact, inaccurate. He also used mirrors in the process of restoring reliable sensory awareness, which he describes in *Use of the Self*.

Fourth, if you want to develop and refine your ability and skill in this area, you could have Alexander lessons with a qualified teacher who will work with you individually. You could also attend Alexander yoga classes if they are available in your area, or at least work with a yoga teacher who has a refined understanding of coordination.

NOTE   1. MCGILL (2009), 70.

CORE STRENGTH

Normal movement does not consist of isolated actions that are cortically (consciously) controlled.
It is a sequence of synergic movement patterns that are functionally related. Evidence shows that
poor movement patterns can lead to low back disorders.

— *Theo Mulder and Wouter Hulstyn*[1] —

The concept of the "core", core strengthening and stability came into vogue in yoga practice in the 1990s. In the three decades prior, I had never heard the term used by any yoga teachers. The idea of working specifically on "core postural muscles" has been widely critiqued since it entered the realm of sports training and rehabilitation. Studies on sports training have been unable to demonstrate that training individual muscle actions enhances skilled, complex movement. The evidence for the usefulness of such training is also contested in the area of back pain treatment and rehabilitation.

Alexander's critique of the remedial physical exercise practiced in his time, and the mindset that underlies focusing on one body part, raises questions that are as relevant today as they were when he was working. Obviously the torso needs to be stabilized to a degree that depends on the activity, but this stability should arise out of sound postural organization supported by natural reflex activity, and it should complement natural functional movement.

Although the idea of strengthening the core muscles is ubiquitous in popular culture, most people have only a very vague idea of what these "core" muscles are, including a limited notion of how they operate and why we would want to strengthen them. There is a common belief that the core muscles are the muscles of the abdomen. The internal obliques are almost always included in the list of core muscles, as is the multifidus. To these are frequently added the muscles of the pelvic floor and the internal and external obliques. Contributors to a Wikipedia article on this topic have included as additional core muscles the rectus abdominis, the erector spinae, and the diaphragm. And for good measure someone has added "minor core muscles": the latissimus dorsi, the gluteus maximus, and the trapezius![2] Indeed, in its popular usage the core is a very vague term.

Senior Anusara yoga teacher Desirée Rumbaugh describes the core as "what supports us spiritually in our lives, and physically in our yoga practice. If our core is weak, the ups and downs of life are much harder to take. A strong core makes us more resilient."[3] Alexander teachers commonly talk about the vital importance of being emotionally and psychologically supported by a strong back, which is a similar concept. The Alexander approach, however, is to indirectly develop the strength and stability of the entire torso by creating proper coordination of the head on top of the spine, and a proper relationship between all the joints from the head to the feet.

The Confusion of Cause and Effect

There is a mountain of research about the deep multifidus muscle demonstrating that wasting of this muscle is *associated with* back pain. It has also been clearly demonstrated that failure to activate the internal obliques, in simple tasks requiring stabilization of the torso, is *associated with* lower back pain. But it is a leap of faith to say that particular muscle weaknesses or the failure of a specific muscle or muscle group to activate, is the cause of the back pain. The Alexander approach would postulate the overall neuromuscular coordination (the use of the self) as a cause, and further identify specific alterations of muscle physiology or function as an effect of that misuse.

Attempts to strengthen the muscles that are believed to be at fault, or asking people to directly tighten, contract, or engage these muscles in their everyday activities, is not going to bring about proper coordination. And even if tightening these muscles relieves a person's back pain, can it be done without further discoordination of the posture? In the long run, is this not likely to create further problems? It is not uncommon for people to attend Alexander lessons for neck pain about a year after they begin to hold on to their abdominals. Bracing may be an excellent strategy for an acute situation, but it is not a long-term solution.

Core Strengthening and Pelvic Floor Exercises After Childbirth

A rationale for core stability after childbirth is that when the pelvic floor and abdominal muscles have been stretched and disengaged, they need to be worked on directly to restore muscle tone. This is not an area in which I have personal experience, so I can only ruminate and offer some provisional conclusions. The question I would ask is, "Did we develop the evolutionary ability for this muscular tone to be naturally restored, provided the use of the self is coordinated?" It seems e ceptionally likely. Alexander teacher Marjory Barlow recounts in her book *The Examined Life* how she regained her muscular tone after childbirth by working with the "monkey" position, thus firing up the overall muscular system in a coordinated fashion by coming into a slight squat. And indeed poses like squatting—a position human beings spent much time in prior to widespread use of chairs and Western toilets—will demonstrably increase abdominal tone. Whatever asanas or approaches are used in restoring abdominal and pelvic floor tone after birth, the focus must be primarily on the overall coordination or balance of the body's weight in an erect stance. Any effort to work particular muscles or muscle groups must be applied in a way that does not interfere with overall coordination.

If a woman's use is poor prior to becoming pregnant, pregnancy will exaggerate this use and it may remain exaggerated even after giving birth. The demands of breastfeeding and carrying a baby for months can exacerbate this poor use. This subject is explored further in Chapter 30, on pregnancy.

The Nervous System Organizes Posture and Movement as a Whole

The attempt to strengthen the core postural muscles comes up against the very same problem that I discuss at length in Chapter 32, on the Mountain Pose or *Tadasana*, where we will look at common suggestions that yoga teachers make to achieve upright posture. The challenge with the approach of strengthening or activating specific muscles is, that the nervous system deals with movement and posture as a whole, not in parts. If one aspect of the coordination is unbalanced (e.g., weak "core" muscles), then the whole body is out of balance. The Alexander Technique approach is to focus on coordination of the whole, starting with the balance of the head on top of the spine and continuing through to the feet on the floor—a process of total neuromuscular reeducation.

"Core" muscles are exactly the same as all the postural muscles of the body in that they are engaged by reflex responses during all activities. As we move the limbs, the natural reflex response of the postural muscles is to stabilize the torso and spine to support these movements. The amount of work required is determined by the demands of the activity in which one is engaged. Running requires a different patterning of the postural muscles from walking. Swinging an axe differs from hitting a golf ball. Picking up a glass of water requires significantly less contraction than lifting a heavy object. If we are well coordinated in our use, and thus have an underlying tone or ready state of play in the muscles, we can rely on all our muscles to respond appropriately when we engage in these activities.

The appropriate muscles will engage at an appropriate level, and negate the need for sudden bracing or consciously maintaining a constant abdominal contraction. Constantly contracting the abdomen interferes with breathing, digestion, and overall coordination. Indeed, any excess bracing interferes with the effectiveness of all our activities, since it tends to produce stiff and unnatural movement. This is very obvious in some activities; just imagine swinging a golf club or tennis racquet or trying to sing with a braced abdomen!

In Alexander Technique lessons, once students are guided into a more balanced posture, I usually observe that they have little difficulty with the core postural muscles holding them up. In initial lessons, well before those muscles could possibly tire, students commonly activate powerful habitual muscular pulls that take them back into their usual, unbalanced posture. The difficulty they have in maintaining or returning to the balanced posture that the teacher is endeavoring to guide them into, is primarily neurological, not muscular. As soon as their attention wavers, or as soon as they attempt to "stand straight," they tend to activate their familiar muscular activity. When they lose the new balanced posture that is so foreign to them, (as will happen in every instance of initially learning the Alexander Technique), they don't have the neurological pathways required to return to it. Indeed, the power of this habitual neurological pattern is, that it underlies all their movements and therefore, is repeatedly engaged in all waking and even sleeping hours. It takes a good deal of repetition of an improved way of using one's self, to lay down the new sensory and motor pathways in the brain.

Eyal Lederman quotes studies which demonstrate that the force level that trunk muscles need to co-contract in order to stabilize the spine, is remarkably low. He comments: "These low levels of activation raise the question of why strength exercises are prescribed when such low levels of co-contraction forces are needed for functional movement. Such low co-contraction levels suggest the strength losses are unlikely ever to be an issue for spinal stabilisation. A person would have to lose substantial trunk muscle mass before it will destabilise the spine!"[4]

Strength Is Different from Stability

As discussed so far, simply having strong muscles doesn't ensure that they will be activated in functional movements. Physiotherapist Glenn Withers writes, "Having worked in various forms of football over the past 10 years, including with Manchester United, Tottenham, Arsenal and Charlton Athletic, the main problem is that most elite footballers actually have very good 'core strength', but very poor 'core stability', a leading cause of injury in elite athletes."[5] Stability relates to the ability of the nervous system to respond appropriately. Coordinated activation of the whole body, rather than specific muscles or muscle groups, is the key.

Strength Is Different from Endurance

It is common to confuse muscular strength and muscular endurance. They are not the same thing and depend on the two different types of muscle fiber that we have already discussed. Endurance is related to the red or slow-twitch fibers, which are able to continue to work over long periods of time, and which predominate among our postural muscles. Strength is related to the white or fast-twitch muscle fibers, which can contract quickly and strongly, but rapidly fatigue.

We need to develop both strength and endurance on the basis of good coordination. Specific exercises focusing on strengthening postural muscles through specific exercises will not be likely to increase endurance. Postural muscles have to work continually for the whole day. To train for endurance, muscles need to be steadily engaged over a long period of time. If muscular endurance has been lost, I would suggest something as simple as well-coordinated walking, as a safe and effective exercise. The standing yoga poses, when practiced in a coordinated manner and held for extended periond, will also develop endurance as well as strength.

In my Alexander Technique and Alexander yoga teaching practice, I find that in establishing improved coordination of the whole body, a muscle group that does in fact fatigue rapidly for many people, is the quadriceps. This occurs in those who habitually stand with their knees locked, using ligaments instead of the quadriceps for support. For some individuals, the erector spinae muscle group in the thoracic area will also fatigue quickly if they are in the habit of hunching forward Tightness and fatigue in the erector spinae muscles of the lower back are very common, but these are almost always the result of discoordination. Improved coordination greatly reduces the extraneous muscular work in the lower back.

Core Strengthening and Stabilization Exercises and Back Pain

Proponents of core strengthening and stabilization exercises may point to their own experience or to studies demonstrating improvement with back pain. However, we know that, on the whole, movement is better for back pain than immobility, and multiple studies have indicated that numerous exercise regimes, including yoga and stretching,[6] aerobic conditioning,[7] and aquatic exercises,[8] (to name only a few), can have positive effects on low back pain. This suggests that the benefit could equally be a result of merely doing exercise, rather than the type of exercise involved.

Summary

In yoga practice, or indeed any type of exercise or rehabilitation, working with an understanding of overall balance and coordination is more useful than focusing on "core" strengthening or stability. This is especially the case, when that focus leaves out the crucial factor of the relationship of the head to the rest of the body. All postural musculature, whether in the feet, ankles, hips, or torso is activated by reflexes, in response to our actions and reactions as we move and exist in a gravitational field. We should aim to remove interferences with those reflexes so that they will function naturally.

If we want to develop strength, endurance, and stability in asana practice, we need to work with poses that develop those qualities while maintaining proper coordination.

Outside of our *asana* practice, if we develop our whole body coordination then the "core" muscles will be naturally worked and developed in everyday activities. The failure of particular muscles or muscle groups to participate adequately in overall postural coordination, is primarily the result of prior neurological conditioning. To this end, fixation on particular muscles or muscle groups such as the "core" deals only with the symptom, and misses the root cause of any inadequate muscular engagement arising in the body.

NOTES **1.** Mulder and Hulstyn (1984). **2.** http://en.wikipedia.org/wiki/Core_%28anatomy%29 (accessed July 14, 2104). **3.** Cited within Brahinsky (2007). **4.** Lederman (2010). **5.** Withers (2010). **6.** Sherman et al. (2013). **7.** Van der Velde and Mierau (2000). **8.** Ariyoshi et al. (1999).

CHAPTER 27

NEUROPLASTICITY

Organic matter, especially nervous tissue seems endowed with a very enormous degree of plasticity . . . so that we may without hesitation lay down as our first proposition the following: that the phenomena of habit in living beings are due to the plasticity of the organic materials of which their bodies are composed..

— *William James* —

In the past decade, the topic of the neuroplasticity of the human brain has been much discussed. The idea that the possibility of change within our neurology does not end in the formative years of childhood and adolescence but extends into adulthood, has been taken up enthusiastically. Books like Norman Doidge's best-seller *The Brain That Changes Itself* documented amazing examples and made huge claims about the possibilities for change. The ongoing development of new technologies for scanning and monitoring brain function has created a huge amount of excitement. Undoubtedly, there is quite a high level of hype in this area, as the marketers follow the researchers. Regardless, Doidge's book popularized the fact that, at least within certain parameters, the brain can change itself. Or is it that we can change our brain? Whichever way, we do understand the many possibilities for growth and development that lie dormant within most adults.

In actuality, except for what has been exposed by the gee-whiz technology we have now, many of the recent discoveries about neuroplasticity are far from new. William James, the nineteenth-century psychologist and father of experimental psychology, introduced the word *plasticity* to brain science in 1890 in the passage that begins this chapter. James was a tremendously influential thinker, and his *Principles of Psychology* is still a relevant and fascinating read today. His speculations as to the actual organic substratum of this phenomenon were remarkably prescient. James was a colleague and mentor of John Dewey, who wrote forewords for Alexander's first three books, which he also assisted in editing. Alexander and Dewey influenced each other's writings. Dewey's ideas provided much of the conceptual underpinning for Alexander's practical discoveries, and Alexander's work furnished Dewey with the means to embody those concepts, especially in his own life.

Education and training of any sort has always depended on this possibility for change. As young children, we can effortlessly pick up other languages. With considerably more effort, we can learn to speak and think in languages other than our native tongue as adults. We can also learn a whole range of new physical skills as adults. People have learned to walk and talk again after a stroke. What the "neuroplasticity revolution" appears to have done, is point out that the possibilities are even greater than we may have imagined—a point Alexander belabored many years ago in his books.

As we have seen, the Alexander Technique is premised on the fact that it is possible to alter deep underlying patterns in the use of the self. This hypothesis was explored in the work Alexander did on himself and his students. In his teaching process, he came to exactly the same conclusions that modern researchers and neuroscientists have reached, a conclusion long known to teachers and trainers in many fields: paying only infrequent attention to one's actions and thoughts is not enough to repattern movement and thinking habits. If we want to learn a new language, the most effective method is to spend time immersed in the culture that speaks the language. In working with people recovering from strokes, it was discovered that applying a much more intensive, long-term, and continuous rehabilitation process than normal, helped even those with a slim chance of recovery to regain a significant amount of function.[1]

Alexander understood that what he called "reconditioning" takes time. This was the reason for his insistence on students' attending lessons five days a week for a minimum of three and preferably six weeks. Over the period, Alexander would consistently ask them to *inhibit* their stimulus to stand or sit, as he guided them through new and unfamiliar movements, gradually laying down new neural pathways. As these new pathways became more established, people developed the ability to choose to implement the new patterns in their daily movements and establish the new pathways and movement patterns more deeply. These new neural pathways could then begin to override the old ones. The idea was, that once the new pathways were thoroughly integrated, people would not relapse into their previous inattention. Indeed, the lessons were also a training in learning how to learn. They were not only training the students' kinesthetic sensibility, but also sharpening their skills of attention, enabling them to observe both physical sensations and mental impulses normally activated below the level of consciousness.

Just as an artist has a heightened sensibility for color, light, and shape, so can we train our kinesthetic sensibilities to make us automatically aware of, and responsive to, perceptions that were formerly ignored.

However, despite all the benefits that we derive from neuroplasticity, it also has negative implications for us. As we saw in the chapter on the power of habit, anything practiced and repeated often enough, whether consciously or unconsciously, will in Doidge's terminology "change our brains," for better or worse.

One of the most troubling changes to the brain and the entire nervous system occurs in relation to pain. The phenomenon known as "central sensitization," occurs when pain sensations go into overdrive with very little connection to actual tissue damage. In these circumstances, sufferers find themselves in a condition of chronic pain, a learned pattern that also stems from our neuroplasticity. As pain researcher Fernando Cervero explains:

> Neuronal sensitization is an intrinsic property of all synapses and a feature of the plasticity of neuronal networks. The molecular modulators of sensitization are present in areas of the brain concerned with cognition, memory and learning, not just in areas concerned with pain. We might even say that the brain learns by a process of sensitization—the same process the brain uses to amplify pain—and that this process can go wrong and result in chronic pain.[2]

NOTES 1. Doidge (2007) covers the topic of recovery from stoke in chapter 5 of his book. One such instance is the remarkable recovery of actress Patricia Neal from a near-fatal stroke, after a very intensive treatment regime instituted by her husband, Roald Dahl, which was described in the book *Pat and Roald* by Barry Farrell. 2. Cervero (2012), 73.

PAIN

These pains you feel are messengers. Listen to them.

— Rumi —

Your brain works for pain perception and for everything else, by producing images and sensations that best help you make decisions about every aspect of your life. Sometimes these images and perceptions are very precise, but often they are not at all direct reflections of the originating stimulus, and occasionally they are far from accurate.

— Fernando Cervero —

Pain, both physical and mental, is part of the human condition. Pain and the avoidance of pain are what bring many people to both Alexander Technique and yoga. For the traditional yogic and Buddhist traditions, escape from the suffering involved in the endless succession of births and deaths is a central aim of the practice. Unlike the more optimistic outlook of most modern people, the concept of rebirth is one in which suffering far outweighs the pleasures of existence.

Scientists and pain researchers have identified three types of physical pain.
1. Nociceptive pain. This is "good" protective pain that causes us to draw our hand away from a hot or sharp object. A nociceptor is the receptor of a sensory neuron that responds to stimuli that may damage us. Intense stimuli to these receptors generate withdrawal by reflex and by sensations of pain.
2. Inflammatory pain. This is of a different kind and quality. If you stub your toe your nociceptors will let you know about it immediately, but the pain will then persist to ensure that you protect the injured area. This also refers to conditions like arthritis, when joints or other types of inflammation cause ongoing and persistent pain.
3. Neuropathic pain. This pain is activated in the absence of any obvious tissue damage. It is pain developed in the nervous system itself. The best-known example of this is phantom limb pain.

Pain is defined by the Association for the International Study of Pain as "an unpleasant sensory and emotional experience associated with actual or potential tissue damage or described in terms of such damage."[1] This definition captures the idea that, contrary to what may be our intuitive undestanding, pain is not necessarily associated with tissue damage. Indeed, pain has three components:

1. Sensory or nociceptive
2. An emotional response that is always unpleasant

3. Cognitive processing and meaning making: What is causing it? How dangerous is it? How can I stop it? How will it affect my life? Pain is a personal and relative phenomenon. An injury to a single finger of a pianist will be much more significant, and almost certainly much more painful, than to someone for whom the finger is not of such key importance.

This multidimensional experience is simultaneously processed by many areas of the brain at once, creating multiple associations between different patterns of activation. The terms "pain matrix" and "neuromatrix" have been coined to describe these sensory, emotional, and cognitive elements that interact to give the total pain experience.

Lobotomy operations were once used to deal with the pain of terminal illness. Although the lobotomy didn't remove the sensation of pain, it removed the normal link between pain and suffering. Dr. James W. Watts and Dr. Walter Freeman wrote in 1945: "Psychosurgery changes the individual's reaction to pain without materially changing his ability to feel pain. Pain may be present, but when divorced from its implications becomes bearable and may be accepted with fortitude."[2] It is the cognitive aspect of the pain experience that transforms it into suffering.

— *Chronic Pain* —

The experience of pain is mysterious, and normal understanding of it as a direct transmission of impulses from bodily tissues to the brain, does not begin to cover its complexity. Chronic pain is an area that, although it has received a great deal of study and inspired many hypotheses, still holds considerable uncertainty.

Both structural and biochemical brain changes are present in patients with chronic pain. However, where the nociceptive inputs have been removed following a hip operation, reduction of gray matter in the brain has reversed, a clear indication that these changes were a result, rather than the cause, of the pain.[3]

Some people are undoubtedly much more sensitive to nociceptive inputs than others. A study of the relationship between pain and the level of arthritic changes in the knee showed only a "modest" connection, with indications that presence and severity of pain did not have a direct correlation to the intensity of the arthritis.[4]

Our thoughts and perceptions have a profound effect on the amount of pain we feel. A number of visual illusions of an affected painful part can strongly modulate the pain experience. Lorimer Mosely reported that "in patients with chronic hand pain, magnifying their view of their own limb during movement significantly increases the pain and swelling evoked by movement. By contrast, 'minifying' their view of the limb significantly decreases the pain and swelling evoked by movement."[5] As already discussed in the chapter on the Alexander directions, creating the illusion of either lengthening or shortening an arthritic finger can significantly decrease pain sensations.[6]

In recent times, central sensitization has become the fashionable explanation for most cases of persistent pain. However, as Cervero remarked in his overview of current pain research:

> Clinicians use sensitization as an all-encompassing term in regard to persistent pain. Patients with fibromyalgia, irritable bowel syndrome or chronic osteoarthritis are said to suffer from conditions caused by sensitization of their nervous system. The idea is that enhanced excitability of parts of the brain concerned with pain perception leads to increased pain sensitivity. Unfortunately these interpretations are hypothetical and it is difficult to establish beyond reasonable doubt that any one of these chronic pain states in question is caused by enhanced brain activity.[7]

— *Meditation, Yoga, Alexander Technique, and Pain* —

Chronic pelvic pain syndrome is notorious for its intractability and for the pain and disability it causes. Like many other chronic pain conditions, no proven medical treatment options to cure or relieve the condition exist. In *Teach Us to Sit Still*, novelist Tim Parks narrated his own journey with this condition, from bizarre medical recommendations and treatments based on treating the problem as a physical or "plumbing" problem, to finding a meditation practice firmly anchored in the body. He attended *Vipassana*, insight meditation retreats where the focus is simply paying attention to sensations arising in the body. The emphasis in *Vipassana* practice is on developing equanimity in the face of whatever arises, removing judgment and any attempts to change or alter the situation.

Reflecting on the journey he went through, he commented: "Just when I seemed to be walled up in a life sentence of chronic pain, someone proposed a bizarre way out: sit still, they said, and breathe. I sat still. I breathed. It seemed a tedious exercise at first, rather painful, not immediately effective. Eventually it proved so exciting, so transforming, physically and mentally, that I began to think my illness had been a stroke of luck. If I wasn't the greatest of skeptics, I'd be saying it had been sent from above to invite me to change my ways."[8]

We will explore this type of meditation further in the next chapter, but for those with chronic pain let's note here that people practicing insight meditation may be able to:

- Calm the nervous system. Stress and anxiety always exacerbate pain. As the nervous system relaxes, there is an increased production of natural opioids, which further dampen pain signals. In the more blissful meditation states, sensations of pain may completely disappear.
- Release excessive muscle tension. Muscle tension can stimulate the nociceptors even in the absence of tissue damage.
- Remove judgment from the sensation of pain. As we have seen, our cognitive judgments and perceptions of pain can create a "top-down" influence by either increasing or decreasing perceived pain sensations.

This approach has many resonances in the Alexander Technique, which, as Alexander described, is "based on inhibition, the inhibition of undesirable, unwanted responses to stimuli, and hence it is primarily a technique for the development of the control of human reaction."[9] The three elements of pain sensation—nociception, emotion, and judgment—interlink and reinforce each other. Any holistic response to pain, particularly chronic pain, needs to address the whole person, which means addressing all three of these elements. Although one of these factors may dominate a person's pain condition, the three are always interlinked. What would be a minor pain stimulus for some will create significant pain for others, so ameliorating the stimulus plays an important role in relieving pain conditions and gradually reducing the oversensitivity of the nervous system. The physical causes of the nociceptive stimuli are often quite obvious to an Alexander teacher. But clinicians, lacking the training to diagnose people's use of themselves, may overlook the physical causes and diagnose "central sensitization" as the problem, and then design cognitive strategies for patients to live with their pain. I have worked with a number of people who were diagnosed as suffering from central sensitization, who subsequently experienced significant pain reduction once their holding patterns were released.

As many have experienced directly, Hatha Yoga practice provides a potent means of dealing with pain issues, which is one reason for its massive popularity. These are some of the ways Hatha Yoga practice helps to overcome pain:

- Regular stretching of contracted muscles of the back may relieve chronic back pain.
- Stretching the body calms the nervous system.
- Mindful focus on moving the body also calms the nervous system.
- General strength and conditioning of the legs can relieve knee issues.
- By applying the Alexander Technique to their yoga practice, those suffering from neck pain and headaches can prevent habitual neck contraction as they work themselves in more active poses. Learning how to move without neck contraction seeps into everyday activities and helps to end general neck pain and tension headaches.
- Dysfunctional breathing patterns deregulate the body chemistry, which may cause constriction of the smooth muscles of the body. For sensitive individuals, this deregulation may be a potent factor in initiating and maintaining pain. Effective yoga practice will begin to regulate the breathing, but it is important to not overbreathe while practicing yoga.

Finally, the asana, mindfulness and meditation practices, are embedded in an overall approach to living as outlined in the Eight Limbs of Patanjali Yoga and the Eightfold Noble Path of the Buddha. These formal practices are based on an approach to living that is underlain with conscious and ethical behavior. Our daily moment-to-moment living needs to support our more formal practice. This integration and constant heightened awareness helps free us from the suffering of pain.

NOTES 1. CERVERO (2012), 16. 2. WATTS AND FREEMAN (1945). 3. RODRIGUEZ-RAECKE ET AL. (N.D.). 4. FINAN ET AL. (2013). 5. MOSELY (2008). 6. PRESTON AND NEWPORT (2011). 7. CERVERO (2012), 71. 8. PARKS (2010), 127–31. 9. ALEXANDER (1942, 1947), 93.

MINDFULNESS AND MEDITATION

My first interest in the Alexander Technique came from a book I read when undertaking several years of intensive immersion in Buddhist mindfulness practice in Thailand. I was immediately intrigued by similarities between the two disciplines and decided that, when I had the chance, I would experience lessons in the Alexander Technique. The practice I was studying is based on the *Satipatthana Sutta—The Foundations of Mindfulness*—the opening lines of which summarize its approach (see the box).

This is the direct way, monks, for the purification of beings, for the overcoming of sorrow and lamentation, for the disappearance of pain and distress, for reaching the Noble Path, for the realization of Nibbana, (full enlightenment) namely, the Four Foundations of Mindfulness.

"A monk dwells contemplating the body in the body, ardent, clearly comprehending and mindful, overcoming covetousness and grief in the world;

"He dwells contemplating the feeling in the feelings, ardent, clearly comprehending and mindful, and putting aside greed and distress with reference to the world;

"He dwells contemplating the states of mind in the states of mind, ardent, clearly comprehending and mindful, overcoming covetousness and grief in the world;

"He dwells contemplating thought and perceptions in the thoughts and perceptions, ardent, clearly comprehending and mindful, overcoming covetousness and grief in the world."

— Satipatthana Sutta — *The Four Foundations of Mindfulness*

The Pali term *Sati*, which is commonly translated as "mindfulness," means paying attention or remembering. Thanissaro Bikkhu explains:

> Mindfulness is what keeps the perspective of appropriate attention in mind. Modern psychological research has shown that attention comes in discrete moments. You can be attentive to something for only a very short period of time and then you have to remind yourself, moment after moment, to return to it if you want to keep on being attentive. In other words, continuous attention—the type that can observe things over time—has to be stitched together from short intervals. This is what mindfulness is for. It keeps the object of your attention and the purpose of your attention in mind.[1]

It is an attention that is deeply grounded in the body, and expanded to include emotions, states of mind, thoughts, and perceptions. The type of attention directed to these "four foundations of mindfulness" may vary, from analytical observation of how psychophysical states develop and disappear, to bare awareness of the sensations arising and passing away. It involves: bringing awareness to whatever is arising in consciousness; and, observing how one is acting and reacting from moment to moment. Clear perception creates space for evaluation, for example, whether to respond or not to respond. Similar to the Alexander Technique, mindfulness focuses on clear observation of impulses prior to their expression, which, in Alexander's terms, frees us up to "give or withhold consent" to those impulses.

In meditation practice, stilling the mind and body begins with focusing on the bare sensations arising from the body and the breath. Then one begins to notice the continuous mental chatter. It is the nature of the mind to think, and the most skillful way of dealing with this is not to try to stop the thinking. One should just notice it, then return to the awareness of the in-and-out movement of the breath or the physical sensations arising in the body. The gentle attention on the breath and body begins to shift the focus away from the habitual flow of thoughts, subsequently focusing on our physicality, thus facilitating deep states of calm.

> *When for you there will be only the seen in what you see, only the heard in what you hear, only the sensed in what you sense, only the thought in what you think, then...there is no you in connection with that. When there is no you in connection with that, there is no you there. When there is no you there, you are neither here nor yonder nor between the two. Just this is the end of suffering.*
>
> *— The Buddha — Malunkyaputta Sutta*

As already stated, meditation may give rise to states of calmness, tranquility, and bliss. Clear, focused, and detached attention may also give insight into how underlying patterns of thinking and feeling are developed and maintained. This insight gives the opportunity for choice, rather than permitting these patterns to dominate our reactions. In recent years, aspects of this type of Buddhist practice have been taken up by psychologists and psychotherapists. Jon Kabat-Zinn has developed a healing modality, Mindfulness Based Stress Reduction, which is now widely used to treat emotional and behavioral disorders, and the psychological symptoms associated with chronic and terminal illnesses. Another similar hybrid used by therapists is Mindfulness Based Cognitive Therapy. In fact, the physical and psychological benefits of mindfulness practices have created so much interest in psychological and a ademic circles, that the amount of research done in this relatively new area of study has already eclipsed the studies done on the Alexander Technique.

Traditional psychotherapy had focused more on cognitive and emotional aspects of mental issues. However, people caught up in vicious cycles of obsessive thinking patterns or in chronic pain, (and the emotions such as fear, rage, and depression that accompany those cycles), can focus on bare physicality in order to ground them in an alternative way of being. This focus on the body may at first give rise to grosser sensations of pain and discomfort. But in deeper states of meditation, this focus can also engender states of pleasure. As the Buddha in a *sutta* from the *Anguttara Nikaya* describes one of the states of meditative absorption:

> the monk permeates and pervades, suffuses and fills this very body with the rapture and pleasure born of concentration. There is nothing of his entire body unpervaded by rapture and pleasure born of concentration.[2]

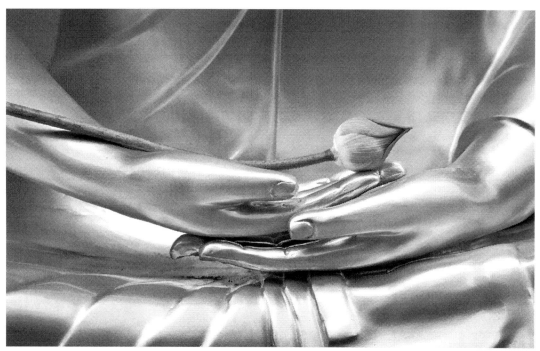

Figure 29.1

Conversely, as anyone who has done more intensive meditation knows, as a person delves deeper into the practice it brings one face to face with aspects of one's self that are not so pleasant. Although brief periods of meditation may be therapeutic and calming for most people, intensive meditation may be challenging or even harmful for those with serious mental health issues. Such people would be better off undertaking meditation as part of one of the psychological or psychotherapeutic practices discussed above.

This practice of attention is not limited to sitting meditation practice. Although the sitting practice is an effective means of developing deep states of tranquility and insight, mindfulness practice, like the Alexander Technique, includes all the activities of daily life. The *Satipatthana Sutta* describes how paying attention is not simply for the purpose of observing what we are doing, but also for understanding the true nature of the psychophysical states that arise. This careful attention allows us to analyze our psychophysical states so that we can overcome harmful ones, prevent them from arising in the future, and learn how to develop positive states.

Practices like Hatha Yoga, tai chi, and Qigong offer highly focused "movement meditations" which may more easily facilitate a flow of focused attention. Having the combination of clear intention and focused attention in the practice makes it easier to avoid the distractions of obsessive thinking. Furthermore this type of practice trains and develops highly focused attention. Alexander comments on the difficulty we all have in maintaining a steady flow of attention and intention in developing new movement habits:

> My daily teaching experience shows me that in working for a given end, we can all project one direction, but to continue to give this direction as we project the second, and to continue to give these two while we add a third, and to continue to give the three directions going as we proceed to gain the end, has proved to be the pons asinorum of every pupil I have so far known.[3]

Meditation

I have given a very brief outline of a key Buddhist mediation practice. In both the Buddhist and Hindu traditions there is such a vast array of writings, philosophies, and meditation approaches that we have no hope of even summarizing them all here. In addition, within the Christian, Jewish, and Islamic religions there are "mystical" traditions that employ meditation approaches. However, in outward form all these meditation practices resolve into sitting and stilling the body. Most types of meditation also involve focusing the attention on a particular meditation object, which may be a mantra, a visualized mandala, the breath, or the body.

Despite the differences among meditation traditions, normally after a period of sitting still, the practitioner will begin to reach some degree of psychophysical stillness. According to Eric Harrison, regardless of the type of meditation people are doing, "All meditations converge on the body map . . . to some degree."[4] Indeed, as you sit, the kinesthetic, proprioceptive, and visceral sensations tend to impinge strongly on the consciousness, as does the incessant flow of thoughts and images. Meditation traditions approach these phenomena somewhat differently, but in all of them the result tends to be a calming of both body and mind, alongside a shift away from the dominance of the sympathetic towards the parasympathetic system.

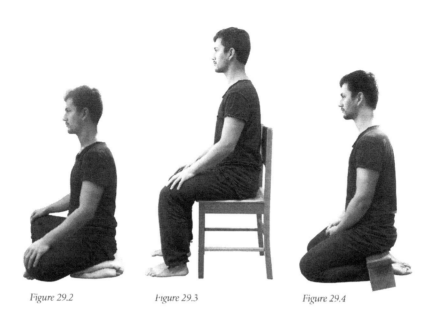

Figure 29.2   *Figure 29.3*   *Figure 29.4*

— *Postural Considerations for Meditation* —

Traditionally one would sit on a floor or cushion with crossed legs for meditation, but many Westerners are unable to sit comfortably in this position. Other options are to sit in a chair or kneel on a stool. For people who are very tight and bound up in the body, sitting still in any position can be somewhat of an ordeal. Both yoga and the Alexander Technique can help one develop flexibility, openness, and expansion so that sitting in meditation becomes much easier.

When people sit in meditation, it is normally recommended that they sit "upright." The intention to sit upright is one thing, however, and the means to do so is another. As can be easily noted in observing pretty much any group of meditators, the ability to sit upright is not as common as one would hope. Paradoxically, the ability to access very subtle kinesthetic information about feelings within the body, does not translate at all into accuracy about the location of body parts in space. Our vision provides considerable information about the position of our body in space, and once we close our eyes we lose this visual information. As we close our eyes we often sink a little deeper into habitual patterns of collapse, or, less frequently, hold ourselves rigidly erect. It is very common to see people moving to relieve tension in their body after a period of meditation. The Alexander Technique can assist us in developing a highly refined kinesthetic sensibility over time, so that we can maintain freedom, openness, and coordination in meditation sitting poses.

If your weight is not centered on your sitting bones, you have no chance of sitting upright easily. As the pelvis rolls back, the torso begins to round forward unless a considerable effort is made to straighten the back. This means that when sitting cross-legged, you should always have enough support under the pelvis so that your weight is fully on the sitting bones, which enables you to rock slightly forward using only the hip joints, not the spine.

The Buddhist Eightfold Path

Samma-Ditthi
Right view, or right understanding

Samma-Sankappa
Right thought or attitude

Samma-Vaca
Right speech, clear, truthful, and nonharming communication

Samma-Kammanta
Right action, based on an ethical framework for living

Samma-Ajiva
Right livelihood

Samma-Vayama
Right effort; the Buddha described the tuning of the string of an instrument, neither too tight or too loose, as analogous to the quality of effort required

Samma-Sati
Right mindfulness, paying attention to one's self in the present moment

Samma-Samadhi
Correct concentration, meditation, and absorption

NOTES **1.** Thanissaro Bhikkhu (2008). **2.** Thanissaro Bhikkhu (trans.; n.d.), 195–96. **3.** Pons asinorum, literally "the bridge of the ass," is used metaphorically to describe a problem that represents a critical test of ability or understanding. Alexander (1932, 1955), 20. **4.** Harrison (2013).

PREGNANCY

Many expectant mothers turn to yoga as a way of relaxing, tuning into and preparing their body for the changes during pregnancy and the rigors of childbirth. Those who already have a yoga practice can modify it as the pregnancy progresses.

Besides fatigue and morning sickness in the first trimester, another common and unwelcome accompaniment to pregnancy is back pain and other musculoskeletal problems. As pregnancy progresses, all the ligaments begin to soften and loosen as the hormone relaxin does its job, preparing the body for the birth. During delivery the joints of the pelvis and sacrum are required to move in ways that are well beyond the norm, and the softening of the ligaments makes this movement possible. We have already seen that ligaments serve the important function of protecting joints from moving out of their healthy range of motion. When ligaments lose elasticity, it is much easier for the everyday pattern of misuse to create extra strain on vulnerable joints. The growing load of the developing baby adds to these strains and tends to accentuate preexisting patterns of use.

The sequence of photos in Figure 30.1 gives a good visual illustration of this process. As we can see at the very start of the pregnancy there is a pattern of overextension of the torso, with the shoulders pulled back, hyperlordosis of the lumbar spine, and hyperextended knees.

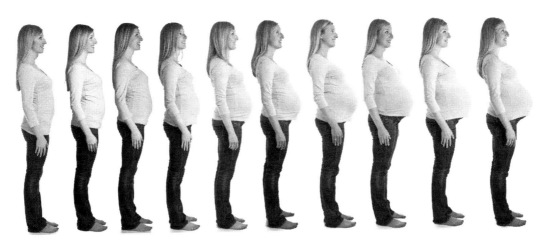

Figure 30.1

Over the nine months of the pregnancy, we can observe accentuation of this postural set. An increasing backward lean to counteract the weight of the baby in the front is extremely common. This obviously puts great strain on the joints of the lumbar spine, sacroiliac joint, and knees. This backward lean may cause or worsen low back, sacroiliac, knee, and hip pain; symphysis dysfunction; diastasis recti (separation of the rectus abdominus muscle into the right and left halves); and pelvic floor dysfunction.

The Alexander Technique focuses on improving overall coordination so that the back supports the extra weight in the front. In Figure 30.2 we can see that the weight of the baby is being supported more from the back than in Figure 30.1. The lower back is fuller and further back, so the weight is carried through the pelvis into the legs and feet.

If the preexisting postural pattern is one of leaning backward, then some training in the Alexander Technique near the beginning can minimize the possibility of musculoskeletal pain as the pregnancy develops.

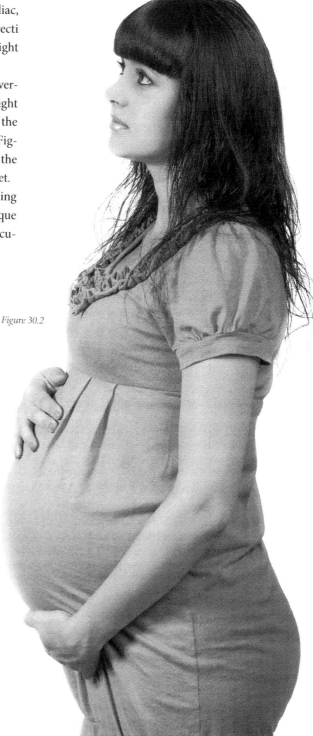

Figure 30.2

Yoga Practice

Increased flexibility caused by the stretching of the ligaments is essential for the birthing process, but it is potentially dangerous. It is of particular importance that you not increase flexibility in ways that contribute to your misuse. Although it is possible to use the heightened flexibility of pregnancy for structurally opening up a fixed area of the spine, this should be done only under expert guidance, as the possibility of overstretching other areas is very high.

Squatting has been used for millennia as a position for giving birth, as it is much superior to delivering the baby from lying down.[1] This allows greater opening of the pelvis than when lying down, and lets the woman generate stronger and more efficient voluntary expulsive forces that are better coordinated with the contractions. Developing the overall flexibility to be able to squat is an important part of practice during pregnancy. Chapter 35, on squatting, goes into this in considerable detail.

Supported by proper coordination, working with the monkey, squatting, and standing poses will help to develop the postural muscles and alignment and thus, will protect the lower back from being pulled into hyperextension. If you don't have a teacher to observe you, then work with mirrors to ensure that you do not reinforce harmful postural habits.

Alterations to Yoga Practice

There is no widespread agreement about appropriate yoga practice during pregnancy, and there is probably no one answer to this question given that women vary in their responses to being pregnant. From observations of those I have taught, I will say it is possible for many to continue with yoga practice from conception right through to the day before delivery.

Yoga may well help to cope with the possible nausea and fatigue of the first trimester, though it is important to practice carefully and mindfully, as this is the stage when miscarriage is most likely.

Here are some generally agreed recommendations for pregnant practitioners of yoga:
- Don't overstretch.
- Jumping in and out of poses should be avoided.
- Avoid deep back bends.
- Don't work twists deeply into the belly.
- Poses such as the Plank, that work the abdominals strongly, should be avoided.

- Vigorous yoga workouts and "hot yoga" should be avoided right from the start of the pregnancy.
- Lying on the belly is unadvised and uncomfortable as pregnancy develops.
- Don't compress the belly; keep the thighs out of the way in forward bends, avoid deep twists, etc.
- There is no agreement on whether or not inversions are good. Certainly avoid them if there is any possibility of falling out of them! Some women continue with them right through pregnancy, but as we know, people differ. Listen to your own body and proceed with caution.
- Lying on the back becomes uncomfortable as pregnancy advances and starts to compress the vena cava veins, interfering with circulation. For some women this happens very early, for others later in pregnancy. An alternative to the semisupine position or the Corpse Pose, is lying on the left side, as pictured in Figure 31.3 on page 127.

NOTES 1. The Cochrane Library has published a review (Gupta, 2012) of twenty-two trials looking at positions for women in second-stage labor. They found that those who used an upright position for birthing were:

- 23 percent less likely to have a forceps or vacuum-assisted delivery
- 21 percent less likely to have an episiotomy
- 35 percent more likely to have a second-degree tear, except when a "birth cushion" is used, in which case there was no additional risk of tearing
- 54 percent less likely to have abnormal fetal heart rate patterns
- 65 percent more likely to have blood loss greater than 500 ml

The authors of the paper questioned the accuracy of the blood loss statistic because it was based on estimates of caregivers, which is not a reliable method of assessment. There were no differences between groups in measuring duration of pushing, Cesarean section rate, third- or fourth-degree perineal tears, need for blood transfusion, admission to neonatal intensive care unit, or perinatal death. The authors' plain language summary of this review concluded that "women should be encouraged to give birth in comfortable positions, which are usually upright. In traditional cultures, women naturally give birth in upright positions like kneeling, standing or squatting. In Western societies, doctors have influenced women to give birth on their backs, sometimes with their legs up in stirrups. This review included 22 studies (involving 7280 women). The review of trials found the studies were not of good quality, but they showed that when women gave birth on their backs there was more chance for an assisted delivery, e.g. forceps, there was a higher chance of requiring cuts to the birth outlet, but there was less blood loss. More research is needed."

CONSTRUCTIVE REST: SEMISUPINE POSITION

The semisupine or constructive rest position (Fig. 31.1) is something I recommend to all my students as a daily practice, whether they are practicing yoga or not. It was taught as an essential part of self-care in a large and well-designed back pain trial published in the *British Medical Journal* in 2008. This trial demonstrated that the technique yielded measurable and long-term relief from chronic back pain.[1] Semisupine is a highly constructive way of reducing tension, by consciously directing and projecting one's thoughts while in a supported resting position. If done regularly (ten to twenty minutes every day is highly advisable), it can help align and elongate the spine and improve overall posture. I always begin and end my yoga classes with this pose. Depending on the length of the class, we will practice it for ten to twenty minutes at the start and four or five minutes at the end, with an invitation to stay longer at the end of the class, if the students wish. It is also the base position for a sequence of reclined poses.

When my first Alexander teacher worked with me in the semisupine position (Fig. 31.1) on the table, I was astounded by the amount of release and opening that took place. There was obviously considerable tension of which I was absolutely unconscious. Even after years of yoga and mindfulness meditation practice, this deeper holding was so ingrained that I had never been aware it was something extra I was doing to myself.

Figure 31.1

The *Savasana* or Corpse Pose (Fig. 31.2) is a standard and very popular part of every yoga class. It is a position in which people can rest, let go of extra muscle tension, and enter a deep state of relaxation. In Alexander yoga classes, however, we have replaced the *Savasana* with the semisupine position, for these reasons:

- The emphasis is on width, expansion, and length throughout the body rather than directly aiming for "relaxation." The "letting go" that occurs in this position is connected to release and opening, which can then be incorporated into our upright coordination.
- For many people, especially those with a contracted lower back, lying with the legs straight as in *Savasana* contracts and puts pressure on the lumbar spine, which may create pain and discomfort.
- The contact of the feet with the floor, particularly the ball of the big toe, stimulates postural reflexes and helps us experience opening and expansion through the legs, hips, pelvis, and entire torso.
- With the head lying on books we can link through the whole of the spine and torso to access an opening and expansion that we don't experience if the head drops back.
- The arms are positioned in a way that allows for balanced expansion through the upper torso and shoulder girdle. This releases the effects of trying to force "good" posture by using contractions such as pulling the shoulders back.

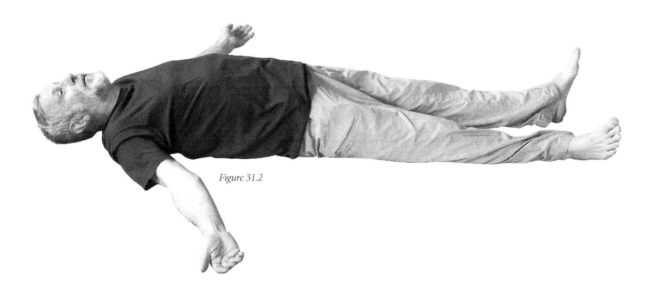

Figure 31.2

Instructions for the Semisupine Position

The description assumes that you have a teacher to instruct you in this pose, and the written instructions are just for reference. Most readers of this book won't have this, so I have added some further information at the end of these instructions.

1. Gather some books for stacking under your head, and find a place to lie on your back on the floor. More information about book height is at the end of these instructions.
2. Make sure you are warm, as you may cool down in this position and tighten up in response to lower body temperature.
3. Lie on a carpet or yoga mat, on a firm surface.
4. Come into this pose, arranging yourself so that your spine and pelvis are as symmetrical as possible.
5. Once on your back, bend your knees toward the ceiling and place your feet flat on the floor.
6. Rest your hands on your torso or by your sides.
7. Be aware of the contact of your back with the floor. Don't use muscles to try to change that contact, but you can send the intention for widening, softening, and expanding through the back and torso.
8. Place the soles of your feet flat on the floor, with the weight evenly distributed between the corners of the feet. Do not let the feet roll in or out.
9. If the legs are tending to fall inward, bring your feet closer together. If they are falling outward, move the feet further apart.
10. The back is resting into the floor, but you are not pushing it or trying to flatten out the natural curves.
11. The arms are relaxed, and there is an intention for breadth through the front and back of the shoulder and chest area (again without pushing).
12. The pelvis is resting and echoes this sense of breadth and expansion.
13. Breathing is normal and through the nose, with the lips lightly closed.
14. Stay awake and alert, which is facilitated by keeping your eyes open. You can gently activate your Alexander directions: the neck softens by undoing any subtle tendency toward contraction, the head releases forward and up, and the back lengthens and widens. Forward and up in this position may be better thought of as forward and away, with the face directed toward the ceiling and the top of the head directed toward the wall behind you. But this is not something you are "doing"; it is just an intention.
15. At first you may like to experiment with a number of methods for directing your thinking during this time. Remain aware of the gentle opening and expansion. Gradually you will learn how to direct this opening without pushing to get it.
16. Move carefully in the process of coming up. In particular, you need to avoid lifting your head and tensing the neck and abdominal muscles. Rather, roll your head and knees to bring you to rest on your side. From here you can use your hand to push yourself up to sitting, rather than tensing your neck muscles. To stand, you can come through a lunge or a squat, again paying special attention to avoiding unnecessary activation of the neck muscles.

— *Book Height* —

The number of books required varies greatly, but the average is two or three. The optimal book height depends on the distance between the back of the head and the most curved point of the thoracic spine. Those with a large curvature of the thoracic spine need many more books than people with a small curvature.

The arrangement of the books is most difficult for people with an overstraightened neck or spine. It is important to ensure that the neck is not overstraightened, and that its natural curve (lordosis) is encouraged in this posture. For some hypermobile people with an overstraightened neck, the C7 and T1 vertebrae may drop back toward the table while they are in semisupine. In those instances placing a folded tea towel under these vertebrae increases comfort considerably, even if the position does not feel consciously uncomfortable prior to that.

— *Back Pain in Semisupine* —

Lying on the back in semisupine puts too much pressure on the lower back and sacrum for some people. In a guided lesson, the teacher can often help the student find relief by moving the pelvis. In my yoga classes, some of my students lie with their pelvis very slightly raised on a foam wedge; a blanket or towel suffices for that modification if you don't have a wedge. The pressure on this area is often caused by a contraction through the lower back, which pushes a tender area into the floor. You may avoid this by stretching out the back, bringing your knees up, and squeezing them toward your abdomen prior to bringing your feet to the floor. For the very few people who can't find comfort in this posture, or for pregnant women, it is possible to lie on the side (Fig. 31.3).

Figure 31.3

Knee and Leg Position

In this position we want to keep the knees releasing up toward the ceiling, releasing not only out of the hips, pelvis, and lower back, but also from the contact with the feet on the floor. There is no way we can "do" this releasing; we simply have to ask for it to happen. For some people there is a very strong underlying muscular contraction that tends to pull the legs off to the side. Attempting to hold the legs upright in the early stage of this practice creates a high level of tension in the hips, gluteals, and lower back, which makes release difficult. If this is the case, it may be useful to tie a belt around the legs to keep them in place, or to rest the legs on the seat of a chair so they are at a right angle to the body.

Alternative Position

For a very few people, this posture may not be comfortable, even with the modifications listed here. This is most common in women in an advanced stage of pregnancy. Some of my students are comfortable lying in semisupine until the sixth or seventh month; others have to use alternative lying positions in earlier months. If you listen to your body, it will be obvious when it is time to stop lying in semisupine, and to move into lying on your side (Fig. 31.3).

Benefits of Semisupine Procedure

- Improves overall organization and alignment
- Gives the intervertebral discs a chance to rehydrate, which will result in increased length through spine
- Elongates any curves of the spine that have been exaggerated through compression without flattening out the natural curves of the spine
- Releases muscular tension and holding throughout the body
- Improves breathing, both capacity and coordination
- Improves circulation because blood flows better when there is less tension in the musculature
- Lessens pressure on nerves, especially if there is an impingement condition present
- Allows the internal organs to move, reorganize, and function more effectively
- Assists overall energy level through resting of the musculature and nervous system
- Can reduce emotional disturbances such as stress and anxiety through combined physical and mental rebalancing
- Helps cultivate greater awareness of one's back, and thus three-dimensionality, which may help expand proprioception[2]

NOTES   **1.** Little et al. (2008).   **2.** Adapted from Brennan (2012), 156. Much of this chapter has been taken or adapted from the *Body Mapping Manual,* written by Fiona Bryant, which is a workbook used by trainees at the School for F. M. Alexander Studies.

PART **FOUR**
YOGA POSES/ASANAS
✦✦✦✦

YOGA POSES/ASANAS

*Being the first accessory of Hatha Yoga, asana [yoga poses] is described first.
It should be practiced for gaining steady posture, health and lightness of body.*
— *Hatha Yoga Pradipika* —

❂

*I have been criticized for "keeping things back," because I would not give in my
book instructions and set exercises that people could do at home by themselves.
In all such instances I point out that I will not be guilty at this stage of my teaching
experience of adding to the mass of literature on the subject of exercises, or take the
grave responsibility for the harmful consequences which are certain to result from
the practice of exercises, according to written instructions, by people whose sensory
appreciation is unreliable and often positively delusive.*
— *F. M. Alexander* —

As you read this section on the yoga poses, it is important to keep in mind Alexander's thoughts on the usefulness and wisdom of following written instructions in the performance of any type of exercise. Anyone with unreliable sensory appreciation will inevitably interpret the instructions using his or her own kinesthetic sensations as a guide. In addition, people often have misconceptions in relation to the concept of coordination, even in "normal" upright posture and in particular yoga poses. This even goes so far as their ideas about the range of healthy movement of the various joints.

I can, perhaps, take some comfort from the fact that in a later chapter in the same book, Alexander succumbs to temptation and is himself guilty of giving a very detailed instruction for a particular exercise, albeit with caveats about how inadequate the instructions are, however he doesn't call it an "exercise".

I am assuming that most of my readers are doing these or similar poses already. My approach to the particular poses discussed in this book, besides simply describing them, is to draw readers' attention to ways of altering the poses to suit those with physical limitations, weaknesses, or restricted flexibility; to identify errors and mistaken ideas that people commonly bring to these poses; and, to look at how optimal coordination can be achieved within the poses.

Some of the chapters also have detailed discussions on the anatomical considerations related to each pose, as well as explanations of how everyday postural habits tend to be affected and accentuated by certain poses.

The sequence of the sections is arbitrary. I have started this section of the book with the Mountain Pose or *Tadasana*, which allows me to engage in an in-depth examination of the idea of good and bad posture, as well as to critique common beliefs about good posture and posture correction.

I hope this book may encourage some readers to seek out a teacher who can give them some direct instructions. As already discussed, Alexander used mirrors so that he could check his kinesthetic sensations against what he could perceive visually. Nowadays, we can also use a video camera linked to a screen to observe ourselves in the moment of moving.

The common theme running through these chapters on yoga poses is, that people differ, and because of this, there is no "correct" way of doing each pose so as to work for everyone. Instead, the so-called "correct" way to approach the poses involves: paying attention to our own unique body; our own flexibility, strength, structural issues, and habitual movement patterns; as well as, the mental and emotional state we bring to the activity. We need to understand what works best for ourselves, using the pose intelligently, as a means to experience openness, expansion, therefore, freeing and adapting it to our body. We want the body to move as a coordinated whole, paying particular attention to the length of the whole spine and the balanced relationship of the head, neck, and back (the primary control).

I always ask my students to be very clear about their intentions in any pose. By this I mean, that they should be clear about the direction and flow of energy that the particular pose opens up for them and toward which they need to aim.

I hope that for some readers the descriptions and issues that are discussed in this section on the yoga poses, in conjunction with the rest of the book, will clarify and improve their thoughts and ideas about how to approach their yoga practice.

This section on postural yoga is laid out in a number of chapters covering several types of yoga poses. I have made no attempt to cover the full range of yoga poses: that would be a formidable task. However, the principles behind the instructions given for the poses in this section, can be applied to many more poses than just those described here.

TADASANA: MOUNTAIN POSE AND GOOD POSTURE

There isn't anything either right or wrong when dealing with co-ordination. There are degrees of movement. Life is really moving from one position to another. We never stop and say, "This is right—this is my posture, this is the way I ought to be." If we do that, we're stiff trying to hold that posture. It isn't natural for our bodies to be held in positions.

— *Marjorie Barstow[1]* —

The Mountain Pose (Fig. 32.1), a staple of many yoga classes, is often described as the "foundation for all standing poses," with the benefits said to include:

- Developing symmetry and balance of body alignment
- Developing internal focus
- Improving the strength of spinal and abdominal musculature

From an Alexander Technique point of view, refining and perfecting upright posture is the work of a lifetime. Indeed, the act of being upright is something that very few people do with good coordination. Although most of us don't spend a lot of time in a static standing posture, this pose represents the starting place from which we initiate all of our movements: in this way it influences us, for good or ill, in all of our activities. The process of learning to finely coordinate one's self in an upright stance—both stationary and in movement—is a major part of the three-year full-time training for Alexander Technique teachers.

Figure 32.1

Once you have lost free and coordinated upright posture, for whatever reason, it is no easy matter to restore it. The philosopher John Dewey, who was had lessons with Alexander, described the difficulty with "standing straight", very clearly:

> A man who has a bad habitual posture tells himself, or is told, to stand up straight. If he is interested and responds, he braces himself, goes through certain movements, and it is assumed that the desired result is substantially attained; and that the position is retained at least as long as the man keeps the idea or order in mind. Consider the assumptions which are here made.It is implied that the means or effective conditions of the realization of a purpose exist independently of established habit and even that they may be set in motion in opposition to habit. It is assumed that means are there, so that the failure to stand erect is wholly a matter of failure of purpose and desire. . . . Now in fact a man who can stand properly does so, and only a man who can does. In the former case, fiats of will are unnecessary, and in the latter useless. A man who does not stand properly forms a habit of standing improperly, a positive, forceful habit The common implication that his mistake is merely negative, that he is simply failing to do the right thing, and that the failure can be made good by an order of will is absurd. . . . Of course, something happens when a man acts upon his idea of standing straight. For a little while, he stands differently, but only a different kind of badly. He then takes the unaccustomed feeling which accompanies his unusual stance as evidence that he is now standing straight. But there are many ways of standing badly, and he has simply shifted his usual way to a compensatory bad way at some opposite extreme.[2]

Try this Experiment for Yourself

Stand side-on to a full-length mirror in what feels to you like a good upright posture. Look to see if what you are feeling, is reflected in what you are seeing. If you are like the average person, you may see that you are:

- *Pulling your head and shoulders back.*
- *Locking your knees and pushing your pelvis forwards.*
- *Arching/hollowing your lower back so that instead of your weight connecting through your pelvis and legs onto your feet, you are holding yourself up by creating tension in your legs, pelvis and lower back.*

The Problem of Faulty Sensory Perception

We all believe that when we feel we are standing straight, we are in fact doing so. Yet for most people nothing could be further from the truth. The reality is, that we are almost certainly, as Dewey explains, simply standing in a different bad way from how we were standing before we decided to "stand up straight."

A major insight of the Alexander Technique is that once people have lost their everyday underlying coordination, they have also lost their ability to kinesthetically sense what they are doing with their body with any accuracy.

The Alexander Technique is, in fact, a process of gradually repairing this unreliable sensory perception. As a result, their sensory perception will eventually match what they are actually doing with their bodies. An implication of faulty sensory perception is, that if a person who no longer stands well, uses kinesthetic and proprioceptive feedback to discern how to change the manner of standing, true coordination will not be found.

In Figure 32.2A you see someone who feels he is standing upright. Figure 32.2B shows him standing once he has been guided manually and verbally by an Alexander teacher. Figure 32.2C shows his internal sense of where the Alexander teacher has guided him.

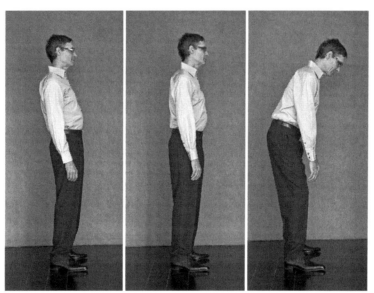

Figure 32.2A   Figure 32.2B   Figure 32.2C

— *How Tadasana Is Commonly Described* —

Instructions given in the yoga books I have reviewed for this chapter share common themes. These are mostly variations and elaborations of the pose described in B.K.S. Iyengar's classic *Light on Yoga*.[3] This description begins with the instruction to "stand erect," followed by a detailed description of the placement of the feet on the ground including: the instruction for the heels and the big toes to be touching each other; for the heads of the metatarsals to be on the floor; and, for stretching all the toes flat on the floor. He then gives specific instructions for the knees, hips, stomach, chest, and the spine being "stretched up" and the neck being "straight." The photo accompanying his description is very similar to Figure 32.1, with the arms being held, extended straight and slightly out from the side of the body.

Descriptions by other teachers also begin from the feet on the floor and they elaborate, often in great detail, manipulations that the yoga practitioner does, to particular bits of her body. For example, John Schumacher describes "gripping with your buttocks as you internally rotate your thighs. The soft openness of your pelvis frees your spine, while the firmness of your buttocks lifts and supports it."[4]

Other common instructions, some of which you may be familiar with, include:

- Contract the muscles of the quadriceps to pull the knee caps up.
- Rotate both thighs inward.
- Lengthen the neck so that the crown of the head moves to the ceiling.
- Slide the shoulder blades down the back.[5]

I won't attempt to make a full list of the large number of specific adjustments suggested for different areas of the body. But a principle behind all of these suggestions is encapsulated in David Coulter's description of how all standing postures are to be organized: from distal (from the ends of the limbs) to proximal (to the center): "Standing postures are . . . constructed from the feet to the hips to the torso, and from the hands to the shoulders and the torso."[6] The head is not even mentioned, in this description.

As we have discussed in the preceding chapters, however, central coordination is of paramount importance in the Alexander Technique. In fact, Alexander refers to this coordination of the head on top of the spine and its relationship to the torso, — as creating the primary control for the whole of the organism.

In this regard, an article in *The Conversation* on what makes a great tennis coach, is instructive:

Through a series of experiments (the results of which haven't yet been published) analysing the gaze behaviour of coaches we have discovered that when watching a player's serve, expert coaches tend to focus on proximal areas (those close to the midline) such as the trunk. Novices spend more time viewing the racquet and ball motion. . . . It is well known that the ability to interpret and use earlier occurring information ("proximal kinematics") is a key contributor to expertise. Proximal segments (such as the trunk) are critically important as they form the foundation of movement. With a greater understanding of the kinetic chain—a sequence of movements, usually proximal to distal, used to create an effective tennis serve—expert coaches are able to identify problems with the player's game.[6]

In cultures whose members have retained more balance and coordination than have people in modern chair-bound cultures, it is common to see people, and particularly women, carrying large loads on their heads. As discussed in Chapter 24, it is imperative that the whole body be optimally organized to support this weight without damaging the neck or spine. Figure 32.3 beautifully demonstrates how to support weight placed on the top of the head. In cultures where this practice is common, you will not see:

- Knee caps pulled up
- Chest raised
- Shoulder blades pulled back
- Contracting of hips or buttocks

Figure 32.3

Do you know how much your head weighs?
Between 4.5 and 5 kilos (9.9–11 pounds)!
Try picking up a 4 or 5kg bag of potatoes.
Try resting it (or if you have a bad neck, think about resting it)
on top of your head. Notice the amount of force it puts through
your body. If we are well coordinated there will be
an expansive response to support that weight.
If badly coordinated the result will be compression.

None of these actions are required to coordinate the body, and engaging them will interfere with easy balance and coordination. In fact, most of these actions would cause the weight to transfer in a way that would immediately put excess pressure on the discs, vertebrae, and all the joints.

On the contrary, what we see is a fine balance of the head on top of the spine, with not the slightest overcontraction through the neck or back. The extra weight is being supported directly to the feet through the bones and deep postural muscles, without any overactivation of the more superficial muscles.

The suggestion that we should progressively align ourselves, arranging the distal body parts first, and progressively adjusting inward, is the exact opposite of how easy coordination should work. As we have seen with the Alexander Technique, we work to gain the freedom of the whole body through the proper coordination of the central axis, which is created by the balance of the head on top of the spine, length through the spine, and expansion and freedom through the torso.

Coordination Is Primarily an Overall Neurological Action

The common theme of all of the suggestions listed above, is about changing the overall posture in bits and pieces, the knees, the feet, the shoulders, the neck, etc.

But how, we must ask, do individuals interpret such instructions? Anyone who teaches yoga, or any physical skill, will understand that even the simplest instruction is interpreted diversely. For example, when a yoga teacher asks students in a class to hold their arms out to the side, parallel to the floor, this will be undertaken in a variety of ways, but each student will believe he or she is accurately following instructions.

Regardless of the accuracy of these suggestions, the question remains: Does a balanced standing posture automatically arise out of correcting and organizing individual parts and areas of the body?

Both the Alexander Technique and neurological science would answer this question with an unequivocal "no." Insisting that coordination is primarily a global/holistic neurological action. The nervous system always deals with movement and posture as a whole gestalt. As Mabel Elsworth Todd puts it, "This automatic process [balance through the body] is interfered with whenever we attempt to force into a new position any particular part without reference to the pattern of the whole."[8] Or as Alexander describes it, we can only set up the conditions to indirectly create balanced posture and poise. And removing the interferences is the beginning of creating those conditions.

The Silken Tent

She is as in a field a silken tent
At midday when the sunny summer breeze
Has dried the dew and all its ropes relent,
So that in guys it gently sways at ease,
And its supporting central cedar pole,
That is its pinnacle to heavenward
And signifies the sureness of the soul,
Seems to owe naught to any single cord,
But strictly held by none, is loosely bound
By countless silken ties of love and thought
To everything on earth the compass round,
And only by one's going slightly taut
In the capriciousness of summer air
Is of the slightest bondage made aware.

— Robert Frost —

We would be well served by removing a number of interferences, and the key one is our very idea of standing upright. "Stand up straight, pull your shoulders back, tuck your pelvis under, pull your kneecaps up, tighten your legs and buttocks, pull your stomach in . . ." are very common instructions for standing upright not only in relationship to the Mountain Pose but just regarding posture in general. Attempts to follow these instructions may be conscious, but they are frequently *unconscious* because the original instruction or impetus has been forgotten, and the instructions are now embedded in postural and movement patterns.

Many disciplines and practices such as ballet, martial arts, and gymnastics have a "home base" standing position. In all cases, this home base is deceptively simple and mostly done with less consciousness than other "more difficult" postures, poses, or movements, which need to be executed with more obvious skill than the seemingly simple base poses. But those base poses inform overall coordination in every subsequent movement within those disciplines; therefore healthy coordination in the base poses is essential for ease and safety in the rest of the discipline. People in these home-base positions frequently overuse the superficial muscles, in particular the extensors of the lower back, thereby contracting the musculature in the neck, back, legs, and feet.

We would do well to cultivate the qualities of ease, balance, and quiet strength outlined in Robert Frost's poem "The Silken Tent." This, of course, is easier said than done. Most of us have developed habits that discoordinate us. As a result, easeful posture, which means being efficiently coordinated, is very likely to feel wrong. Many people will need one-on-one Alexander Technique lessons to be able to achieve true ease and balance.

Finding Balance Without Stiffness

As previously discussed, we have two types of skeletal muscles: postural and movement. In a position like the Mountain Pose, we want to turn off the movement muscles and allow the postural muscles to do their work. There is no need to stiffen the arms and legs, to pull the shoulders back, or to contract the back. Most of the instructions listed above are to turn on movement muscles that are not actually required for maintaining easy upright posture. Indeed, once these more superficial movement muscles are turned on there will always be an accentuation of the various twists and kinks in the structure.

I would suggest that *Tadasana* simply be our normal easy standing, what we revert to in between poses, and that we pay particular attention to identifying and undoing the tightening habits that we bring to our everyday standing.

NOTES 1. BRENNER (1987). 2. DEWEY (1922), 28–30. 3. IYENGAR (2001), 40. 4. SCHUMACHER (1990), 70. 5. ELLSWORTH (2010), 32. 6. COULTER (2001), 228. 7. GIBLIN (2013), 5. 8. TODD (1937, 1980), 102.

FLOOR STRETCHES

I normally start my own yoga practice lying for some time in the Alexander Technique semisupine position, before practicing a number of lying-down poses. This allows time to notice any subtle tightening, and undo any extra tightness or imbalance in the muscles. While lying there I ask for an expansive release, which sets up the system for effective movement.

I will cover a few of these poses in this chapter, though the twists have a dedicated chapter later in the book.

These may appear to be quite simple poses, but there are some things that require our awareness if the poses are to be safe and effective:

- Our primary intention must be to coordinate the whole body. Frequently people do a number of things in these poses: tighten their neck, tense the shoulders, or grip the jaw or tense their ribs, whether by restraining their breathing or pushing the chest toward the ceiling. It is common for people to tense their neck to lift their legs. Those with a habitually tight neck use their neck muscles to hold their legs up!
- There is such a thing as too much flexibility. Hypermobile people with a large range of movement should work with poses that promote strength and stability, as listed below.
- It is important to differentiate the sensation of muscle stretch from nerve irritation. In particular, those who have had sciatica—pain caused by irritation or pressure on the sciatic nerve that runs through the buttock and back of the leg—need to be mindful of stimulating nerve pain. Sciatic pain and impingement is particularly likely in stretches that work the hamstrings.
- Those with hip issues need to avoid movements that irritate the hip joint, and focus on releasing the leg out of the hip socket in all these poses. They should avoid any poses that cause them to contract the leg into the hip socket, and many people with hip problems have a strong habit of doing exactly that.
- The ligaments around the knee joint perform a very important function in stabilizing a joint that is easily injured. Overstretching these ligaments causes an unpleasant sensation and increases the potential for injuring the knee, so this should be avoided.

— *Preparation: Bringing the Leg Up* —

The poses listed in this section all begin from lying in the semisupine position (Fig. 33.1) and raising one or both legs (Fig. 33.2). Many people habitually activate this movement by tightening the neck, contracting the back, and slightly twisting the torso, which interferes with their freedom and coordination.

Instead, we need to send the Alexander directions, and thus, inhibit the immediate impulse to tighten the neck and contract the back, that is triggered in response to the intention to raise the leg. It may initially appear that there is no way to accomplish this movement without those contractions. One strategy people may use to prevent the back contraction, is to tighten the abdomen and push the lower back onto the floor. This may prevent some of the tightening, but it is not the coordinated response we want to develop in this movement. As discussed in the chapter on the core, we want the activation of the abdominals to occur as a reflex within our movement patterns. This involves: paying focused attention; catching the critical moment just prior to the movement; and, making a very clear and conscious choice in that moment not to give consent to the impulse to tighten.

One can gain extra stability for the torso by pressing the supporting foot into the floor as the other one is raised. If you are raising both legs it is easiest to raise one at a time. It may help to bend the knee of the first leg you raise toward your torso, and hold on to that knee to help stabilize the torso as you lift the other leg.

Some people find this process difficult or impossible, even with the aid of a teacher. In this case, this process is helpful as an exercise in its own right. You can begin with your feet raised on a block, or with feet pressed into a wall with your pelvis close enough to the wall that you can lift one foot without any gripping (Fig. 33.3). As you develop the ability to refuse consent to the gripping in these supported positions, you can gradually work with the feet lower until you are able to lift them from the floor without the excess gripping.

It is equally important to release excess gripping, in the process of bringing the legs back onto the floor.

Figure 33.1 *Figure 33.2* *Figure 33.3*

Reclining Hamstring Stretch: Supta Padangusthasana

Place a belt around the sole of one foot and take that leg into the air.

Points of focus:

- It is not necessary to straighten the knee, and it certainly should not be hyperextended. As noted already, it is important to not overstretch the ligaments that support the knee joint, which would eventually lead to lack of stability in the knee joint and consequent knee problems. The stretch should be felt in center of the hamstring muscles rather than behind the knee, so the knee needs to be bent enough that the ligaments around the knee are not stretched; those with very tight muscles may need to bend their leg a lot.

- The leg needs to be very slightly rotated laterally (away from the midline; Fig. 33.5) as it extends out of the hip joint. Most people rotate it medially (inward; Fig. 33.6), which jams the femur into the hip socket.

- Be aware of the foot. It should be angled so that the foot is squared off, angled as it would be if you were standing on the ceiling (Fig. 33.7). But many people collapse the whole foot inward (Fig. 33.8). These people normally have collapsed arches, so the use of the foot in this pose mirrors how they use it when standing. In those cases, attempting to square the foot may strongly stretch the muscles on the inside of the lower leg, which need to regain their length to be able to support the foot. Care should be taken to not rotate the whole leg inward while doing this, so straighten the foot only as far as you can while keeping the leg centered.

- If the nerve is being irritated by this stretch, bend the knee as much as necessary to avoid this irritation. You will still stretch the muscle with the knee bent, but if you don't then you shouldn't be doing this pose.

- Make sure the movement is from the hip joint, and that the lumbar spine is not rounded or pushed into the floor. If you are quite flexible, you may need to work strongly to avoid this. It may help to actively extend the opposite leg, even pushing the foot that will be slightly raised into a wall. If it's not comfortable to have the other leg stretched out along the floor, you can bend that leg.

Figure 33.4

Figure 33.5

Figure 33.6

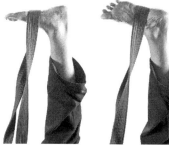

Figure 33.7   *Figure 33.8*

Wide-Legged Reclining Stretch: Salamba Supta Upavistha Konasana

Place a separate belt around the sole of each foot and extend both legs straight up into the air; then spread the legs apart (Fig. 33.9).

Points of focus:
- Make sure the legs are rotated slightly outward from the hip socket.
- If you have hip problems, you need to inquire whether this rotation of the legs is good for you: if it hurts, this means it may be further damaging your hip joint.
- If you have high mobility, then in this pose you shouldn't attempt to increase flexibility in this pose, but instead practice a strengthening posture (below).
- A variation of this pose is to bring the pelvis close to the wall and spread the legs apart, with the legs supported by the wall.

Figure 33.9

Reclining Leg Side Stretch

Place a belt around the sole of your right foot and lift the right leg while keeping the left leg down on the floor. Then take the right leg across the torso to the left at approximately a 45-degree angle (Fig. 33.10).

Points of focus:
- The same considerations regarding the previous poses also apply to this one.
- Keep the pelvis fairly flat on the floor; this is not a twist.
- The position of the stretch along the leg will differ considerably from one person to another. It is important, once again, to not stretch the knee ligaments, and to differentiate between muscle stretch and nerve stretch.
- This posture should be avoided if it aggravates lower back or hip pain. (This caveat, of course, applies to *all* poses.)

Figure 33.10

Strengthening Poses

There are a number of poses that involve lifting the legs without support from the arms. If chosen appropriately for our own strength and flexibility and if done well, they will reflexively activate and tone the postural muscles. For some people this is a relatively easy action, but if the postural muscles are not strong enough or the requisite coordination to support the weight of the legs, is lacking, then we may lift them at the expense of the integrity of the torso, particularly by gripping the neck, tightening the shoulders, and hollowing the lower back. In working with these poses mindfully, we can begin to train our motor system by catching, then inhibiting the impulse to tighten and discoordinate in response to extra muscular work. We learn to keep our neck free and apply the Alexander directions to coordinate ourselves, while doing stronger muscular work, something we can take into everyday activities. People with a tight, sore neck typically tighten it in any activity that calls for extra effort—even just thinking hard, which was illustrated in the famous statue of *The Thinker* in Chapter 6.

When we lift our legs without the support of the belt, the muscles of the torso and neck activate to support the legs as well as maintaining the integrity of the torso. This activation needs to balanced; often the activation tends to be more in the neck or lower back.

Leg Lowered and Raised

From the semisupine position, lift one leg as described above. Then, maintaining it reasonably straight or slightly bent, slowly lower that leg toward the floor (Figs. 33.11 and 33.12). Lower the leg only as far as possible without activating excess tension through the neck or pulling the lower back off the floor; all the postural muscles of the torso must work in unison to support the weight of the leg. If the leg can go all the way to the floor without excess tension, hover it just above the floor for a full breath, and then raise the leg. This can be repeated three or four times on each side, but not so many times that you become fatigued and begin to discoordinate yourself.

Figure 33.11   *Figure 33.12*

Both Legs Lowered and Raised

Similar to a single leg lift except done with both legs.

Warning: most people can't do this without severely compromising their coordination. In fact, to teach this in a general yoga class is positively dangerous.

Both Legs Apart and Together

This is a medium-intensity strengthening pose, and it is not suitable for those with lower back pain.

Bend both knees toward the sky, extend both legs, and then very slowly spread the legs apart and bring them back together a number of times. Practice only enough repetitions that you can still maintain proper coordination through the torso, and do not contract the neck (Figs. 33.13, 33.14, and 33.15).

Come out of this pose by bending the knees to bring the feet to the floor, and keep your neck free throughout this movement.

Figure 33.13   Figure 33.14   Figure 33.15

— Arms Above the Head —

- From the semisupine position raise both arms into the air, keeping the neck free as you lift them.
- Actively extend through the arms in the direction of the floor behind you.
- Go only as far as your flexibility allows you, to maintain the length, opening, and expansion throughout the torso, and to feel only a moderate stretch in the shoulder area.
- Ensure that the arms are a connected part of your Alexander directions and the overall active expansion of the torso.

Comments:
- The most common thing people do in this pose is overstretch themselves, which tightens and pushes the ribcage forward and hollows the lower back.
- This pose gives an indication of the true range of motion of the arms and shoulder girdle. If people are restricted in this movement of their taking their arms back from lying down, then when they raise their arms in standing poses they are likely to lift their chest, narrow their back, and contract their lumbar spine in the attempt to put the arms up above their head. It will be useful for them to work in the standing poses in exactly this same coordinated way, making sure that the arms are connected into the overall length and expansion of the torso.

Figure 33.16

Arms to the Side and Bent

- Extend the arms at about a 90-degree angle out from the torso while intending to expand out of the shoulder (glenohumeral) joint.
- Bend at the elbows as you move the back of your hands toward the floor. Many people will find this quite easy, but some will find they have insufficient range of motion for one or both hands to reach the floor. In this case they should not try to push, but rather place support under the hand(s).
- Continue to send the directions for opening and expansion through the entire torso and arms. Direct the elbows away from the shoulder with the intention for more space in the shoulder joint.
- If there is restriction, notice how it connects from the arms into the torso. Without muscularly doing it, simply send the intention for opening and expansion through the lines of holding.

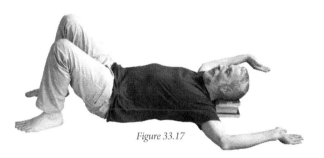

Figure 33.17

MONKEY: POSES BASED ON THE POSITION OF MECHANICAL ADVANTAGE *(UTKATASANA)*

The reeducational work, done with an Alexander teacher, in the process of getting into and out of a chair prepares people for going into Alexander's "position of mechanical advantage," which is commonly known as "the monkey." It involves the whole body coming down in space and bending forward while maintaining openness and expansion through the torso, and neither rounding nor hyperextending the spine.

People habitually bend forward, from the same particular point in their spine. If this single point is constantly and consistently stretched in this way, the habit is reinforced and physical damage gradually accumulates. Constantly hinging from one point in the spine is a bit like bending a piece of wire back and forth at one point; eventually it will give. This will be discussed in more detail in the chapter on forward bends.

Unlike the individual joints between our vertebrae, our hip joints have a great range of movement, and effective bending makes use of these mobile joints. Developing our ability to work with the monkey teaches us how to bend without putting pressure through the spine. Not only that, when done well this pose helps us access extra length and flexibility through the spine.

Stuart McGill carried out a study in which a subject's lower back muscles were measured in a pose resembling the monkey. The measurements were compared to those taken taken when the subject was bending with a fully flexed spine. There was a massive reduction of force through the lower back in the monkey-type position compared to when the spine was flexed.[1]

Developing students' ability to bend efficiently in this way is a common part of Alexander Technique lessons.

Figure 34.1   F.M. Alexander teaching the monkey to a young girl

Looking at these pictures of simple monkey positions (Figs. 34.1 and 34.2), you might expect this would be quite easy for you. In my experience, however, it is initially beyond many people's ability to move into this simple posture without either hyper-flexing or hyperextending the spine. In addition, people will tend to throw their weight forward and onto the inside of their feet, which means they have to overwork their leg, buttock, hip, and back muscles to maintain balance. We want to include the monkey as a habitual part of our daily movement, but most people need to relearn it.

When done accurately and precisely, it activates a pattern of mutually balanced antagonistic pulls through the musculature and connective tissue of the body. In this position it is possible to take the torso out of its habitual contraction or collapse, so that we can activate a widening of the back, a freeing of the floating ribs, and an opening of the breathing. Care must be taken to ensure that the weight is supported directly through the feet and there is no gripping through the lower back, buttocks, or legs. The entire lower body does the minimum work required to maintain this posture.

In the first two photos, the monkey is being demonstrated as an exercise, divorced from any practical activity; but Figure 34.3 demonstrates its use in daily life. Figures 34.3 and 34.4 show the difference in ease between the two options we have while doing work that requires forward bending—whether it is the deep bending required for this type of work, or simply bending forward over a counter in preparing food.

Figure 34.2

In Figure 34.3 the forward bend is coming primarily from the hip joint, while the spine maintains length and the torso remains open and expansive. By contrast, in Figure 34.4 we see that the spine is being flexed from the middle of the back and the torso is compressing.

You may have had the experience of bending over at some point, perhaps to pick up something quite light from the floor, or to tie up your shoelaces, and experiencing a sharp and intense burst of pain followed by persistent pain and immobility that may last for some time. In some more serious cases, the cause of the pain is a fracture of the end plate of a vertebra, which may be accompanied by an audible popping sound, though nothing will show up on a scan or X-ray.

Figure 34.3 Hard work

Other potential causes of the pain include rupture of, or damage to a vertebral disc, or the sense of electric shock caused by sudden pressure on a nerve exiting the spine. Whatever the cause, the muscles of the back then go into spasm to protect the spine, and one is sore and restricted in movement for some time. This bend can be looked at as "the final straw," with years of faulty body use culminating in physical damage. In some cases this pain and spasming can become either an ongoing chronic condition, or one that improves for a time but then recurs at intervals.

Lifting heavy weights without good body use is obviously going to damage the back very quickly, and weight lifters talk about lifting with "neutral spine." Neutral spine refers to every joint being held in an optimal position to permit equal distribution of force through the spine. This positions the spinal column and pelvis in a safe midpoint between the extremes of flexion and extension.

Figure 34.4   Back-breaking work

In yoga classes here is how I teach the bend, which is based on the monkey (Fig. 34.5):

1. Stand close to the back of a chair.
2. Using the Alexander directions, come to a point of easy upright balance with the feet apart and angling slightly outward. Use a mirror to ensure that you are not leaning backward in an attempt to "stand up straight."
3. Continue to direct to free the neck and send the head forward and up, with the back lengthening and widening as you send the knees forward over the center of your feet. You should not press down into the legs while doing this.
4. Lightly take hold of the back of the chair.
5. Continue to lengthen through the torso as you begin to tilt the chair forward.
6. Continue with the directions and make sure the head is leading the movement. Tilt the chair further forward while rotating forward from the hip joint.
7. Move forward until your torso is at a right angle from your hip joint, or until tightness in your hamstrings prevents any further forward movement of the pelvis. Make sure, using a mirror or feedback from a teacher, that you are neither flexing nor overcontracting the spine (Fig. 34.5).
8. Stay in the pose for ten to twenty breaths, provided it is easy to do so and you can maintain your coordination; continue to send the directions. Identify any subtle tightening, and release it as you gradually experience more opening and expansion.
9. Resend the directions and gently bring the chair back toward you while returning to standing. This is the point when many people overstraighten themselves. Make sure you don't overextend as you come upright.

Some people find that as they hinge forward the pelvis doesn't continue to rotate and instead, they round forward through the torso. This may be for one of three reasons. First, although the physical flexibility exists, the person does not have a movement pathway in the motor cortex for this to happen. Many people feel that knees bending forward and pelvis rotating forward are contradictory movements, and they will automatically straighten their legs as the pelvis rotates forward, or they will rotate the pelvis backward as they bend their knees. The second potential impediment to the pelvis hinging, is a faulty sensory awareness, that guides people somewhere other than where they believe they are going. And the third possibility may be tightness in the hamstrings, so that even though the knees are bent, the pull of the hamstring prevents the pelvis from rotating further forward.

In the next chapter we will look at using this position as our starting point for squatting.

Figure 34.5

— *Utkatasana: Lightning Bolt Pose, Half Squat* —

Similar principles apply to entering *Utkatasana*, except that you are not using the chair and are not coming so far forward. The most common error in this posture is for the lumbar spine to be contracted and hyperextended into a backbend. The torso needs to be fully extended and expanded.

Take care to release and lengthen through the legs, as gripping the legs is common in this pose. As the knees bend and the torso angles forward, lengthen through the muscles of the upper and lower legs. Both hamstrings and quadriceps lengthen, while simultaneously working to support the angled body.

Likewise, the muscles of the torso are also lengthening, as the curves of the spine are slightly or considerably lengthened. As the muscles are lengthening, they are also working a little more strongly to support the torso, just like the legs. We need to ask for elasticity within these working and lengthening muscles.

As the weight of the head shifts further forward in this pose, the muscles of the neck are called on to increase their tone and to support the head. Once more we need to access freedom and elasticity within the extra work.

Figure 34.6

NOTES 1. "The fully flexed spine is associated with myoelectric silence in the back extensors and strained posterior passive tissues and high shearing force on the lumbar spine (both from reaction shear in the upper body and interspinous ligament strain)," whereas "a more neutral spine posture recruits the pars lumborum muscle groups and aligns the fibres to support the shear forces." In the example that Stuart McGill used, the fully flexed posture resulted in 1900 N of shear load on the lumbar spine, while the other reduced the shear load to about 200 N—a massive reduction. (McGill, 2007, 102)

SQUATTING

Galen Cranz told this story in *The Chair*:

> In 1852 an English colonialist working in India voiced his complaint about the local workmen. He was particularly indignant that blacksmiths, carpenters and masons squatted to work, complaining indignantly "All work with their knees nearly on a level with their chin." He noted that this posture suggested "indolence and inefficiency . . . especially irritating to an Englishman", but even more so to one who hires and pays such workmen.
>
> As the workmen ignored his orders to cease working in this way, he bolted their anvils to a table, but within a day or two his workers had taken to squatting on stools in order to reach their anvils. At this point the colonialist gave us reasoning that he could not get them to stand because of "a deficiency of muscular power in the lower limbs" which he attributed to their not using chairs.[1]

Figure 35.1   F.M. Alexander

The hip joint, or acetabulofemoral joint, is a ball-and-socket joint that includes the head of the femur (the ball) and acetabulum (the socket) of the pelvis (Figs. 35.2 and 35.3). Its major function is supporting the weight of the body, in both stillness and movement. The weight of the trunk is connected through the pelvis to the femur, legs, and feet via this joint. There is an optimum angle of the pelvis that transmits the trunk weight in line with the design of this joint, and indeed all the weight-bearing joints.

It is also our major joint for bending forward. In yoga poses like the seated forward bend, *Paschimottanasana*, if we fail to use this joint through its appropriate range of movement, we inappropriately flex the spine and stress the sacroiliac joints, the facet joints of the vertebrae and the discs. In fact, even not practicing yoga, this is what most people do in the numerous day-to-day activities that involve bending forward.

The terms *hip* and *hip joint* are generally vaguely understood. If we ask a group of people the location of their hip joints, we will get a number of responses. Some will point to the top of their iliac crests, others to their greater trochanters, and others in the general direction of the pelvis. When yoga or movement teachers ask people to bend from their hip joints, people will interpret this instruction in different ways. It is important to have a clear idea of the exact location of the hip joints in order to learn to use them efficiently.

This joint is not palpable through the muscle and connective tissue. We can get an idea of the width and location of these joints by placing the hand over the pubic symphysis as it spans the distance between the two joints. As we can see in Figures 35.2 and 35.3, the pelvis is a very deep joint. In Figure 35.4, we see the index fingers placed in the closest point to the joints on the surface of the body.

LEFT HIP JOINT

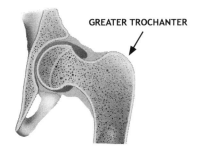

GREATER TROCHANTER

Figure 35.2

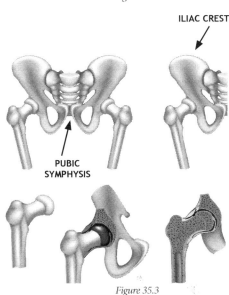

ILIAC CREST

PUBIC SYMPHYSIS

Figure 35.3

Figure 35.4

Squatting has been universal throughout 99.9 percent of human history and prehistory. It is a movement that works the hip joint through most of its range of motion (Figs. 35.5 and 35.6). Similar to the Monkey Pose, what we can see in these squats is a lengthening of the muscles of the legs and the torso. However, after a lifetime of sitting on chairs and modern toilets, most people have lost the ability to squat with any degree of comfort or coordination. Yet this is a posture that human beings have used since the dawn of time. As children begin to walk they are constantly moving from standing to squatting (Fig. 35.5), but they quickly lose their familiarity with squatting in our modern world.

By contrast, people who have been brought up in cultures where squatting is the norm are able to squat with their heels planted firmly on the ground, the arches of their feet activated, their knees abducted (moving away from the midline), and the torso and spine lengthening. We also know that in cultures in which squatting is part of daily life there are fewer cases of osteoarthritis of the hip joint and back problems, than in Western countries.

What is the effect, then, on people who never exercise this major part of their flexibility, a movement that was used daily by their ancestors over millions of years? I believe that the ill effects on posture, movement, and well-being are both profound and widespread. When we sit in a chair, the most common tendency is to slump through the whole torso, either by poking the head forward and rounding the upper back or by tilting the pelvis so the weight moves toward the sacrum. Almost equally common is the compensatory movement called "sitting up straight," where the extensor muscles, particularly of the lower back, are overused to maintain uprightness. At the same time, the legs are commonly held tightly, often being adducted (pulled toward each other), contracted and pulled into the hip joints, or one leg (always the same one) is crossed tightly over the other.

Figure 35.5

This distortion of the body puts pressure through most of the joints, muscles, and organs, which predisposes us toward a whole range of symptoms including; back and neck pain, headaches, repetitive strain injuries (RSI), knee pain, and hip problems. It also sets us up for a concomitant restriction of the breath, and it places pressure on the internal organs.

Restoring Our Ability to Squat

In the classical yoga texts there is no *asana* that incorporates squatting. It was so much a part of daily life that there was no reason to either practice it, or to develop the ability to squat. Today, however, most of us need to practice diligently to restore the ability to squat with our heels on the floor; maintaining a slight but lengthening curve through the spine, finding ease in the neck, back, and shoulders, and with the knees angling out over the feet in such a way, that the feet maintain a full healthy arch.

Modern people attempting this pose often cannot keep their heels on the floor, or if they can, their legs collapse inward, which collapses the arches of the feet (Fig. 35.10). In addition, the few who are able to keep their heels in contact with the floor, usually find that their back rounds strongly forward, as this is the only way they can avoid falling backward in the pose.

There is not just one muscle or muscle group that must be released to regain the ability to squat. Some people will notice a marked restriction in their ankle joints, others in their calf muscles or hip flexors; but in fact it is a whole-body restriction. Some people who are quite flexible find they can't squat as far, or as comfortably, as others who have overall stiffer muscle tone. The problem is how to coordinate the whole body in this movement. It doesn't require great flexibility, just properly coordinated flexibility, and this coordinated flexibility can gradually be developed.

Figure 35.6

Here is a procedure for developing the squat:

- As described in the previous chapter, come into the Monkey Pose and tilt the chair forward, lengthening the whole torso as you fold and extend from the hip joint.
- From here, keep hands in contact with the chair and slide them to the edges of the seat as you move; continue to lengthen the torso while coming into a full squat with heels on the floor and knees pointing out over the center of the feet (Figs. 35.7, 35.8, and 35.9).
- *Warning:* you should never feel strain or pain in your knees, in this or any other yoga pose. If it feels as if you will strain your knees, then go only as far as is comfortable. You may find over time that you will be able to move further without jeopardizing your knees.
- Once your legs are fully bent, if you have the necessary flexibility then move your pelvis toward the floor and come toward a more upright squat. If you have to round your back to do this, then stay further forward; more flexibility will slowly develop.
- If this is quite impossible, you can place support under your heels, such as a wedge or a book, rather than risk falling over or completely distorting the whole body.
- Another way of working with this movement is to do supported squats, holding onto a door handle or heavy object such as a table when squatting to keep from falling backward.

The Benefits

Gradually, if you continue working with good coordination from the monkey to squatting, the whole body will begin to open up. The tendency to either collapse or overcontract the back will gradually reduce as the back muscles release. As the back lengthens and widens, the quality of its tissue and musculature changes, allowing the ribs to move freely with the breath. The diaphragm, which was previously restricted by the lack of movement in the floating ribs, is able to move easily in response to the demands of breathing, and pressure is taken off the abdominal organs.

Figure 35.7   *Figure 35.8*

Figure 35.9

Also the hip joints are exercised through their full range of flexion when we squat, and for most people it becomes easier to maintain natural foot arches. Provided the knees are directed out over the center of the feet, the movement of the knee joints remains in accordance with those joints' design; muscle imbalances in the hip rotators and leg muscles, (which would predispose incorrect tracking of the knees and yield collapse or overcontraction of the feet), will be corrected (Figs. 35.10 and 35.11).

Incorporating Squatting into Our Everyday Life

Of course, there are many ways to incorporate the squatting position into our daily life. We could replace the old toilet with a squat toilet. Or, if that might be too much for visitors in your one-toilet household, you can squat on the seat or purchase a platform to place over the toilet. Ideally, we can develop ourselves in our ordinary everyday activities without the need for special exercises.

Figure 35.10   Squat with knees coming in and feet collapsed

Figure 35.11   Squat with feet activated

NOTES   **1.** CRANZ (2013), 35.

STANDING POSES

The Warrior and other standing poses listed in this section, if done well, are dynamic strengthening poses offering an opportunity to work strongly with your legs, while maintaining openness and expansion through the upper body. Gradually increasing the time you spend in these poses will help you develop strength, stamina, and balance.

Make sure that you never get to the point of tightening your neck or interfering with your coordination in order to maintain the pose. Hypermobile people, who work these poses well, will learn to use their muscles appropriately and transform the habit of collapse. For the unwary, the habit of hyperlordosis will be accentuated in these poses.

Warrior Pose One: Virabhadrasana One

1. Stand at the front of the mat in an easy upright pose. Release the right knee forward a little and incline the torso slightly forward from the hip joints.
2. Taking care to maintain freedom in the neck, allow the head to release forward and up and expand through the torso as you step the right leg back. Place the ball and front of the right foot on the floor with the whole foot facing forward. The leg will be straight, or as straight as you can make it.
3. Angle the left foot very slightly out to the side and bend the left leg, pointing the knee out over the center of the left foot. The knee may bend to a right angle if you have sufficient flexibility, but do not discoordinate yourself trying to do this. The knee should not be flexed further forward than a position directly above the ankle.

Fig. 36.1 Warrior Pose One

4. Direct the neck to be free and the head to release forward and up, making sure that the whole torso is lengthening and expanding without contracting the lower back.

5. Maintaining the full length of the torso, raise both arms into the air. Be certain the movement comes from the flexibility of the shoulder joint and not from arching the back (Fig. 36.2).

6. Let go of any excess tension or holding through the neck or torso, and simultaneously counterbalance the forward direction of the bent front knee by sending the rear of the back foot back, while keeping the heel off the floor.

7. Only those who can fully and comfortably lengthen the spine and extend the whole torso should move into a back bend. Ensure that the movement is initiated from the head, which creates an extension through the upper back, instead of beginning the movement in the lumbar area. There should be no sense of compression in the lumbar area (Fig. 36.3).

Fig. 36.2   Take arms up only as far as is possible while keeping the full length through the torso.

Fig. 36.3   Moving into backbend while maintaining full expansion.

Comments:

- I first learned this pose with the back foot being angled sideways at about 90 degrees and then rotating the pelvis, so that it was facing forward. My observation of doing the pose in this way is, that it tends to put pressure on the back knee; very few people can actually get their pelvis facing forward, and it is rare for each side to be angled precisely the same as the other. This asymmetry then accentuates any habitual twisting pattern through the body.
- A common error in this posture is to put the lumbar spine into undue extension and contraction (Fig. 36.4). Discomfort or compression in the lumbar region is a sure sign that you are overarching this area.
- People with a strong habit of accentuating the lumbar lordosis may need to angle forward from the hips in this posture. (See the third person from the front in Fig. 36.1).
- Those with unstable ankle joints may find it difficult to find balance with the back foot facing forward. It is fine to hold on to a chair next to you or place one hand on the wall to assist with your balance.
- It is common for people to send the front knee inward, which jams the femur into the hip socket. Make sure that the knee is directed out over the center of the foot (Figs. 36.5 and 36.6).
- It is important to keep the legs active. Hypermobile people tend to sink into the pelvis and hang on the ligaments. Muscles, not ligaments, should be supporting you.

Fig. 36.4 *Lumbar overcontracted.*

Fig. 36.5 *Knee and foot collapsed.*

Fig. 36.6 *Sending the knee over the foot allows the foot to retain its arch.*

Warrior Pose Three: Virabhadrasana Three

1. Move into Warrior Pose One.
2. Bend the front leg and angle the whole torso forward over the front thigh.
3. Straighten the bottom leg and simultaneously lift the back leg.
4. Your pelvis should be level. If you have the flexibility, your back leg will be parallel to the floor. If your flexibility is more restricted, lift your leg only as far as you can without twisting the pelvis.
5. Remain in the pose for several even breaths.
6. Return to Warrior One by bending the bottom leg and returning the back leg to the floor with a controlled movement.

Variation/Preparation

1. Stand in front of a wall and hinge forward from the hips until the hands are supported by the wall.
2. Come forward from the hip joint, at a right angle if you have the flexibility to do so, while lengthening the torso. If you don't have sufficient flexibility, come to a lesser angle, going only as far as you can while maintaining length.
3. Raise one leg backward. Take it backward only as far as can be done while keeping the pelvis level.

Comments:

- When our balance is challenged it is very easy to tighten. Make sure you catch and prevent any tendency to contract your neck, hold your breath, and generally tighten your whole body. With the aid of the Alexander directions, continue to direct into openness and expansion, against the habit of tightening.
- Keep your torso square. If you can't get your leg back and up, it will help to work with poses that stretch the quadriceps and hip flexors.
- Do not hyperextend the lower back.

Fig. 36.7   Warrior pose Three

Warrior Pose Two: Virabhadrasana Two

1. From an easy standing pose, spread the legs apart sideways.

2. Rotating the leg from the hip joint, turn the right foot sideways to a 45-to-90-degree angle. The amount of turn will depend on your hip flexibility.

3. Turn the left foot slightly inward. The exact angle of the left foot will vary from person to person. Turn the leg only so far that the arch of the left foot does not collapse. Make sure to position the leg so there is no stress on the left knee joint.

4. Bend the right leg with the knee pointing toward the center of the right foot. Bring the thigh toward a position that is parallel to the floor, but do not let the knee bend further than a right angle. This is when the posture becomes tricky, because we want to make sure that bending the right knee out over the right foot does not collapse the arch or distort the torso. This may mean taking the right foot forward of the front plane of the torso and the left leg, or taking the left hip further forward. The right foot needs to be angled appropriately for the bend in the leg and the direction in which the knee is moving.

5. Return to your Alexander Technique directions for overall coordination, and bring both arms up and out to the side.

6. Activate the legs so that you have two opposing directions of rotation, out from the hip with each leg. This means there is a rotation in the right leg that is taking the knee out in the direction of the center of the foot, and a rotation in the left leg that sends the outside of the foot to the floor and maintains an arch in that foot.

7. Rotate the head to look over the right arm. This rotation must be completely free. Do not force it; the rotation must come out of the free alignment of the head, neck, and back.

Fig. 36.8   Warrior pose Two

Comments:

- Make sure the arms are coming out of the total length and width of the torso. Most people take the arms too far back, thus narrowing the upper back and tightening the muscles of the neck. If you think of taking both arms out to the side for balance as if you were on a tightrope, this is the appropriate place for the arms. If you were to pull your arms too far back when you need them for balance, you would fall.
- Avoid lifting your shoulders as you lift your arms.
- Energize the directions out through the arms, wrists, hands, and fingers. This is more of an energetic action than a muscular one.
- As with all the standing poses, people with an exaggerated lumbar lordosis need to ensure that they don't accentuate it in this pose.

Fig. 36.9   Warrior pose Two

Side Angle Pose: Utthita Parsvakonasana

1. Move into Warrior Pose Two (Figs. 36.8 and 36.9).
2. With the right knee bent, fold your torso sideways to the right while taking the left arm up, in such a way that there is a line of lengthening directly from the outside of the back foot, through the leg, the side of the body, and the arm, to the hand. The underside of the body should also be extended.
3. The distance you move into this posture will be determined by your flexibility (Figs. 36.10 and 36.11).
4. Ensure that there is not the slightest compression in the hip joint. Be sensitive to this, and don't push it.

Fig. 36.10   Side Angle Pose   Fig. 36.11   Side Angle Pose

Triangle Pose: Utthita Trikonasana

Go only as far as you can while maintaining length through both sides. Figures 36.12 and 36.13 demonstrate working with the pose while maintaining this length, but in Figure 36.14 the attempt to get the hand on the floor is distorting the torso.

1. From an easy erect stance, step the feet about a meter apart.
2. Turn left foot slightly in, around 30 degrees.
3. Turn the right foot out close to 90 degrees. The turnout will depend on your flexibility.

4. Engaging your Alexander directions, raise your right arm to the side and extend your torso to the right while moving the pelvis to the left. It is sideways movement out of the hip joint. Do not compress the right hip joint, which is common when people end-gain in this movement. At the same time ensure that the right knee is not hyperextended; the leg will be straight with a micro bend in the knee and the kneecap in line with the foot such that the arch of the foot is maintained.

5. Go on extending out to the side as far as you can go while keeping both sides of the torso lengthening, and then, depending on your flexibility, bring your right hand to rest on your thigh, knee, lower leg, foot, or the floor.

6. Take the left arm up into the air, and keep width and expansion through the upper back between the two hands.

7. Turn the head to look at the left hand, if this can be done with complete comfort.

Comments:

- This is a complex pose that requires precise instruction for most people to do it without discoordinating themselves. People commonly do one, several, or all of these things when they overextend into the pose: they collapse the lower side whilst rounding round the upper side of the torso, or they lock and inwardly rotate the right leg, which puts pressure on the knee joint and jams the femur into the hip socket, or they collapse the arches of the feet, or narrow and compress the back in lifting the arms, or position the head in a way that makes turning it painful or impossible.

Fig. 36.12   Fig. 36.13   Fig. 36.14

Half Moon Pose: Ardha Chandrasana

1. Begin standing easily, and then move the feet apart in the same way as for the Triangle Pose.
2. Bend the right knee, making sure it is moving out over the center of your right foot. Arrange the position of the foot to allow this to happen.
3. Bring the right hand onto a block or the floor, while making sure both sides of the torso are extending.
6. Keep both legs active and rotate your pelvis away from your standing leg, but don't compress the lower back.
7. Rotate your head to gaze at your left hand in the air. To do this without strain, your head will need to be in line with, and coordinated with, the torso. If you can't fully achieve this, keep looking forward.
8. Remain in the pose for several breaths. Gradually increase the time you stay in the pose (Fig. 36.15).

Fig. 36.15

Comments:

- This is an easier pose than the Triangle, but most people will find that they lose awareness of the position of their head and are unable to comfortably rotate their head.
- While learning this pose, you can use the wall for support if your balance is challenged.

One-Legged Extension

The emphasis in this pose (Fig. 36.16) is on energizing the entire body through its' overall length and expansion. That is, from the foot on the floor through the torso and head, and thus, releasing forward and up, and into the arms and hands above the head.

For many, the pose will stretch the hamstring of the raised leg. If there is no stretch, the leg can be raised further by placing a block on top of the chair under the foot. If there is still no stretch, you can hinge forward from the hip joint. Be sure to maintain the length and expansion within the pose.

Comments:

- In Chapter 33 we explored lying on the floor with the arms stretched overhead (Fig. 33.16). In that position, it is easy to see when there is interference in the length and expansion through the torso, as the back tends to pull away from the floor. We need to take this awareness into this pose, with the arms being raised sufficiently to connect into the overall extension and with the back still integrated into the body. In this pose the arms are frequently pulled too far back, which tightens the neck, pulls the shoulder blades back, and narrows and shortens the back.
- Never stretch forward to the point where openness and expansion are lost.
- Keep the pelvis squared.

Fig. 36.16

One-Legged Twist

This twist can be done as pictured (Fig. 36.17), or with the leg out in front as in (Fig. 36.18), which is more difficult to coordinate, but which will also put a stretch through that leg.

Once more, the arms are fully connected into the overall opening and expansion of the body. You can think of the arms connecting into the whole width and length of the torso, expanding out like the wings of a bird. They will be slightly forward of your midline. Avoid pulling the arms back, which would tighten your neck, narrow your back, and tense the shoulder muscles.

Fig. 36.17   *Fig. 36.18*

TWISTS

A s we have seen, a major difficulty many face in practicing yoga, is having faulty ideas about how the body is designed to move. If their ideas about the body's movement possibilities are incorrect, then they will inevitably run into problems as they attempt to do the impossible! Incorrect ideas about what is possible and how to safely move in twists are definitely prevalent.

Think about this question regarding your spine: What are the possibilities for rotation in the several regions of the spine—the lumbar, thoracic, and cervical vertebrae? (Fig. 37.2)

Lumbar vertebrae have virtually no rotation available, but people commonly attempt to twist this area of the spine, which results in compression in the lower back, shortening and contraction through all the back muscles, and stiffening in the rib cage. For ease and safety, the whole lumbar spine needs to lengthen in twists. This creates support through the entire spine and enables freedom in the rib cage and rotation in the thoracic spine.

David Gorman records the rotational range of motion of the areas of the spine as 5 degrees in the lumbar spine (or 1 degree between each pair of vertebra), 35 degrees in the thoracic spine, and 50 degrees in the cervical spine (neck).[1] These figures are an approximation, of course, as actual rotation is difficult to measure and there is considerable variation among people. But the thing to note is, that the orientation of the articular facet joints of the lumbar spine makes rotation in that area extremely limited.

Fig. 37.1

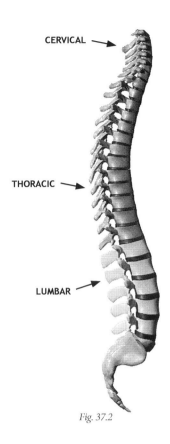

CERVICAL

THORACIC

LUMBAR

Fig. 37.2

The thoracic vertebrae are where the ribs attach, at the costovertebral joints (Fig. 37.3). The structure of and connections between the thoracic vertebrae permit considerably more rotation than is possible in the lumbar spine. What restricts the rotation in this area is the rigidity with which most people hold their rib cage. As is pictured in Figure 37.4, the front part of the rib cage, which attaches to the sternum, is made of cartilage. Cartilage has a significant amount of flexibility, but that flexibility can be reduced by years of misuse in fixing or collapsing the rib cage.

There are twelve ribs. The top ten ribs attach to the sternum (breastbone), and there are two "floating ribs." It is very common for people to restrict the rib cage, either by habitually collapsing or by trying to stand or sit "straight." When they try to be "straight," they pull back the shoulders and push the chest forward, thus narrowing the back and creating rigidity in the rib cage. The flexibility of the rib cage is a major determinant of the range of rotation of the thoracic spine. Overcontraction and narrowing of the back also restricts the mobility of the floating ribs, subsequently severely limiting the movement of the diaphragm, as we explored in Chapter 22.

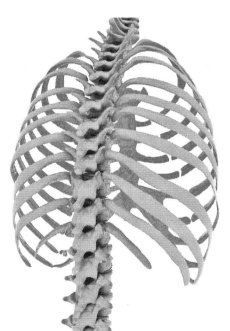

Fig. 37.3   Rib Cage Rear

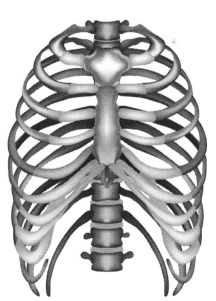

Fig. 37.4   Rib Cage Front

It is essential for any healthy twisting movement to maintain length throughout the spine, thus providing optimal space between the vertebrae. When twisting, we want to activate the very deepest layers of postural muscles (rotatores, interspinales, and intertransversii), as well as the multifidis (Figs. 37.5 and 37.6). These are all postural muscles that span one, two, or three joints between the vertebrae and help stabilize the spine. This stabilizing function is very important, as the larger or more superficial "movement" muscles will be recruited to stabilize the spine, if the postural muscles lose their elasticity from tension or collapse. This leads to tiredness and often pain and discomfort in these muscles. After a first Alexander lesson, people frequently have a floating sensation of lightness and length. This release is possible only if we stop overusing those more superficial muscles, which are better adapted for movement than for stability.

It is essential that twists access these deep postural muscles around the thoracic vertebrae. This means the whole torso needs to be freely lengthening and expanding. That requires letting go of excess holding in the rib cage, whilst *directing* into length and expansion.

When doing a twisting pose, it is quite common for people to contract the lumbar spine, in an attempt to both lengthen and twist that part of the spine, thereby pulling one of the shoulder blades back. This subsequently contracts and shortens the muscles of the back and puts stress on the intervertebral discs. People doing this feel the sensation mainly through the superficial muscles of the back, a much less pleasant experience than if the deep postural muscles are the focus of the movement.

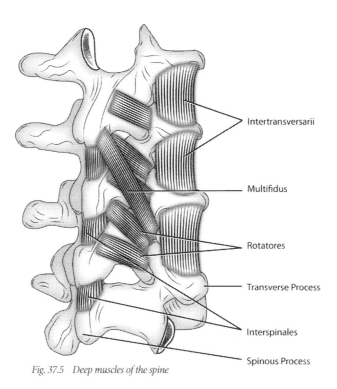

Intertransversarii

Multifidus

Rotatores

Transverse Process

Interspinales

Spinous Process

Fig. 37.5 Deep muscles of the spine

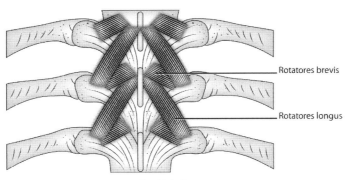

Fig. 37.6   Rotatores

Figures 37.1 and 37.7 demonstrate seated twists in which there is freedom of the neck, length through the spine, width through the back, and openness through the whole torso. It is possible to work very deeply within this pose when we have lengthening of the spine in concert with flexibility in the rib cage. Then we can twist all the way into the internal organs of the abdomen as well. In doing this, we can contract the muscles of the abdomen inward, but only to the extent that we do not tighten the neck or shoulders. We can usefully work to this depth only if we are not compromising free coordination of head balance and the length and freedom of the spine, whilst still maintaining the overall expansion of the primary control.

In Figure 37.8 we can see that the torso, instead of lengthening and expanding, is moving into collapse. Rather than having the weight on the sitting bones, he is rolling back toward the sacrum. The spine is being rounded and the abdominal organs compressed.

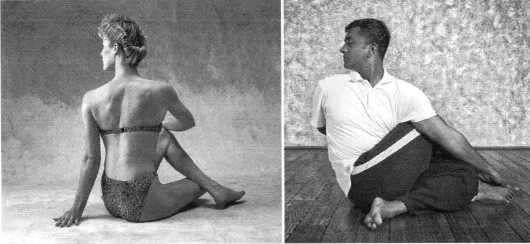

Fig. 37.7   *Fig. 37.8*

Many people lack the flexibility to sit on their sitting bones (ischial tuberosities), and so effective twisting while sitting on the floor is impossible. Unless the sitting bones are in contact with the floor and provide the fulcrum of the body's weight, there is no possibility of accessing length through the spine. If we cannot comfortably center ourselves over the sitting bones, then we need to furnish enough support under the pelvis so that length through the spine is possible. This may be simply a folded blanket, as in Figure 37.1, or a tall block, as in Figure 37.9.

The second reason for the collapse in Figure 37.8 is that he is reaching his left arm too far over his bent knee, which increases the collapse through the torso. In Figure 37.1 we see a practitioner with almost complete access to the rotation of her spine, which enables her to wrap the arm around her knee and hold her other hand behind her back.

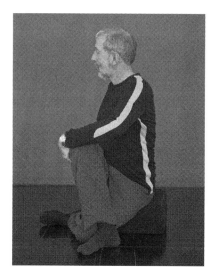

Fig. 37.9

This is often considered the "correct form" for this pose, but probably fewer than one in a hundred people have the flexibility to do this without collapsing. In most cases people attempting this will simply discoordinate themselves. In Figure 37.7 we can see that the practitioner, rather than discoordinating herself by trying to use her arms as in Figure 37.1, is using the contact of the hand with the leg to assist with the twist, thus keeping the integrity of her head, neck, and back.

Another version of the sitting twist can be done in a chair (Fig. 37.10). For people who have limited flexibility when sitting on the floor, sitting on a chair can be especially helpful. It is necessary, however, to avoid the tendency to overextend and narrow the back in this. That is in contrast to seated twists on the floor, where the tendency is to flex and collapse the torso as in Figure 37.8.

Fig. 37.10

Points of Awareness in Twists

As in all yoga poses, it is good to have an Alexander yoga teacher to observe and give you feedback and guidance. Lacking this support, here are some points of awareness to help you practice usefully and safely:

- Twisting poses have a reputation for worsening sacroiliac pain by overstretching the ligaments in this area, which should not be twisted. There should never be the slightest pain in this area. If you work with proper coordination, and especially avoid overcontracting the lumbar spine, you will avoid this problem.
- I have occasionally worked with students with disc problems who have been told by their doctor or other health care practitioner, that twisting is not good for them. Indeed, some have developed rigid use of themselves by restricting normal twisting activities in daily life. Certainly discs do not appreciate the spine being both twisted and shortened, which is very common. However, twisting while lengthening is quite a different matter, and if done carefully with the aid of an experienced teacher, virtually everybody can receive benefit from these poses.
- In addition to the problems mentioned above, if you have pain in the neck, back, knees, hip joint, or around the shoulder blades, then you are probably discoordinating yourself in the pose and need to rethink what you are doing.
- Both sitting bones should be equally grounded in this pose. If you find that they are uneven, it means you are shortening yourself on the side of the more grounded buttock, and instead of rotating and lengthening you will be corkscrewing your spine into compression.
- In a well-coordinated twist, you will notice that your breathing frees up effortlessly. If you are collapsing or narrowing and tightening your back, your breath will be restricted. If we find our breath constricted in any yoga poses the answer is not to try to get more breath in, but to remove the constriction that is preventing the breathing from working freely.

Lying Down Twists: Jathara Parivartanasana

Twists from a supine position are a staple in many yoga classes. It is essential that twists be carried out with the spine fully lengthened. For some people, however, the lower back becomes contracted as they twist. This creates tension through the large superficial muscles of the back and puts pressure on the discs and joints of the spine. If you put a hand over the lower back while in this posture, you should find it to be more or less flat. For some people, the underlying structure or pattern of tightening doesn't let this happen, at least not the in the way these twists are normally taught.

Figures 37.11 and 37.12 demonstrate a couple of ways of working with these twists. In Figure 37.12 a block is being used to support the leg so that the lumbar spine isn't overtwisted. It can also sometimes be helpful to have the arm away from the twist resting on a block, in order to help lengthen the muscles through the back. Stress in the lower back or the big muscles of the back may be removed by bringing both knees up, then twisting.

Fig. 37.11

Fig. 37.12

Twist from Prayer Position

Some people have a strong pattern of pulling in the lower back, so none of the supine twists on the floor will work very well. However, twisting from the Prayer Pose may enable them to experience the benefits of twisting. Go into the Prayer position (Fig. 37.13), which is described in the next chapter, on forward bends, making sure the whole torso is fully lengthened. Then extend the right arm across the underside of the body toward the left. Turn the head in the same direction as the arm. Return to the center and repeat on the other side (Fig. 37.14).

Fig. 37.13   *Fig. 37.14*

NOTE   1. GORMAN (1981), 56.

FORWARD BENDS

I n forward bends, as in all poses, everyone has a unique range of motion. In Figure 38.1 you can see that the child's major point of flexion is the hip joint. In the adults (particularly the man), there is much less movement from the hip joint, so whatever bend they are able to reach comes predominantly from rounding the spine. If they bent their knees, they would get more hip joint movement. But most people will try to do forward bends with their legs straightened, which fully extends the hamstrings. If the person's hamstrings are even just reasonably tight, bending with straight legs will prevent the pelvis from being able to rotate forward around the hip joint.

Forward bends are normally done with the intention of stretching the hamstring muscles. The hamstring group consists of three muscles, all of which originate from the ischial tuberosities (sitting bones) and attach onto either the tibia or fibula, just below the knee joints (Figs. 38.2 and 38.3). This means they cross two articulations: the pelvis around the femur, and the knee joint. Tightness through the hamstrings is a major reason for restriction in forward bends. Tight hamstrings can prevent rotation of the pelvis when the legs are straight, and Figure 38.4 demonstrates the resultant collapse through the torso. Figure 38.5 demonstrates how more flexible hamstrings will favor more length through the spine in this position. There are, though, some people with quite flexible hamstrings who also have difficulty going into a forward bend without rounding the spine. In these cases the tightness is in the lumbar spine, which tends toward a reverse curve and therefore can't lengthen out and bring the pelvis with it.

In fact, the ability to fully move into such a pose is affected by tightness through the large superficial back muscles, the deeper layer of muscles, and particularly the ligaments around the spine. The person in Figure 38.6 has a great amount of flexibility in the hamstrings and throughout the spine, which is fully lengthening within the forward curve. In Figures 38.7 and 38.8 we see reduced mobility.

Fig. 38.1

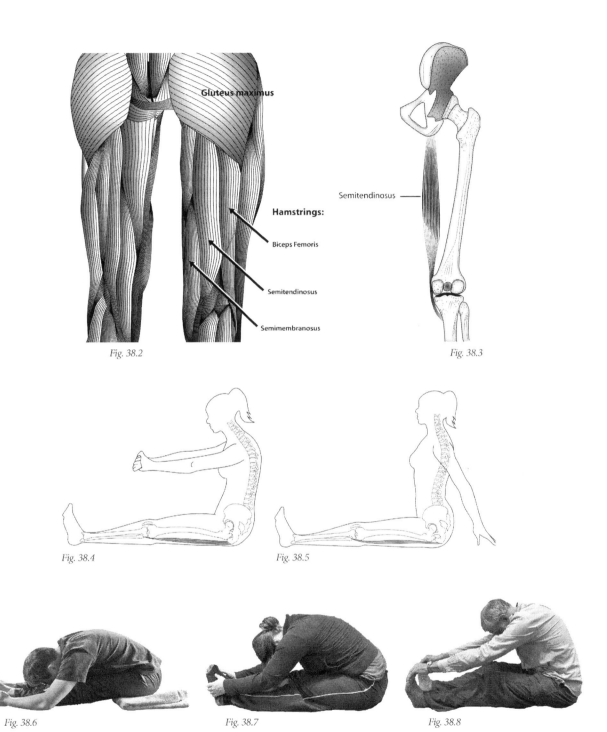

Fig. 38.2

Fig. 38.3

Gluteus maximus

Hamstrings:

Biceps Femoris

Semitendinosus

Semimembranosus

Semitendinosus

Fig. 38.4

Fig. 38.5

Fig. 38.6

Fig. 38.7

Fig. 38.8

The Importance of Ligaments

The importance of ligaments in helping us maintain upright posture and providing stability to our joints, is often overlooked. Anatomical discussion of yoga poses tends to focus on working with particular muscles or muscle groups, but we also need to be aware of the role of ligaments. The sensation in ligaments (and tendons), when we overstretch in a pose, is quite a different feeling from stretching (lengthening) muscles. When stretching muscles along an opening line of expansion, the feeling is pleasant. When overstretching ligaments (which connect and stabilize joints) and tendons (which attach the muscles to the bones), the feeling is not a pleasant one. It may be felt as strain, which could continue once we come out of the pose.

The intervertebral discs and facet joints furnish a level of mobility to the spine: there are a total of twenty-four articulations from the top of the spine to the pelvis. At the same time, they are tightly bound together by a fascial network of ligaments that imparts stability and protects against excess movement, which could damage the discs or the facet joints. There are two ligaments running the length of the spine—the anterior longitudinal ligament and the posterior longitudinal ligament—as well as ligaments around the facet joints.

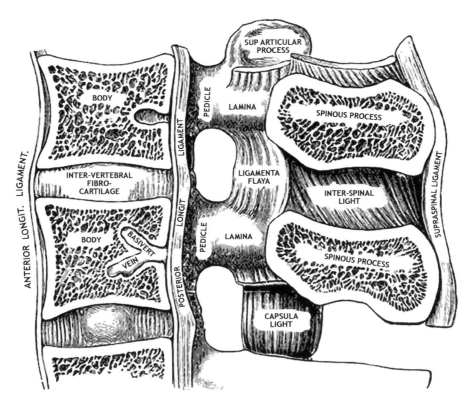

Fig. 38.9 Medial sagittal section of two lumbar vertebrae and their ligaments

The supraspinal ligament runs from the spinous process of the seventh cervical vertebra down to the sacrum. The ligamentum flavum connects adjacent vertebrae all the way from the second cervical vertebra to the first section of the sacrum, connecting between the laminae of the vertebrae. All these ligaments resist movement in a number of directions, including forward bending. In a forward bend, the elastic fibers of the ligamentum flavum, in conjunction with other ligaments, supply a strong returning force and maintain the relative positions of the vertebrae (Fig. 38.9). The elasticity of the ligamentum flavum is an essential element in enabling effortlessness in upright postures.

The vertebrae of the spine, and indeed every joint of the body, are designed such that there is a range of movement and a relationship between them that is healthy. Movement outside of this range is likely to damage discs, facet joints, or ligaments, and if the curves of the spine are habitually accentuated or over-straightened, then pain and dysfunction can be a common consequence.

In everyday living most people do not use the spine optimally. Think of the office worker hunching over her desk for most of the week. In such a situation, the fibers of the ligamentum flavum and other ligaments are constantly overstretched and gradually lose their elastic potential to return the spine to its healthy "upright" curves.[1] There is also a gradual overcontraction of the muscles and connective tissue that taken together, flex the torso, including the supraspinal ligament. Consequently, the supporting ligaments and muscles that assist with extension are weakened, and the ligaments and muscles that assist with flexion of the torso increase in tone. Furthermore, there is also a change in the nervous system. Gradually this stooped posture begins to feel natural and becomes the default posture. In this scenario, a conscious effort needs to be made to "straighten up," but this is generally followed quickly by a return to the default posture once conscious effort and attention cease. Thus the individual will be oscillating between "sitting up straight," which is tiring, or on the other hand collapsing, which involves less muscular effort but puts a number of other pressures on the body.

The Role of Habit

As we discussed in the chapter on the Monkey Pose, when most people approach a forward bend, they will inevitably begin bending from those same points in their back as they always have in the past. This accentuates and deepens the existing pattern. Even if they try not to bend from those points they usually won't be aware of doing so anyway, thanks to the phenomenon of "faulty sensory awareness."

In addition to overstretching this hyper-bendable area of the spine, the rest of the spine is pulled in a way that may create strain and injury in the lower back and sacroiliac joints. Looking at Figure 38.8, we can see that a habitual pattern of bending from the spine joints overstretches the ligaments in the back of the spine, as well as the small deep postural muscles that assist with maintaining spinal extension: the spinalis thoracis, transversospinalis, interspinalis, and multifidus (see Figs. 37.5 and 37.6 on page 174 and 175). In fact, these are the very muscles that we ideally want to keep constantly and subconsciously toned, in order to maintain upright posture. Therefore, if this over-activation of all the flexor muscles - and the attendant ligaments and connective tissue - become habitual and continuous, then easy upright posture will become difficult to attain.

Kneeling Forward Bend: Prayer Pose

This forward bending pose (Fig. 38.10) is one in which it is easy to work with the full length of the torso, because there is no constriction on the tilt of the pelvis from the hamstrings.

From a kneeling position, come forward from the hip joint, lifting the pelvis high enough that the entire back, front, and sides of the torso can be fully lengthened, and rest your forehead on the floor. Make sure your neck is not compressed, by ensuring the forward and up direction of the head on the atlanto-occipital joint. As with all poses, varying levels of flexibility means that for some people the pelvis may be on, or almost on, the heels, while for others the thighs will be at a right angle from the knee joint.

Fig. 38.10

Standing Forward Bends

In Chapter 34 we explored the Monkey Pose. If you feel a stretch in your hamstrings when you practice this pose with the chair forward, then this is your ideal pose for cultivating coordinated flexibility in a forward bend. In this case, poses like the seated forward bend, *Paschimottanasana*, will be well out of your range, as you will not be able to coordinate usefully in them.

Standing Forward Bend: Uttanasana
The standing forward bend is similar to the position of the family in Figure 38.1. As we can see, the adults are not getting a lot out of this pose and are straining their backs. This pose is effective and safe only for those who are reasonably flexible, and should always be done with a bend in the knees. Those who tend to hyperextend their knees should, even if they have a lot of flexibility, make sure they keep the knees at least slightly bent in this pose.

To come into the pose, think of directing the torso to come up off your legs, as you release the knees and hinge forward at the hip joint. The feet will be fairly close together and pointing forward. Activate a line of lengthening up through the legs, rotating the thighs slightly inwardly, without contracting your quadriceps. There needs to be space for the pelvis to rotate forward as the spine expands throughout its total length. It is essential not to bend from the habituated part of the spine, as you will simply accentuate hyperflexion of the spine at this point. For those who habitually hold the lumbar are contracted, a slight rounding of this area will give a feeling of relief, but for others it may do the opposite.

If the back is overly rounded in this pose, it may be useful to work more with elongation of the spine, by coming forward to the seat of a chair or a block on the floor. The emphasis should remain on extension rather than rounding the back. If there is still insufficient flexibility, then work with the Monkey Pose.

Wide-Legged Standing Forward Bend: Prasarita Padottanasana

This forward bend is similar to the *Uttanasana*, but for many people spreading the legs reduces the restriction in the hamstring muscles and allows more rotation of the pelvis. For most people, this will work best when the feet are facing straight forward.

The same considerations apply as for the *Uttanasana*.

Forward Bend Extension from the Wall: Padahastasana

This pose is a good one for those with moderate flexibility. It is somewhat similar to the Monkey Pose with the chair forward (Fig. 34.5), except that in this pose, in addition to maintaining the length through the torso, you can also work a strong stretch into the hamstrings.

Stand with the feet a little out from the wall, slightly bend the legs, and bring the pelvis to the wall. Without straightening the legs further, rotate the pelvis by moving the sitting bones up the wall. It can help to take hold of the sitting bones with your hands to manually rotate the pelvis.

A common mistake in this posture is to overcontract the lumbar spine in an attempt to maintain length. An even more common error is to collapse the whole torso forward. We certainly don't want to round the lumbar spine in coming forward, but rather to lengthen it through the natural curves of the spine.

As in all poses, we want to prioritize lengthening of the spine. This is always more important than stretching the hamstrings. The model in Figure 38.11 is reasonably flexible, and many people will not be able to go this far forward with good coordination. Remember, the legs, especially the hamstrings, can be stretched in a multitude of other ways without having to discoordinate the whole body.

Fig. 38.11

Sitting Forward Bends

Paschimottanasana

The *Paschimottanasana* is an advanced forward bending pose in which the expansion is through the whole backline of the body, which includes the network of muscles and fascia that connect from the soles of the feet to the ridge of the brow. The stretch should be continuous through this backline. It is important for those with hyperextension of the knee joints to be mindful in all forward bends, and to make sure they are not accentuating this habit thus overstretching and weakening the knee ligaments. It is fine to bend the knees to the extent necessary to allow full spinal extension.

The flow of the pose should follow through the legs, the forward tilt of the pelvis, and the length and expansion of the back. It is particularly important to ensure that we do not accentuate a forward curve through the spine by bending at its habitual bending point, therein breaking the flow of the pose. In no way do we want to train the flexors to contract, as that cuts off the flow of energy through the front of the body and compresses all the internal organs. Practiced effectively, this pose is a powerful way of accessing flow, energy, and expansion through the whole spine and torso.

On page 181 the person in Figure 38.7 has good hamstring flexibility but is not as flexible through the spine as the person in Figure 38.6. The person in Figure 38.8 has even less spinal flexibility alongside more limited hamstring flexibility. The problem with having less spinal flexibility, is that when getting into position, we tend to favor those few vertebrae of the spine that do move forward. In the process, we overstretch the muscles and ligaments in that area. Those few vertebrae of the spine do bend, but not in harmony with the rest of the spine as in Figure 38.6.

In fact, if you find that you practice forward bends by primarily flexing one area of the spine, then that area will normally feel tightest to you. This will be the area you habitually bend from while sitting at the computer, cooking, picking up a child or a bag of groceries, gardening, and indeed most of the activities of daily life. This is the area of the spine in which you have too much flexibility in flexion, and conversely very little ability for length and extension in everyday upright posture.

Fig. 38.12

How to Work in the Pose

Firstly, we need to make sure that however far forward we fold, we are extending and lengthening in concert with, along, and through the natural curves of the spine. Only after we have full length and expansion in the spine do we want to move further into the pose and curve, as in Figure 38.6. Most people may never get that far, but they will still benefit enormously from the processes of lengthening their spine and folding just a little way forward.

We want the seated forward bend (*Paschimottanasana*) to work in a way that is not hyperextending already overstretched ligaments, but rather lengthening and toning those ligaments. In Figure 38.12 we can see that the practitioner is sitting on a blanket to raise her pelvis. This allows her to be on her sitting bones, which gives the possibility of forward movement of the pelvis. Also, rather than rounding her back over, she is lengthening her spine and folding to a chair, which stops her from end-gaining by restricting her to a safe range of motion. This can be quite hard work, especially for those with weakened back muscles and ligaments. If people are too tight in the hamstrings to be able to sit on their sitting bones, they will have to elevate their pelvis for the pose to work for them. In any type of sitting forward bend, it is essential that we begin centered over our sitting bones. If we already have the pelvis rolled back, we have no chance of rotating it forward.

— *Other Seated Forward Bends* —

Many of the same considerations apply to other seated forward bends. We always want to give priority to the primary control by coordinating the head, neck, and torso and to ensure that we are not hyperextending the knee joints and ligaments.

Single Leg Forward Bend: Triang
Muka Eka Pada Paschimottanasana

- This can be done sitting on a block or a blanket, depending on your flexibility. Even if you are very flexible, you ought to use a blanket under the buttock of the bent leg to help keep the pelvis even.
- Make sure your pelvis is square; this will be facilitated by keeping the knees close together.
- It is fine to bend the straight leg, as in Figure 38.13, depending on your flexibility.

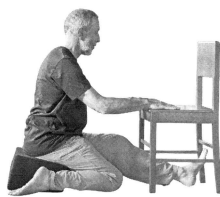

Fig. 38.13

Wide Legged Forward Bend: Upavista Konasana

- Start with your weight fully on your sitting bones. If your pelvis rolls back when you sit on the floor, elevate it on a blanket or block (Fig. 38.14).
- Support your hands with a block or chair if your flexibility does not allow you to place your hands on the floor without collapsing through the torso.
- Rotate the legs outward from the hip joints. The legs must not rotate inward.
- The knees may be somewhat bent. They should definitely not be locked.

Fig. 38.14   *Fig. 38.15*   *Fig. 38.16*

Cross-Legged Forward Bend: Adho Mukha Sukhasana, Adho Mukha Padmasana

The problem for most people who sit in a chair all day is, that when they attempt to practice cross-legged poses, the joints that need to open to sit comfortably, namely the hip joints, don't have sufficient flexibility. This means the knees are potentially endangered. The knee joints' healthy range of motion is primarily flexion and extension, also known as bending and straightening. They also have a very minor degree of internal rotation and a slightly larger degree of external rotation. But the knee joints do not appreciate being fixed in rotation, which is what happens in sitting cross-legged when there is not full hip joint flexibility. Crossing the legs and bending forward increases the rotation through the knees. A common yoga injury to the knees is often caused by people being too enthusiastic about getting into, and working with, cross-legged poses. The way to deal with this problem is to sit so as to maintain a fair amount of opening of the knee joint:

- Sit on a blanket or a block with your weight centered directly over the sitting bones.
- Organize your legs so that your feet are out some way forward and your knees will fold at a point close to the level of your hip joints (Fig. 38.15).
- Give your directions for the neck to free, the head to move forward and up, and the back to lengthen and widen.
- Bend forward as you activate a lengthening and expansion through the whole of the torso.
- Go only as far forward as you can without discoordinating (Fig. 38.16).

Because the hamstring muscles don't prevent forward rotation of the pelvis in this position as they do when the legs are straight, many people can fold further in this pose. For some people with an apparently fixed kyphosis, moving into this pose has a remarkable effect on allowing it to lengthen out—though I'm not quite sure how that works.

The stretch will be felt on the outer side of the hip joints along the outside of the legs. It certainly should not be felt in the hip joint.

Some people with hip issues have problems with this pose, and even with the legs bent in this fashion, a small number of people with knee injuries cannot do this without further damaging their knees. Alternative poses are covered in Chapter 43, on hip openers.

Other Seated Forward Bends

As in all the sitting poses, you need to start with the sitting bones on the floor, on a blanket, or on a block. Most people will need to be elevated. Compare Figures 38.17 and 38.18 with Figure 38.19, and you can see what happens to overall coordination, when people who lack the flexibility needed for the sitting bones to contact the floor, do not elevate the pelvis. Those who are more flexible can round through the torso once the full hip flexion is reached, as in Figure 38.17. But note that this is with an overall lengthening and expanding curve through the entire torso.

Bring the soles of the feet together and move the knees in the direction of the floor, making sure you do not lose length in the process. If you have the flexibility, you can then fold from the hip joint, maintaining length and openness through the torso.

Fig. 38.17   Fig. 38.18   Fig. 38.19

NOTES 1. Moshe Solomonow describes how ligaments can be adversely affected through ongoing stresses created by faulty patterns of posture and movement: "Loading or stretching a ligament over relatively short periods induces changes in its length-tension behavior that may last twenty to forty times longer than the duration of the loading/stretching. This phenomenon has significant implications for the ability of a ligament to protect and stabilize joints in workers who are subjected to sequential periods of static or cyclic activities during a given day. As the work-rest periods go on, the ligament exhibits cumulative creep and reduction in its ability to protect the joint, causing the later part of a work period (or day) to be more prone to injury. Since full recovery of the creep with rest also requires more than twenty-four hours, there would be a cumulative creep from the previous work day at the beginning of a new work day. . . . Overall, the decrease or loss of function in a ligament from rupture or damage leads not only to compromise of its mechanical contributions to joint stability but also to sensory loss of kinesthetic perception and fast reflexive activation of muscles and the forces they generate in order to enforce joint stability" (Solomonow 2004, 53).

DOWNWARD FACING DOG POSE:
ADHO MUKHA SVANASANA

The Downward Facing Dog Pose is one my favorites, and anyone who has practiced yoga is probably familiar with it. It is a half-handstand, a forward bend, an inversion, a stretching pose, and a strengthening pose all in one. It has a number of benefits if it is worked correctly. It gives a whole body stretch and wonderful lengthening from the feet through the legs to the entire spine and torso. It develops overall strength, in particular in the arms, and tone in the postural muscles. This helps to strengthen bones, which is a key to preventing osteoporosis. In addition, it also develops flexibility and gives us the benefits of inverted yoga *asanas*.

It is commonly described and illustrated in yoga books and classes, as being practiced with the heels fully on the floor. In the pictures below we can see two people in this pose with heels fully on the floor.

The model in Figure 39.1 is lengthening and expanding beautifully in this pose. But do you have the same flexibility? If you don't and you try to copy her, what do you imagine will be the result?

In Figure 39.2, instead of having the lengthened torso of the first example, the model's torso is shortened and compressed, though even she has above-average flexibility. The spine is shortened, the breathing is restricted, and the abdominal organs are compressed.

Fig. 39.1　　　　　Fig. 39.2

So what is the answer for those of us with less-than-full flexibility? Look at Figure 39.3. She has pretty good flexibility, but not enough to be able to lengthen her torso and completely straighten her legs by bringing her heels right down to the floor. So to maintain the integrity and openness of her torso, she is slightly bending her legs. Although lifting her heels from the floor, she is still working with a good stretch into her calves and at the same time activating the spine into length and the torso into expansion. Look at the beautiful length through her spine. Her torso is expanded, her breathing is unrestricted, and the organs of the abdominal area fully supported without the slightest compression.

Fig. 39.3

People with much less flexibility will need to bend the knees considerably more than this to work with the full length through the torso. They will also need to bring the torso further up through the arms to get a lengthened connection through the spine from the head to the sacrum (Fig. 39.4).

Now let's look at a very flexible person in this pose (Fig. 39.5). From the perspective of the Alexander Technique, this is not an ideal way to coordinate that flexibility in this pose. Instead of the back being rounded out, as we see in less-flexible people (Fig. 39.2), the back is shortened and contracted in the opposite direction, particularly the upper back, while the whole shoulder girdle is overstretched.

Fig. 39.4

We would need to have both the head and upper back in the same relationship to the arms as we see in Figures 39.1 and 39.3, for this pose to offer the possibility of length and expansion through the torso, open space for breathing, and unimpeded energy flow through the spine.

Fig. 39.5

The Problem of Asymmetry in This Pose

One very common problem with the Dog Pose is people accentuating asymmetry in their bodies by entering the pose unevenly. In this pose, it is easy to unintentionally exaggerate scoliosis, a sideways curvature of the spine, and end up with twists ingrained even further. This is a difficult thing to observe in oneself, as it can't be felt and often cannot be seen in a mirror. The most obvious manifestation of lateral distortion, is a twist through the pelvis and a shortening through one side of the body.

It is not always associated with scoliosis. Many people go into the pose with their hands or feet unevenly placed. Another tendency is, to sinking the upper back through the shoulders, when one shoulder is more flexible than the other, which is frequently the case. Indeed, the more one sinks into the chest, as in Figure 39.5, the more exaggerated a pre-existing asymmetry becomes. Usually, lifting and broadening the upper back and shoulder area will undo the distortion. If this unintentional twist is at all exaggerated, one will need the assistance of a teacher to be guided out of this pose.

How Can I Use This Information in My Own Yoga Practice?

Having information about a more efficient and effective way of practicing a pose is not enough for us to be able to apply it to ourselves. Ideally, we would find a teacher who can observe us and guide us through the pose.

However, the founder of the technique had no one to guide him in the process of developing more effective posture, movement, and vocal habits. He was unable to rely on the accuracy of his kinesthetic information, so he used mirrors to observe what he was doing with himself in activity. Because it can be quite difficult to notice that you are moving into a habitual twisting contraction, placing a video recorder in front of you may help you see it.

Indeed, in a yoga class, when I guide people into more length and expansion in the Downward Facing Dog Pose, their kinesthetic sense of where I have moved them compared to what they are actually doing with themselves rarely correlate.

Therefore, if you want to experiment with the information in the absence of a teacher, I strongly recommend that you use a mirror to overcome your "unreliable sensory appreciation." Your brain will believe your vision over your kinesthesia, and gradually you will begin to educate and refine your proprioceptive and kinesthetic senses.

Warnings About This Asana

The most common injuries people experience from this pose are caused by hyperextending. You should never feel strain in the shoulder joint while practicing this pose. The work in the arms should be felt principally through the deltoids, the big muscles at the top of the arms.

Some people strain their neck in this pose, especially those who tend to tighten their neck muscles in their normal daily activities. If you cannot remain in the pose with a free neck, you should immediately come out of it. Otherwise, you are simply practicing and reinforcing the habit of tightening your neck and discoordinating yourself.

People may also feel strain in the back, especially if they are not lengthening and expanding through the torso. Figures 39.1, 39.3, and 39.4 show the pose, demonstrating a range of flexibilities, whilst maintaining length and expansion. Back pain is a sure sign that you are compressing your spine, and you don't want to repeat and thus, reinforce the habit. You need to come out of the pose immediately and rethink what you are doing with yourself.

People with wrist problems should approach this pose with care. Often wrist tightness begins to free up while working in this pose. However, this is not guaranteed, and I advise that people start by practicing the pose quite briefly, then checking after a yoga session to confirm that their wrists feel OK.

Dog Pose from Forearms

Here is a modification of the pose (Fig. 39.6) that may be useful for those with wrist or elbow injuries, but be aware that this requires a reasonable level of flexibility. It is also a useful alternative to the Dog Pose for strengthening and toning the triceps, instead of working the biceps, as happens in the full Dog Pose.

Forearms are placed on the floor parallel to each other. You need to make sure that you are able to lift right up off your arms, with the length of the torso being supported by the arms, rather than the weight of the torso collapsing onto the arms.

Fig. 39.6

Preparations for Downward Facing Dog Pose

There is no yoga pose that benefits everybody, and this pose is no exception. Some people are too stiff to be able to work the pose effectively and need to develop more flexibility first.

Preparatory poses for this one are the Prayer Pose, the Monkey Pose taking the chair forward, and poses that work with flexibility through the hamstrings and calves. The body is also prepared for this pose by continually working into length and expansion in all the poses and, of course, in the activities of everyday life.

BACK BENDS

Back bends are the most difficult poses to teach in a group class, because of the variety of structures, limitations, and patterns of use among people. Some people have a weakness in the fifth lumbar vertebrae, called spondylolysis, that predisposes them toward stress fractures. A stress fracture of the pars interarticularis, the small part of the vertebra that connects the facet joints, can progress to a forward displacement of the vertebrae, a condition called spondylolisthesis, which is common among gymnasts and people engaging in activities that involve frequent back extensions (Fig. 40.1).

For people with this problem, back bends are positively dangerous. When we consider that about 5 percent of the population has this condition, and that not all are diagnosed, this is something all yoga teachers need to take into account. People with this condition will feel discomfort in the lumbar spine, but often they are so used to it that they simply ignore it until things get really bad. At the same time, almost everybody can benefit from at least some back bend poses. Most of the daily activities people do involve directing the attention forward and often downward, and when we don't use ourselves well, we frequently curve forward throughout the day.

Years of activities such as computer work, cooking, and gardening may result in flexor muscles being habitually shortened, thus working with back bends can help to lengthen them. So back bend yoga poses, along with postural and movement reeducation in our daily activities, can assist us in finding greater comfort and ease.

When considering back bends, it is useful to have an idea of the structure and function of the major extensors of the spine, the longissimus group, and the iliocostalis group. The longissimus and iliocostalis work together, but can be functionally separated into thoracic and lumbar portions (Fig. 40.2). The thoracic section contains approximately 75 percent slow-twitch fibers and the lumbar section is normally evenly mixed between slow- and fast-twitch fibers.

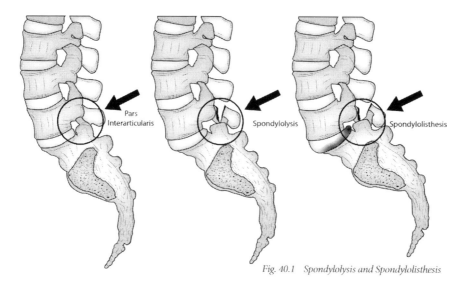

Fig. 40.1 Spondylolysis and Spondylolisthesis

The fiber proportion indicates whether the muscle's function has been adapted more for postural support (more slow twitch muscle fiber), or more for movement (more fast twitch muscle fiber). The line of action of the thoracic portion is such, that those muscles produce the greatest amount of extension with the minimum compression of the spine. The line of action of the lumbar portion is such, that it generates strong compressive shear forces between the lumbar vertebrae in extension, something that many will directly experience as a sensation of pain or pressure in back bends.

In most people, the extensor muscles of the lumbar portion of the spine are already overworking. Some people live in a constant back bend (Fig. 40.3), In fact, in my own yoga classes, its not unusual to have a few who choose to work on forward bends, whilst the rest does back bends. The most common misuse by people when in upright standing or walking positions, is that they lean back. (see Chapter 32, on the Mountain Pose). This tends to happen even if they are collapsing forward with the upper back forming their spine into an S-shape curvature (Fig. 40.4). One major factor in the current epidemic of low back pain is the fact that discs and facet joints of the lumbar spine, are already under severe pressure from this overcontraction. Attempts to counter the collapse by "sitting up straight", simply overcontract the lumbar spine even more. So-called "lumbar supports" normally overemphasize the lumbar lordosis.

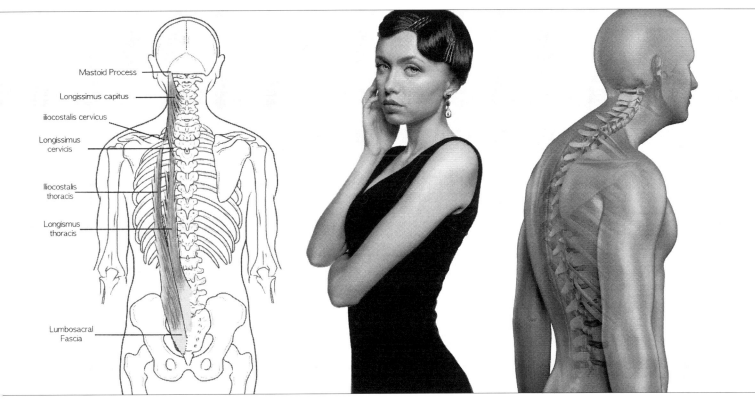

Mastoid Process

Longissimus capitus

iliocostalis cervicus

Longissimus cervicis

Iliocostalis thoracis

Longismus thoracis

Lumbosacral Fascia

Fig. 40.2   Fig. 40.3   Fig. 40.4

It is essential to approach any back bend with the understanding that, as in all other poses, the intention is to move into openness and expansion. In back bends the opening and expansion is through the front of the body. This opening and expansion should not, under any circumstances, be obtained at the cost of compression through the back and spine. For many people, there is already narrowing and compression between the lumbar vertebrae, so almost any attempt to move into a back bend risks putting more pressure in that area.

The question here, is which back bends will be safe and effective for which individuals. One of my basic principles in deciding the usefulness or danger of a particular pose or way of moving is that it needs to feel "good." In my classes I am constantly encouraging people to develop discriminating awareness of the bodily sensations, so that they can begin to differentiate "good" from "bad." For the watchful yoga teacher or the practitioner observing via a mirror or video, it also needs to look good. (See Fig. 40.7 for a back bend that doesn't look good.)

In this chapter I'll cover a number, but by no means all, of the back bends. Similar principles can be applied to back bends not mentioned here.

— *Passive Back Bends* —

These passive back bends work very well for people with an exaggerated bend (kyphosis) in the upper back. The back bend can help them gradually open and expand without unduly compressing the lumbar spine. However, for those with a hollow or flat upper back, it doesn't do much. And for those with a chest that has been stiffened by pushing it forward, with the subsequent flaring of the lower ribs, this pose will accentuate that fixation and should be avoided. The pose in Figures 40.5 and 40.6 is sometimes described as a "chest opening" pose, but the idea that the chest is opened by pushing it forward is mistaken. In fact, for people who habitually hold their rib cage in this way, this pushing forward, is how they make their ribs rigid and inflexible. In Figure 40.7 we can see how this type of use is harmfully exaggerated in this pose.

Fig. 40.5

Fig. 40.6

Fig. 40.7

A rolled blanket is placed under the middle of the upper back. The head may be unsupported, but for those with a fairly fixed thoracic spine, it is useful to place books under the head; otherwise the neck is bent back too severely. As the upper torso gradually extends, some people may be able to remove the books, depending on the degree and flexibility of their kyphosis. Normally people will stretch out their legs, but if this puts pressure in the lower back, then the legs should be bent. The arms can be stretched out toward the floor above the head, creating extension from the hands to the feet (Fig. 40.5). If taking the arms back hyperextends the shoulder area, then the hands may be supported on a block or chair.

Another variation of this, is to lie over two blocks (Fig. 40.6). We have blocks made of very firm foam with a slight angle at the top of the block.

Active Back Bends

Bridge: Setu Bandha Sarvangasana

The bridge is a back bend that will work for many people.

Bring your feet close to your buttocks, level with each other and pointing straight forward. The emphasis when lifting into the bridge is on sending the knees away to ensure the maximum length through the back. There should be no sensation of pressure in the lower back. If you feel any compression through the lower back, you have gone too far. Imagine the vertebrae of the spine coming off the floor and back onto the floor, one at a time.

Occasionally people with knee problems experience pain while practicing the bridge, which may be alleviated by placing blocks under the feet. They also need to watch that they are not squeezing the legs together as they lift.

Cautions:

- As with the shoulder stand, this is not a good pose for those with an overstraightened neck. For people with nerve impingement in the neck area, it is positively dangerous and should be avoided.
- Holding the ankles with the hands causes narrowing between the shoulder blades and overcontraction and pressure in the lumbar spine. Keep your arms to the sides to encourage the maximum width through your back, or you can take the arms back onto the floor over the head.

Fig. 40.8

Cobra: Bhujangasana

The cobra pose doesn't work for many people as it tends to overcompress the lumbar spine. In the classic version of this pose the extension is done with the front of the pelvis mostly on the floor, as the practitioner extends upward and backward with the help of the arms. Sometimes the instruction is given to strongly contract the buttocks as a way of "protecting" the lower back. But my thoughts on this, from an Alexander Technique perspective, are that we need to be working in an open extension that doesn't require muscular work in the buttocks beyond what happens reflexively in this posture. If we have to work to "protect" the lumbar spine, then we are probably extending it too much.

We want a line of extension moving through the front of the torso and neck (Fig. 40.9). This line of extension needs to extend through the lower torso to avoid overcontraction of the lumbar area. There should be no sensation of compression in the lumbar spine. Those who have the flexibility to do this pose, commonly break the line of extension by overcontracting the neck. It may be difficult to apply the Alexander direction of the head, that is, releasing forward and up in this posture, unless we understand that the direction is not about a position of the head. This direction leads the lengthening extension of the whole spine in any position. What more frequently happens in this pose, as in ordinary upright poses, is that the balance of the head creates a downward and contractive pressure through the spine as it is pulled back. Another common pattern is that the shoulders get contracted and pulled up around the ears. The shoulder girdle should be expanded and overcontracting the upper back, avoided.

One way of practicing this is, to elevate the front of the pelvis on a blanket; this reduces the likelihood of contracting the lower back.

Fig. 40.9

Sphinx: Salamba Bhujangasana

The Sphinx gives the benefits of the Cobra Pose with less danger and fewer contraindications. Once again, the emphasis is on length through the front. You may go up a fair way or hardly at all. Listen to your body; the aim is opening and energizing, not putting yourself into the "right position."

Lie on your front and send the Alexander directions for length and expansion through the body. Don't begin by lifting the head, but rather think of it lengthening the spine as you send the top of the head forward along the floor. Then you can begin to slowly lift the head and the top of the torso off the floor, all the time maintaining the length. Activate the extensors through the thoracic spine rather than the lumbar. Then begin to bring your arms into the movement to assist with the upward extension, going only so far as permits you to continue opening and expanding. Any compression through the lumbar spine is an indication that you have gone too far.

Fig. 40.10

Upward Facing Dog: Urdhva Mukha Svanasana

This pose raises the pelvis and spreads the extension through the body into the legs, thus allowing more opening of the hip joint, and a less extreme extension of the lumbar spine than the cobra (Figs. 40.11 and 40.12). In this pose, the extension begins in the feet, which are placed with the tops of the feet on the floor. If this foot position is difficult, you can tuck the toes under and extend from there. Many of the same considerations apply to this pose, as the Cobra Pose.

Fig. 40.11 *Fig. 40.12*

Prone Back Stretches: Shalabhasana Variations

This is not a pose I would teach in my classes. For most people, it puts a huge amount of pressure on the lower back. Our model here shows considerable activation of the extensors of the upper back, and she can practice this without harm. But for at least 95 percent of the population, this pose should be banished—along with abdominal crunches—from yoga or exercise routines. Stuart McGill, in referring to loads on the low back during extension exercises, wrote, "Even worse is the commonly prescribed back extension class in clinics, in which the patient lies prone and extends the legs and outstretched arms: this again activates all four extensor sections but imposes up to 6,000 N (more than 1,300 lb.) on the hyperextended spine. This is not justifiable for any patient!"[1]

He continues: "Several variations of exercise technique can preserve activation in portions of the extensors and greatly spare the spine of high load. E.g. kneeling and extending one leg back generally activates one side of lumbar extensors to 20% & imposes only 2,000 N of compression. Bird dog extending the opposite arm and opposite leg also activates thoracic extensors & contains spine load to about 3,000 N." (The Bird Dog Pose is included in Chapter 42, on poses from kneeling.)

Fig. 40.13   Fig. 40.14

Bow Pose: Dhanurasana

The Bow Pose (Fig. 40.15) may work for more people than the other prone back stretches. While you work quite actively in the pose, the extension through the spine is partially passive, because you are using the arms to assist with the extension.

Points of awareness:
- There should not be even the slightest hint of compression through the lumbar area.
- The focus is on lengthening through the front.
- It is helpful to think of lengthening out through the front of the thighs as you lift the legs.
- Some people with knee problems feel this pose in their knees. If there is any pain in the knees, don't practice this pose.

Fig. 40.15

Camel: Ustrasana

This pose (Fig. 40.16) requires considerable length through the lumbar spine, with the bulk of the extension coming from the thoraco-lumbar junction and above, to avoid excess compression of the lumbar spine. By placing the toes on the floor so that you don't have to fold so far back to reach the heels, or even by bringing hands to a chair placed behind you, you can make the pose more accessible. Like many back bends, this posture is not good for those with a habitually raised chest or flared lower ribs. And this pose is not effective and safe for people who are highly contracted in the lumbar area.

Fig. 40.16

Wheel or Upward Bow: Urdhva Dhanurasana

This is a wonderful back bend (Fig. 40.17), but it is accessible to only a few people. Just because we can put our body into this position doesn't mean we *should*. For most people, this pose puts an unacceptable amount of compression through the lumbar spine.

In classes we will sometimes assist people into this pose so that they can work it with more length through the spinal extension (Fig. 40.18).

Fig. 40.17   Fig. 40.18

NOTE   1. MCGILL (2007), 91.

SIDE BENDS

S ide bends are wonderful poses that assist in: opening the breathing and the ribs; finding more freedom though the shoulder girdle, and, expanding and opening the sides of the torso. There are a number of side-bend poses and I will cover just a few, but the same considerations apply to others not covered here.

Seated Side Bend: Parivrtta Janu Sirsasana

The seated side bend is practiced sitting on the floor. As with all floor-seated poses, most people will need some support under the buttocks (Figs. 41.1 and 41.2). This entails raising them enough for the sitting bones to be fully supported. This is necessary for the spine to be able to lengthen.

Normally, one leg will be bent and the other taken out to the side. Those who can't fold their legs because of knee problems may do this with both legs out to the side (Fig. 41.3). As in all poses, begin by giving the directions for freeing the neck and gaining optimal length, openness, and expansion through the torso. With the left leg bent and the right leg out to the side, rotate the torso to the left and raise the left arm in such a way, that the back widens. Then, with the intention to lengthen and expand directly through the left side, move to the right.

Your depth in this pose depends on your flexibility (Figs. 41.1–41.4). However far you move, the stretch should be along the left side. In people who are very tight, simply taking the arm into the air will provide sufficient stretch through the side. Care must be taken to not compress the right side. It will bend, but should not feel compressed. The left arm does not have to be held absolutely straight. If you are not very flexible, this will be just a very slight curve, but as you move further the hand can begin to move in the direction of the right foot. Avoid end gaining; make sure to not overreach to grab the foot.

Fig. 41.1

Fig. 41.2

Here are some common errors and points of awareness in this pose:

- The most common error is that the arm is taken too far back behind the head, which narrows and contracts the shoulder girdle and back. This places the stretch into the superficial back muscles, rather than directly up the side. Once the arm is repositioned the stretch will be felt directly up the side. A "correct" angle for the arm cannot be given, as this may vary considerably with the individual. For those who are very tight or held in the shoulder area, the arm may need to come a long way forward. An indication of the arm being in the right position, is that the stretch is clearly felt up the side.
- As in all poses, we need to keep maximal expansion and width through the entire back. If we shorten and contract the back, we can end up putting a good deal of pressure on the discs thus increasing tightness in the muscles of the lower back.
- People with tight hamstrings may feel the stretch only in the hamstring of the right leg and won't be able to move sufficiently to experience the full stretch up the side. If this is the case, they should bend the right leg enough to allow the stretch to move into the side. Those whose knees have a tendency to hyperextend should put a blanket under the knee of the right leg, so that pressure is taken off the knee joint and so avoid further development of their knee's flexibility (Fig. 41.1).

Fig. 41.3

. Fig. 41.4

Variation of Sitting Side Bend

People who are quite stiff, may find it easier to do this side bend sitting in a chair (Fig. 41.5). It helps to have a second chair, on the side you are bending toward, to use for support as you move into the pose.

The same considerations apply, with the aim being to work the stretch completely up the side and to maintain openness through the back.

Fig. 41.5

Standing Side Bend: Chandrasana

As in all standing poses, beginning with a coordinated upright posture, is essential. Stand easily erect with the feet slightly apart, and facing forward. If you are moving to the right, slightly rotate the torso and pelvis to the left, and raise the left arm in a way that connects into an extension through the whole torso. As with the sitting pose, when you move to the right, ensure that the stretch is felt directly through the left side. Do not lock your knees.

This may be done by supporting the lower hand on a chair (Fig. 41.6), or sliding the left arm down the side of the legs (Fig. 41.7).

A version of this pose that requires a little more strength, is to reach both arms up as you come to the side (Fig. 41.8).

Here are common errors and points of awareness in this pose:
- As with the sitting posture, you need to ensure that the position of the arm gives a clear line of stretch directly through the side.
- You also need to ensure that you are not hyperextending the back. This is particularly dangerous in the standing posture, and it can cause you to overcontract the muscles of the lumbar spine and put pressure on the facet joints and discs of the lower spine.

Fig. 41.6   Fig. 41.7   Fig. 41.8

Gate: Parighasana

Here is another upright version of the side bend (Fig. 41.9).

- From the kneeling position, step the left foot out to the side. This pose is often taught with the left foot pointing directly ahead and the entire foot on the floor. If you can do this without twisting and hyperextending the knee, that's fine; otherwise adjust your foot and leg so there is no strain in your knee. For most people, the foot will be pointing slightly to the front.
- Lift your left arm and extend it out to the side, making sure to find an angle that does not compromise the width of the back or shoulder girdle.
- Begin to extend out to the right, taking the hips slightly to the left and bringing your hand onto the left leg. The relationship of the head to the left arm should not change significantly, as you move into this pose.

Fig. 41.9

Lying Side Bend: Supta Chandrasana

I normally call this one "bananasana," for obvious reasons. This is an easy pose that can be practiced by most students for whom the other side bends don't work so well because of neck or back injuries.

Fig. 41.10

POSES FROM KNEELING

The Cat: Bidalasana

This is a pose that is said to increase the flexibility of the spine. However, the way these bends are commonly performed, strengthens the habitual curving forward from only one part of the spine, and it overcontracts the lumbar area in the back-bend part of this movement.

It is a pose that will work well for some people (but by no means everybody), provided they work with the intention to mobilize the whole spine in the movement. Any attempt to do the maximum movement in both directions, will accentuate existing faulty patterns of use.

- Begin the pose in a position that fully lengthens the whole spine (Fig. 42.1). Hands will be directly under the shoulders with the fingers pointing forward, and knees under the pelvis. The ability to fully lengthen the torso is more important than the exact position of the limbs.
- Begin to move forward into a curve, emphasizing the areas of the spine that tend to be immobile in this direction. For most people, this will be through the lumbar area (Fig. 42.2).
- Move back to the starting point and continue through into a slight back bend. Emphasize the bend through the less flexible area in this direction, as well. For most people, the focus will be on extending the thoracic spine, while minimizing extension through the lumbar area (Fig. 42.3).
- Return to the starting position and repeat five times.

Fig. 42.1   Fig. 42.2   Fig. 42.3

Bird Dog

This is a pose that has entered yoga classes from strength training and Pilates, and is commonly used to strengthen "the core." As already mentioned, any exercise coordinating ourselves from the head through the whole body, will strengthen "the core." Attention needs to be given to working the spine, fully lengthened through its natural curves from the head to the sacrum. If done well, this extension will work to strengthen the extensor muscles of the back, without overcontracting the lumbar, in addition, it will give extra work to the abdominals and deep postural muscles of the torso.

- The starting position is the same as for the cat, ensuring full length and expansion of the torso (Fig. 42.1).
- Send the directions for the head to continue to release forward and away, and for the whole torso to lengthen and widen. Slowly extend the back leg backward, lengthening it until it is both long and strong, and then lift it. It should not be lifted above hip height, and you should not twist the pelvis to bring it up or sink through the back.
- Slowly raise and straighten the opposite arm. If it is possible to do so without lifting the shoulder girdle or losing your length, you can lift the arm until it is parallel to the floor. Otherwise lift as far as you comfortably can, without discoordinating yourself.
- Gently return your arm and leg to their starting positions, making sure to maintain your length throughout this process.
- Repeat with the opposite limbs.

Comments
- It is very common for people to lose their length in this pose and collapse their lower backs. If you don't have a teacher to observe you, it is useful to use a mirror.
- Raise the leg and arm only so far as is possible without losing the expansion through the torso. As you can see in Figure 42.5, although the leg has been raised just parallel to the floor it is too high, because it has been raised at the expense of the stability of the lumbar spine. Figure 42.4 demonstrates better coordination.
- As you develop your coordination you can work initially by raising just the arm or just the leg. Make sure that you have good coordination in the pose before raising the opposite limb.

Fig. 42.4   Fig. 42.5

CHAPTER 42

Quadriceps Stretch

This pose (Fig. 42.6) produces a powerful stretch through the front of the thigh. The intention and focus should be on connecting that opening through the torso. The line of stretch will extend from the front of the thigh, through the torso and extended arm.

- Take the right foot onto the wall behind you with your knee close to the wall. Use a blanket to soften the contact of the knee with the floor. The extension through the ankle of your left foot should be such that, as much as possible, the foot is angled with the toes pointing toward the ceiling. Your left foot will be placed in front of you on the floor, with the knee bent to about a right angle. With the strong stretch through the thigh of the leg up the wall, there is a tendency to shorten that side. Raising the arm on the same side, will assist in maintaining an openness and expansion through that side of the body.
- Move your pelvis and torso toward the wall. Another variation of this pose is to take the front foot further forward and then to lunge forward, which will put a somewhat different stretch through the front of the right thigh.

Fig. 42.6

Observations and Cautions

- It is essential that you not feel pain or pressure in your knee. If a blanket under your knee does not prevent pain or pressure, then don't attempt this pose. The First Warrior Pose, as it is described in this book, will work a somewhat similar stretch, as will the Dancer Pose (Fig. 42.7).
- Make sure to not hyperextend the lumbar spine in an attempt to get your back toward the wall. Think of your pelvis moving toward the wall. People who are quite tight in this area may not move very far toward the wall.

Fig. 42.7

CHAPTER 43

MORE HIP OPENERS:
MOVING TOWARD CROSS-LEGGED SITTING

P art of the challenge many people have with sitting in a cross-legged position is a limited range of motion in the hip joints, which makes it difficult for the legs to externally rotate without putting excess pressure on the knees. These poses increase flexibility in this rotation.

Pigeon: Eka Pada Rajakapotasana

This is the basic version of the pose. There is also a gymnastic version, which I will not cover in this book.
1. Begin kneeling on the ground.
2. Rotate and bend your left leg so that your foot is in line with your right thigh, and extend the right leg straight out behind you. Keep the bend of the knee joint as open as possible (Fig. 43.1).
3. You now have the option of folding forward as far as you can, without collapsing the torso (Fig. 43.2), or extending up without overcontracting the lower back.

Comments
- It is imperative that this pose be done without putting the slightest bit of pressure through the knee joint. Many people with knee problems find they can't do this pose. If it causes pain in your knee, find an alternative pose.
- The pose is most commonly felt as a strong stretch through the buttock of the bent leg. If you are feeling a pull in the groin, or pain in the hip, the pose is most likely injuring you.
- If you don't feel the stretch, extend the back leg further behind you.

Fig. 43.1   Fig. 43.2

Standing Pigeon

The pigeon can also be done from standing, by people who find that the floor pose strains the knee joint. The bent leg is placed on a table or chair. Practicing this pose from standing allows you to have a wider angle in the knee joint, with less possibility for strain or damage.

- Standing next to a table or chair, bring the left leg onto it with the knee bent. Place the foot in line with the right thigh. Place the foot forward to allow for a wide angle in the bend of the knee.
  Make sure that the foot of the right leg is facing forward (Fig. 43.3).
- Send your directions for: the neck to be free; the head to move forward and up; and, the whole torso to lengthen and expand as you begin to fold forward. If you already have a strong buttock stretch, you don't need to fold. Fold forward from your hip without allowing the knee joint to bend as you come forward.
- Arms can be raised to enhance the length and expansion of the torso (Fig. 43.4), but if this is too tiring you can leave the arms down.

Comments
- Once more, it is essential that there not be the slightest pain or pressure in the bent knee.
- People often hinge forward initially from the ankle of the standing leg rather than the hip joint, thus lessening the angle of the bend of the knee. Make sure you remain standing directly over your foot.

Fig. 43.3

Fig. 43.4

Wall Gluteal Stretch

This pose is another option for those who still experience knee pain in the two variations of the pigeon described above. The stretch will be around the buttock, and you need to make sure there is no pressure in your knee.

- Lie on your back a little way out from a wall, with your head supported on books; lift the right leg up the wall.
- Lift your left foot and place it on the right thigh.
- Bend your right leg (Fig. 43.5), toward your torso while activating to keep your pelvis square and rotated forward so that your lumbar spine is not being pushed into the floor.

Fig. 43.5

INVERTED POSES

"'You are old Father William' the young man said
'And your hair has become very white;
And yet you incessantly stand on your head—
Do you think at your age it is right?'
'In my youth', Father William replied to his son
'I feared I might injure the brain;
But now that I'm perfectly sure I have none,
Why, I do it again and again'."

Inverted poses are, strictly speaking, the group in which the head is below the torso. This description covers a number of poses, including the Downward Facing Dog and Standing Forward Bend. But in this chapter, I want to discuss the headstand and shoulder stand, and modifications of those poses. I will also cover some handstand poses, which don't include the risk of damage to the arteries, joints, nerves, and other delicate structures of the neck, that is possible with the head and shoulder stands for vulnerable individuals.

Unlike Old Father William, in the poem above we do have a brain, and as mentioned in the chapter on injuries, head and shoulder stands may have the rare, but severe side effect of damaging that wonderful organ. To understand why this should be, look at a typical cervical vertebra (Fig. 44.2) and particularly at the small foramen (hole) in the transverse process. The vertebral artery is threaded through these foramina from the sixth (and in some cases the seventh) vertebra all the way up to its entrance into the skull (Fig. 44.3). Disruptions to the flow of blood or tears in the vertebral arteries can create a blood clot, which can cause a stroke when it reaches the brain. This is well known to occur after neck trauma, or in very rare cases after cervical manipulation therapy.

Fig. 44.1

Headstand: Sirsasana

Iyengar, quoting from the Hatha Yoga texts, refers to the headstand as the "king of all asanas."[1] However, in recent times the considerable dangers of this pose have become apparent to yoga practitioners. Indeed, some styles of yoga leave the headstand completely out the practice (Kripalu, Bikram, Viniyoga, Kundalini Yoga, and Alexander Yoga). And Iyengar's suggestion that the weight be fully borne on the head alone[2] is something that I was, very wisely, not taught in any Iyengar classes I have attended.

Iyengar gives an impressive list of mental and physiological benefits from the headstand, but until now there has been little experimentation to identify the precise physiological mechanisms involved. The original Tantric explanation of the pose describes how *amrita*, the nectar of immortality that resides in the seventh crown *chakra*, drops through the center of the body and is consumed by the fire in the abdomen. Practicing inversions helps us retain this *amrita*, thus prolonging life and preserving *prana*. Whatever we make of this traditional explanation or physiological explanations of the benefits of the poses, there is no doubt that inversions, if practiced with ease and comfort, do have a noticeably calming psychophysical effect.

The headstand may be highly beneficial, for a relatively small minority of people. However, because I find that it does not work for me or most of the people I teach, I won't describe it here.

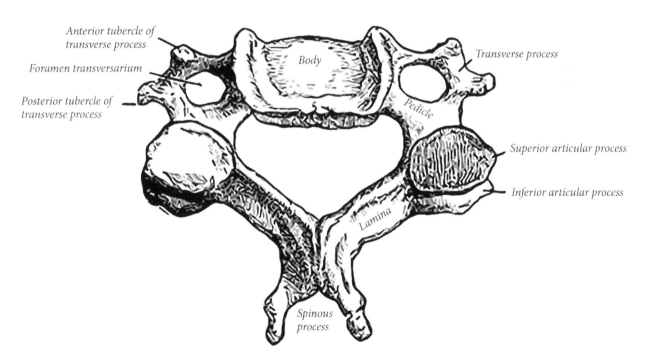

Fig. 44.2   Cervical spine: Superior View Vertebra

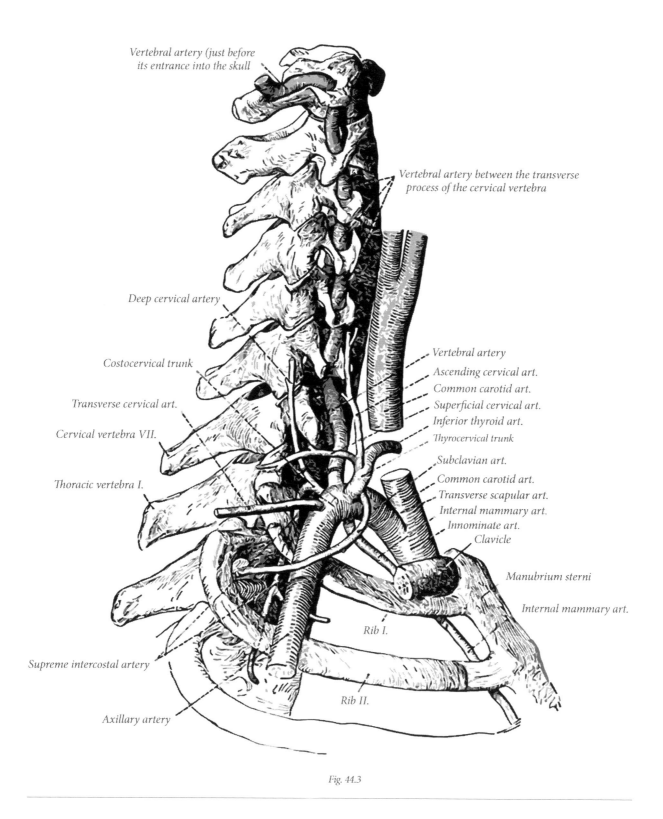

Vertebral artery (just before its entrance into the skull

Vertebral artery between the transverse process of the cervical vertebra

Deep cervical artery

Costocervical trunk

Transverse cervical art.

Cervical vertebra VII.

Thoracic vertebra I.

Vertebral artery
Ascending cervical art.
Common carotid art.
Superficial cervical art.
Inferior thyroid art.
Thyrocervical trunk
Subclavian art.
Common carotid art.
Transverse scapular art.
Internal mammary art.
Innominate art.
Clavicle

Manubrium sterni

Internal mammary art.

Rib I.

Supreme intercostal artery

Rib II.

Axillary artery

Fig. 44.3

Shoulder Stand: Salamba Sarvangasana

The shoulder stand is the second classic pose, and it is described by Iyengar, again quoting from the ancient texts as "the mother of asanas" and "a panacea for most common ailments."[3]

The shoulder stand is also very problematic in terms of potential injuries to the delicate vertebrae, discs, nerves, and blood vessels of the neck. As with the headstand, if done inappropriately, the shoulder stand creates a (very low) risk of catastrophic brain injury. As described by Iyengar, and as is still taught in some yoga classes, the pose is done with the torso rising vertically up and the weight through the fully stretched neck. In Iyengar yoga classes I attended, this pose was practiced with the neck resting over three folded blankets and the head on the floor, which somewhat reduces the severe straightening of the neck. However, if the torso is raised vertically from this posture the neck is still overflexed, which can lead over time to damage to this area.

Fig. 44.4   Fig. 44.5   Fig. 44.6

Any form of shoulder stand should be avoided by those with neck problems and those with over-straightened necks. But some people can work with a less severe form of the pose to receive its benefits safely. This involves using blankets under the neck as the head rests on the floor, and taking the torso up at less than a right angle, with the bulk of the weight through the shoulder area, rather than the neck (Fig. 44.4). While doing this, it is important to listen to the messages from your body. This should be an extremely comfortable pose. Unlike with the other groups of poses (forward bends, back bends, side bends, and twists), we are not stretching or working though a particular line of opening or expansion. The practitioner needs to be aware of the effect of the pose on the physiology of the whole body, and notice the slightest feeling of any excess pressure in the neck or back. A chair may also be used for support in this type of shoulder stand (Fig. 44.5).

Another modification of the shoulder stand that will work for most people, is to lift the legs into the air with the pelvis raised on a pile of blankets or a block (Fig. 44.6). However, some people with neck problems will find that even this modification puts pressure on their neck, and so, should be avoided.

Fig. 44.7

Fig. 44.8

Fig. 44.9

Legs up the Wall: Viparita Karani

This can be done with the pelvis on a block or blankets, or with the pelvis fully on the floor. Even those with neck problems can do this with their head resting on books, as in the semisupine position (Fig. 44.7).

Handstand

The handstand is not a classic yoga pose, but is commonly used in the more acrobatic forms of yoga as part of sequences. This dynamic pose develops strength in the arms and activates the whole system, in much the same way as the stronger back bends.

Initially, you can practice the handstand against the wall. The main difficulty with this pose, apart from the difficulty in balancing, is the risk of collapsing into the lower back. Activate so that your legs are coming up as vertically as possible, rather than their weight dropping into your back.

Half Hand Stand

You can estimate the hand position in this pose by first sitting with your back against the wall and your legs straight out. The approximate hand position when you are inverted, will be where your feet are with your legs straight out. Placing your hands on the floor, begin to walk your feet up the wall until the legs are at a right angle from your torso. Press the feet into the wall and straighten your legs, while pushing up strongly through your arms.

In this pose (Fig. 44.9), one can work very strongly with the length and extension through the spine. If they have the strength to do it, it can work very effectively for people with scoliosis. For some people with scoliosis, coming into this pose appears to confuse the brain so that it no longer knows how to hold the spine in its usual position, allowing it to unravel somewhat.

In my yoga classes I frequently support people in this pose until they develop strength and confidence.

Blood Pressure and Inversions

There is considerable discussion in yoga circles about the issue of safety in regard to inversions and high blood pressure. In the headstand and shoulder stands, the blood pressure does rise initially, but in experienced practitioners it falls after some minutes to just slightly higher than the initial resting state. Swami Kuvalayananda published his studies on this topic in 1926. Figure 44.10 shows the blood pressure readings of healthy and experienced practitioners practicing the headstand. Similar measurements were gained for the shoulder stand, slightly higher initially and slightly lower after five minutes. Of course, the blood pressure also rises in any type of aerobic activity, and those with high blood pressure are encouraged to do aerobic exercise. However, the concern is probably that inversions increase blood pressure within the brain. For people with uncontrolled blood pressure issues, it would be prudent to avoid them.

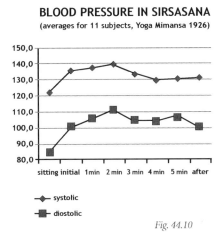

BLOOD PRESSURE IN SIRSASANA
(averages for 11 subjects, Yoga Mimansa 1926)

Fig. 44.10

The Eyes and Inversions

Those with a tendency to experience retinal detachment should avoid inverted poses, probably including the Downward Facing Dog, as the pressure in the eyes is raised in these poses. The *Viparita Karani* with legs up the wall and no support under the pelvis, should be safe.

There is general agreement that inversions should be avoided by those with glaucoma. One exception is a *Yoga Journal* article published in 2007, quoting Sandra Amrita McLanahan, MD, director of the Integral Health Center in Buckingham, Virginia, and longtime yogi. The article suggests that inversions increase blood circulation and lymph flow to the eyes, which helps both glaucoma "caused by impaired circulation of fluids" and cataracts "formed by the build-up of free radicals in the lenses." She does, however, warn those with narrow-angle glaucoma, against practicing headstands.[3] But most other yoga experts hold the opinion that the rise of interocular pressure, particularly in headstands or handstands, means these inversions are contraindicated for glaucoma. *The British Journal* of Ophthalmology published a case study of wide-angle glaucoma worsening with the practice of headstand and improving once the practice was stopped. Their advice is that "patients suffering from glaucoma should be advised against practicing postural (head-down) yoga exercises."[5] A number of other cases have also been published, that give the same advice.

NOTES 1. IYENGAR (2001), 151. 2. IBID., 149. 3. IBID., 171. 4. YOGA JOURNAL STAFF (2007). 5. DIMITER ET AL. (2007).

PLANK VARIATIONS

This chapter focuses on some poses that, like the Dog Pose and handstands, develop arm strength and call on the postural muscles of the torso to support the body in a variety of positions. Strength and weight bearing exercise is important because, among other things, the pressure put through the bones stimulates the osteoblasts (bone-building cells) to make new bone. As people age, the tendency is for the bones to lose density. In old age this can reach a critical point known as osteoporosis, a condition that makes it is easy for bones to fracture. The hip, forearm, and thoracic vertebrae are the most common sites of those fractures. Around 50 percent of women over fifty will fracture a hip, wrist, or vertebra during their lifetime!

A range of upright weight-bearing exercises, if done well, will help maintain bone density in the legs, hips, and spine. It is also useful to incorporate into practice, poses that develop strength in the arms and wrists. Because the whole torso needs to be stabilized in these poses, they also develop the postural muscles of the torso.

For those with wrist weakness, some of these poses may be dangerous. They will need to be approached with caution, and in some cases avoided or modified.

Fig. 45.1

Four Legged Staff Pose: Chaturanga Dandasana

The four-legged staff (Fig. 45.1) is one of the positions of the classic sun salutation, as practiced in the Ashtanga yoga series, but it can be done as an individual pose.

- Start in the higher plank (Fig. 45.2).
- Slowly lower both torso and legs to just a few centimeters above, and parallel to, the floor.
- Maintain the expansion and length through the torso, and keep your elbows close to your side. This means you have to keep the lumbar area expanded. You also need to keep width between your shoulder blades.
- Hold for several breaths, and release before you begin to tighten your neck, or you will lose your length and expansion within the pose.
- Lower yourself in a controlled manner to the floor to release the pose. Or, maintaining the freedom of your neck and the length and expansion through the torso, you can move into the Downward Facing Dog Pose.

Points of Awareness

It is very common for people to collapse their lower back, or tighten the neck while pulling the head forward, or contract the upper back by bringing the shoulder blades together in this pose. It is better to practice one of the easier plank poses, if you are unable to work in a way that prevents these things from happening.

The collapse of the lower back and tightening of the neck, normally happens as a result of either faulty kinesthetic awareness, or lack of muscular tone in the arms and torso. Both of these problems can be worked on over time, and good form can be developed in the pose.

For those who narrow the upper back, the issue is often structural and more difficult to avoid. These people tend to have a more concave thoracic curve, and they should avoid this pose unless they can do it without accentuating the concavity.

The Plank: Phalakasana

The plank (Fig. 45.2) is an easier pose than the four-legged staff. Again, the focus is on working on the length, openness, and expansion within the pose. Hold only as long as you can without compromising your coordination. Breathe deeply and fully.

Fig. 45.2

Plank Variations

Those who find the full plank too difficult can begin with a modified version with the knees on the floor. It is slightly easier balancing on the forearms (Fig. 45.3), and even easier with the knees on the floor and the weight on the forearms (Fig. 45.4).

There is no point in doing a more difficult version of this pose, if you end up tensing your neck and collapsing through your lumbar area.

Fig. 45.3

Fig. 45.4

Side Plank: Vasisthasana

You can come into this pose in one of two ways.

1. You can move into the side plank directly out of the Downward Facing Dog Pose, by shifting onto the outside of your left foot and placing your right hand on your right hip, while you rotate to the left and support your weight on the outer left foot and left hand.

2. Sitting sideways and with the left hand on the floor, you can straighten out your body so that you rise into the pose. Rather than placing the right foot on top of the left foot, the balance will be easier, if you have it just in front of the left foot when you lift.

Some comments:

- The supporting hand should be slightly in front of the shoulder, not directly under it. The arm should be straight but without locking the elbow.
- The whole body should be aligned in a diagonal from the head to the feet.
- Raise the right arm up into the air with the intention of keeping width and expansion between the shoulder blades and widening the back. It is common in this pose for people to narrow the back.
- If it is completely comfortable to do so, you can rotate your head to look at your top hand. Otherwise, keep the head facing forward.
- Hold the position for six breaths, less if fatigue means that you are losing your length, expansion, and freedom. Then return to your starting point, either the Downward Facing Dog or sitting on the floor.
- People with scoliosis should practice this pose on only one side. A recent study demonstrated that by doing daily practice, to asymmetrically strengthen the convex side of the primary curve, it is possible to significantly reduce the scoliosis.[1]

Fig. 45.5   Starting position.   *Fig. 45.6   Easier version with foot in front.*   *Fig. 45.7   Full version with top foot on top of bottom foot.*

Reverse Plank: Purvottanasana

- Sit upright on the floor with legs in front and your hands behind, fingers facing forward.
- Shift the weight into your arms and raise the torso off the floor while aiming the soles of your feet toward the floor. Most people won't get the soles of the feet fully on the floor, but that is not important.
- Keep looking forward. Take your head back only if it is completely comfortable to do so.

Version Two

- This is similar to version one, except that you begin with the feet standing on the floor and raise the torso with the knees bent.

Considerations

- In the plank there is the danger of collapsing the lower back, but in the reverse plank you need to avoid hyperextending, and so, pushing the belly forward and hollowing the lower back. Make sure to maintain a firm but easy line of expansion through the whole body, with the legs extended, or from the torso to the knees with the legs bent.
- Although these poses are often taught with the head dropped backward, this does not work for most people. For almost everyone, letting the head drop back will bend the neck excessively. Take stress off the neck by keeping the head up with the gaze straight forward.
- This pose puts a strong extension through the wrist. Proceed with caution, if you have wrist problems.

Fig. 45.8   Reverse Plank Version 1   *Fig. 45.9   Reverse Plank Version 2*

NOTE   1. According to this study (Fishman 2014), doing this pose for an average of only 1.5 minutes a day, six days a week for two months, reduced idiopathic scoliosis curves for adolescent and adult patients an average of thirty-two percent. The twenty-five-participant trial was evaluator-blinded and x-ray based, and it used the standard Cobb method for measuring results. Given that most sufferers of idiopathic scoliosis can expect a gradual worsening of their curvature, this is quite a remarkable result.

CONCLUSION

It's been quite a journey getting these words down on paper, as well as getting the photos and diagrams organized to create a cohesive learning experience. For many years, I have had the intention of writing such a book, and at the start of 2014 it became clear to me that unless I made a very firm commitment and created a time-table toward doing this, it would never happen. It is the nature of this work that final definitive conclusions are impossible, so there is no easy way for me to wrap up this book. The great thing about practicing and teaching both yoga and the Alexander Technique is, that new understandings and insights are constantly arising. Some of these understandings then refine or even supersede one's previous understanding. I like the definition of an expert as, "a person who has gone so deeply into a subject that he is fully aware of the immensity of what he doesn't know about it." That is the sort of expert that I am.

My Alexander Technique training gave me the invaluable skill of being able to convey very subtle kinesthetic information through my hands to my students. This is a skill that I have developed and refined over the past thirty years, and I rely on it greatly in my teaching. But in writing, I am deprived of this tool, and forced to use language and pictures to attempt to describe this work. The act of writing down these ideas forced me into a process of clarification It also brought me up against the limitations of language to convey the kinesthetic dimensions of the work. Here is how Aldous Huxley describes his challenge in being able to adequately communicate the Alexander Technique to his readers:

> No verbal description can do justice to a technique which involves the changing, by a long process of instruction on the part of the teacher and of active co-operation of that of the pupil, of an individual's sensory experiences. One cannot describe the experience of seeing the colour red. Similarly one cannot describe the much more complex experience of improved physical co-ordination.[1]

In addition to Alexander's four books, there is a wealth of titles on the Alexander Technique. Some of them are very good, but there is no really in-depth writing on the application of the Alexander Technique to yoga practice. I am hoping that this book may help to fill that gap, and will be of use to yoga and Alexander Technique teachers, as well as to those who are seriously exploring these disciplines.

Alexander's work and writings were informed by the scientific understandings in medicine, anatomy, psychology, neurology, and evolution, that were current in his time. His first book was written more than a hundred years ago, and almost sixty years have passed since his death. Since then there have been many discoveries that shed further light on his work. It's not so much that these discoveries alter the basic nature of how we approach the project of change, but many do shine further light on the processes by which this discipline works. I've followed many of these developments over the years. It has been great fun getting up to date on some of the very latest literature and research, and making connections from a range of disciplines to the Alexander Technique, yoga, and meditation practices.

And yoga practice itself has evolved over millennia, out of a prescientific world view that is profoundly different to today. As with the Alexander Technique, yoga's key insights and conceptual framework arose out of deep self-study and investigation. But the philosophy and conceptual framework of both systems are secondary to the practice, which turns their focus back to the psychophysical processes and the flow of our attention and volition; the processes that underlie the quality of our lives, and over which these practices do give us a measure of control.

As for the actual amount of control that we do have over our lives, I believe that we have to approach the subject with somewhat more humility than some of the Hatha Yoga texts, and some of the more exuberant claims of Alexander, as well as the claims of many self-help texts. These all suggest virtually superhuman possibilities for health and well-being. The Muslim propensity to qualify any statement of an expected outcome with the term "God willing", seems to me to express the requisite level of caution in this regard.

The Alexander Technique came into my life after a considerable exploration of yoga and Buddhist mindfulness and meditation practices, and it was a missing piece that provided a way into both awareness and control of my body that I hadn't previously imagined possible. It gave me the tools for a training focused on awareness of the interaction of mental and physical processes, which supported existing practices, and could be applied in the everyday activities of life. Although previously my spinal curvature had been getting worse every year, here was a practice that began to reverse this process. I have no doubt that my fitness, good health, and freedom from any significant bodily pain at the age of sixty-nine is in great part because of my practice of yoga and the Alexander Technique.

I feel very fortunate that my return to Australia, coincided with the opening of the first Alexander Technique teacher training course in Sydney, and that I was able to put aside three years to immerse myself in this training. And I was further fortunate in having the skills to set up a private practice, Alexander Yoga classes, and then a teacher training school, and to have the great privilege of working with a huge number of people.

My students came to the Technique for a wide variety of reasons. For many a major focus was getting rid of pain. Often, attending just a few lessons was sufficient to help them identify a pattern of use that caused and maintained their pain, and that information was sufficient for them to undo the worst of their patterns and resolve their issues. Others came to improve their posture, so as to avoid future problems; to overcome voice problems; to learn tools for dealing with chronic illness; to improve their skill in one of the performing arts, public speaking, or sport; or to support their existing spiritual or personal growth practices.

It has been my great privilege to work with these people and to see major transformations in many cases. At the start of Alexander Technique lessons most people want to know, "How long does it take?" It's sometimes difficult to explain that there is, in fact, no end-point to this work. I may be able to estimate how long it will take for them to significantly reduce their pain or regain improved vocal functioning, but the point at which people really "get" the technique is when they are "stuck" with it. That is, when they can no longer go back the to a previous state of unawareness of what they are doing with themselves, because this heightened awareness and kinesthetic sensibility have become second nature to them. Increased sensibility and awareness is not an unmixed blessing, as it brings our shortcomings into sharper focus, but it is the essential requirement for the process of change, development, and refinement to occur.

I have not listed case studies or remarkable "cures" or transformations, which are the staple of many self-help books. I have witnessed seemingly miraculous cases, like the Parkinson's patient who walked out of the room forgetting that he needed his walking stick; people being able to return to occupations and activities that they loved, but had given up due to injury; people with chronic pain conditions who learned essential strategies for living and functioning with reduced suffering; asthma sufferers who have been able to reduce or go off their medication, and much more. I have also had the privilege of training many teachers of the Technique who are now colleagues and friends, some of whom have taken it into their areas of expertise, such as: occupational therapy, education, yoga, music, voice, drama, horse riding, and many other fields.

I am passionate about the potential of the Alexander Technique to work on many levels: physical, mental, emotional, spiritual. I hope that this book will assist readers in their own personal journeys through life, and point them in the direction of further possibilities for growth and development.

NOTES   **1.** HUXLEY (1941), 223.

REFERENCES

Alexander, F. M. *Aphorisms*. London: Mouritz (2000).

Alexander, F. M. (Fischer J editor) *Articles and Lectures*, London: Mouritz (1995).

Alexander, F. M. *Constructive Conscious Control of the Individual*. Bexley, Kent: Integral Press (1923, 1955).

Alexander, F. M. Introduction to a New Method of Respiratory Vocal Re-education. (1906). Reprinted in Alexander, F.M. Articles and Lectures, London: Mouritz (2001).

Alexander, F. M. *Man's Supreme Inheritance*. London: Chaterson (1910, 1946).

Alexander, F. M. *Universal Constant in Living*. London: Chaterson (1942, 1947).

Alexander, F. M. *Use of the Self*. Bexley, Kent: Integral Press (1932, 1955).

Ariyoshi, M., et al. "Efficacy of Aquatic Exercises for Low Back Pain." *Kurume Medical Journal* 1999, 46: 91–96.

Australian Institute of Sport. *The Warm Up and Cool Down*. Canberra: Australian Sports Commission (2010).

Australian Yoga Journal. "Mountain Pose." http://www.yogajournal.com.au/pose/mountain-pose/ (accessed May 1, 2015).

Barlow, M., and T. A. Davies (eds.). *An Examined Life: Marjory Barlow and the Alexander Technique*. Berkeley, CA: Mornum Time Press (2002).

Barstow, M. "Aphorisms." http://www.marjoriebarstow.com/aphorisms/ (accessed Jan. 9, 2015).

Batchelor, S. *Buddhism Without Beliefs*. London: Bloomsbury (1998).

Bergman, R. A., and A. K. Afifi. *Illustrated Encyclopaedia of Human Anatomic Variation*. http://www.anatomyatlases.org/AnatomicVariants/AnatomyHP.shtml (accessed Nov. 2, 2014).

Bhikkhu, T. Handful of Leaves. Vol 4: An Anthology from the Anguttara Nikaya. Metta Forest Monastery (n.d.).

Bhikkhu, T. "Mindfulness Defined." *Access to Insight* (Legacy Edition), Dec. 1, 2012. www.accesstoinsight.org/lib/authors/thanissaro/mindfulnessdefined.html.

Binkley, G. *Expanding Self*. London: STAT Books (1993).

Brahinsky, R. *Core Purpose Yoga Journal*. Aug. 28, 2007.

Brennan, R. Change Your Posture, Change Your Life. London: Watkins (2012).

Brenner, W. "Practical Marj." *Direction Journal*, 1987, 1(2).

Broad, W. J. *The Science of Yoga*. New York: Simon and Schuster (2012).

Bryant, B. *Body Mapping Manual*. Melbourne: School for F. M. Alexander Studies (2014).

Carrington, W. Thinking Aloud: Thoughts on Teaching the Alexander Technique. Berkeley, CA: Mornum Time Press (1994).

Centers for Disease Control and Prevention. Asthma in the US: Vital Signs, May 2011. www.cdc.gov/vitalsigns/asthma (accessed 1 June 2015)

Cervero, F. *Understanding Pain*. Cambridge, MA: MIT Press (2012).

Coghill, G. Letter. Quoted in Alexander, *Universal Constant in Living*. London: Chaterson (1942, 1947).

Cole, J. *Pride and a Daily Marathon*. Cambridge, MA: Bradford Books (1995).

Cranz, G. The Chair: Rethinking Culture, Body, and Design. New York: Norton (2000).

Coulter, D. H. Anatomy of Hatha Yoga: A Manual for Students, Teachers, and Practitioners. Honesdale, PA: Body and Breath (2001).

Cramer, H., et al. "Adverse Events Associated with Yoga: A Systematic Review of Published Case Reports and Case Series" *PLoS One*. Oct 16, 2013, 8(10): e75515 doi:10.1371/journal.pone.0075515 .

De Beer, G. R. "How Animals Hold Their Heads." Presidential address, *Proceedings of the Linnean Society of London*, vol. 159 1947.

Dewey, J. *Human Nature and Conduct.* New York: Holt (1922).

Dewey, J. *Introduction to Use of the Self.* Bexley, Kent: Integral Press (1932, 1955).

Dimiter, R. B., et al. "Yoga Can Be Dangerous: Glaucomatous Visual Field Defect Worsening Due to Postural Yoga."
      British Journal of Ophthalmology, Oct. 2007, 91(10): 1413–1414.

Doidge, N. *The Brain That Changes Itself.* Melbourne: Scribe (2007).

Ederman, A. "The Fall of the Postural-Structural Model in Manual and Physical Therapies: Exemplified by Low Back Pain."
      CPDO Online Journal, Mar. 2010.

Ellsworth, A. *Anatomy of Yoga.* Heatherton, Vic, Australia: Hinkler (2010).

Farinatti, P. T., et al. "Acute Effects of Stretching Exercise on the Heart Rate Variability in Subjects with Low Flexibility Levels."
      Journal of Strength & Conditioning Research, June 2011, 25(6): 1579-85

Farrell, B. *Pat and Roald.* New York: Random House (1969).

Feuerstein, G. *Psychology of Yoga: Integrating Western and Eastern Approaches of Understanding the Mind.* Shambhala,
      Kindle ed. (2014).

Feuerstein, G. *The Yoga Tradition: Its History, Literature, Philosophy and Practice.* Chino Valley, AZ: Hohm Press (2001).

Finan, P. H., et al. "Discordance Between Pain and Radiographic Severity." *Arthritis and Rheumatism,* Feb. 2013, 65(2): .:363-72

Fishman, L., et al. "Serial Case Reporting for Idiopathic and Degenerative Scoliosis." *Global Advances in Health and Medicine,*
      Sept. 2014, 3(5): 16-21

Flemons, T. "The Bones of Tensegrity." 2012. www.intensiondesigns.com/bones_of_tensegrity.html. (accessed 15 May, 2015)

Giblin, G. "Keep Your Eye off the Ball: Secrets of Elite Tennis Coaching." *The Conversation,* Jan. 21, 2013.
      theconversation.com/keep-your-eye-off-the-ball-the-secrets-of-elite-tennis-coaching. (accessed 15 May 2015)

Gorman, D. *Body Moveable. Vol. 1: Trunk and Head.* London: David Gorman (1981).

Gupta, J. K., et al. "Position in the Second Stage of Labour for Women Without Epidural Anaesthesia." Editorial Group:
      Cochrane Pregnancy and Childbirth Group. *Cochrane Library,* Published online May 16, 2012. (accessed 15 May 2015)

Habal, M. J., et al. "Variability in Muscle Size and Strength Gain After Unilateral Resistance Training."
      Medicine and Science in Sports and Exercise, June 2005, 37(6): 964–72.

Harrison, E. *Mindfulness 101.* Perth Meditation Centre (2013).

Hasenbring, M. I., C. Rusu, and D. C. Turk (eds.). From Acute to Chronic Back Pain: Risk Factors, Mechanisms,
      and Clinical Implications. Oxford: Oxford University Press (2012).

Hickmott, R. "Joint Hypermobility Syndrome." *Medical Observer,* Australia, June 4, 2013.

Huley, A. *Ends and Means.* London: Chatto and Windus (1941).

Iyengar, B.K.S. *Light on Yoga.* London: Thorsons (2001).

James, W. Principles of Psychology. Vols. 1 & 2. (1890). Kindle ed.

James, W. *Talks to Teachers on Psychology.* New York: Holt (1925). Kindle ed.

Katzmarzyk, P. T., et al. "Sitting Time and Mortality from All Causes, Cardiovascular Disease, and Cancer."
      Medicine and Science in Sports and Exercise, May 2009, 41(5): 998–1005.

Kellow, J. *Alexander's Preterm Birth.* 2008 Congress Papers of the 8th International Congress of the F. M. Alexander Technique
      Vol 2. London: STAT Books (2009).

Langford, E. *Mind and Muscle.* Antwerp, Belgium: Garant (1999).

Lederman, E. "The Myth of Core Stability." *Journal of Bodywork & Movement Therapies,* 2010, 14: 84–98.

Levin, S. M. *Biotensigrity and Dynamic Anatomy*. DVD. Stephen S Levine (2006).

Levin, S. M. "Tensegrity: the new biomechanics." http://www.biotensegrity.com/tensegrity_new_biomechanics.php (accessed Nov. 14, 2014).

Levin, S. M. *Tensegrity Wikispaces* www.http://tensegrity.wikispaces.com/Levin,+Stephen+M. (accessed Mar. 17, 2015).

Little, P., et al. "Randomised Controlled Trial of Alexander Technique Lessons, Exercise, and Massage (ATEAM) for Chronic and Recurrent Back Pain." *British Medical Journal*, 2008, 337: a884.

Macdonald, P. *The Alexander Technique: As I See It*. Brighton, UK: Ahpha Press (1989, 2006).

Magnus, R. "Of Some Results of Studies in the Physiology of Posture." *The Lancet*, Sept. 11 and Sept 18 1926.

Mancini, F., et al. "Visual Distortion of Body Size Modulates Pain Perception." *Psychological Science*, Mar. 2011, 22(3): 325–30.

Mannino, D. M., et al. *Surveillance for Asthma—United States 1960–1995*. Division of Environmental Hazards and Health Effects National Center for Environmental Health, and Council of State and Territorial Epidemiologists, USA (1998). http://www.cdc.gov/mmwr/preview/mmwrhtml/00052262.htm (accessed May 21, 2015).

Mansour, A. R., et al. "Brain White Matter Structural Properties Predict Transition to Chronic Pain." *Pain*, 2013, 154: 2160–2168.

Mascaro, J. (trans). Bhagavad Gita Penguin Classics (2003)

Masi, J., et al. "Human Resting Muscle Tone (HRMT): Narrative Introduction and Modern Concepts." *Journal of Body Work and Movement Therapies*, 2008, 12(4): 320–32.

McCall, T. Yoga as Medicine: The Yogic Prescription for Health & Healing: A Yoga Journal Book. New York: Bantam Books (2007).

McGill, S. M. *Low Back Disorders*. Champaign, IL: Human Kinetics (2007).

McGill, S. Ultimate Back Fitness and Performance. 4th ed. Backfit (2009).

Merton, T. *Way of Chuang Tzu* New York: New Directions (1965)

Morgan, L. (Fischer, J.M.O. ed.). *The Philosopher's Stone: Diaries of Lessons with F. Matthias Alexander*. London: Mouritz (1998).

Mosely, G. L. "Visual Distortion of a Limb Modulates the Pain and Swelling Evoked by Movement." *Current Biology*, 2008, 18(22): 1047–48. Miller, B.S. *Yoga: Discipline of Freedom: the Yoga Sutra Attributed to Patanjali* Bantam 1998

Mulder, T., and W. Hulstyn. "Sensory Feedback Therapy and Theoretical Knowledge of Motor Control and Learning." *American Journal of Physical Medicine*, 1984, 63(5): 226–44.

Myers, T. W. *Anatomy Trains: Myofascial Meridians for Manual and Movement Therapists*. Churchill Livingstone (2001).

Myers, T. W., in S. Sieden (ed.). *A Fuller View: Buckminster Fuller's Vision of Hope and Abundance for All*. Studio City, CA: Divine Arts (2012). Kindle ed.

Nietzsche, F. *Will to Power*. New York: Vintage (1968).

Parker, P. J. Courage to Teach: Exploring the Inner Landscape of a Teacher's Life. 10th anniv. ed. San Francisco: Jossey Bass (2007).

Parks, T. Teach Us to Sit Still: A Sceptic's Search for Health and Healing. London: Harvill Secker (2010).

Preston, C., and R. Newport. "Analgesic Effects of Multisensory Illusions in Osteoarthritis." *Rheumatology*, 2011, 50(12): 2314–15.

Ramanujan, A. K. *Speaking of Siva*. Harmondsworth: Penguin Books (1973).

Rhode-Barbarigos, L., et al. *Deployment analysis of a pentagonal tensegrity-ring module*. in CSMA 2011: *10e colloque national en calcul des structures*.

Rodriguez-Raecke, R., et al. "Grey Matter Decrease in Chronic Pain Is the Consequence Not the Cause of Pain." *Journal of Neuroscience*, 2009, 29(44): 13746–50.

Roberts, T.D.M. *Neurophysiology of Postural Mechanisms*. London: Butterworths (1967).

Schumacher, J. "Preparing for Inversions." *Yoga Journal*, July & Aug. 1990, 91: 60-77

Sherman, K., et al. "Mediators of Yoga and Stretching for Chronic Low Back Pain." *Evidence-Based Complementary and Alternative Medicine*, 2013.. Volume 2013, Article ID 130818

Sherrington, C. S. *The Brain and Its Mechanism*. Oxford University Press (1933).

Sherrington, C. S. Quoted in Alexander, *Universal Constant in Living*. London: Chaterson (1942, 1947).

Singleton, N. Yoga Body: The Origins of Modern Posture Practice. Oxford University Press (2010).

Sjoman, N. E. The Yoga Tradition of the Mysore Palace. New Delhi: Abhinav (1999).

Solomonow, M. "Ligaments: A Source of Musculoskeletal Disorders." *Journal of Bodywork and Movement Therapies*, 2009, 13 (2) 136 - 54

Tinbergen, N. "Ethology and Stress Diseases." 1973 Nobel Lecture, Science, 1974 185 (4145): 20-27.

Todd, M. E. *Thinking Body*. New York: Dance Horizon Books (1977, 2007).

Van der Velde, D., and G. Mierau. "The Effect of Exercise on Percentile Rank Aerobic Capacity, Pain, and Self-Rated Disability in Patients with Chronic Low-Back Pain: A Retrospective Chart Review." *Archives of Physical Medicine and Rehabilitation*, 2000, 81 (11): 1457-63.

Watts, J. W., and W. Freeman. "Psychosurgery for the Relief of Unbearable Pain." *Journal of the International College of Surgeons*, 1945, vol. 9. 679 - 83

Weppler, C. H., and P. Magnusson. "Increasing Muscle Extensibility: A Matter of Increasing Length or Modifying Sensation." *Physical Therapy*, 2010, 90 (3): 438–49.

Withers, G. A. "Scientific Response to the Article: The Core Stability Myth." *Times* newspaper, Aug. 10, 2010.

Yoga Journal Staff. "A Closer Look at Inversions." *Yoga Journal*, 2007, Issue 203

Yogi Svatmarama. *Hatha Yoga Pradipika* (trans P. Sinh). (No publisher or date.)

ATTRIBUTIONS FOR PHOTOS AND ILLUSTRATIONS

PART ONE

OPENING PAGE
Andes Huayhuash, Peru © David Moore

YOGA
Shiva as Lord of the Dance. Benjamín Preciado Centro de
Estudios de Asia y África de El Colegio de México

PART TWO

OPENING PAGE
Lifting Fog © Martin Thurnheer, 2008.

CHAPTER 2: Yoga
Fig. 2.1: Patanjali. jpl design/dreamstime.com

CHAPTER 4: The use of the self
Photo of Alexander as a young man (ca. 1890s)

**CHAPTER 5: The Interrelationship between Use,
Structure, and Functioning**
Fig. 5.1: *Direction: A journal of the Alexander Technique.*
ISSN 1039-3145. www.directionjournal.com
Fig. 5.2: Use/Structure/Functioning. David Moore

CHAPTER 6: Psychophysical Unity
Fig. 6.1: Rodin's *The Thinker*. Rob Wilson/Shutterstock

CHAPTER 12: The Primary Control
Fig. 12.1: Mannan Rao © Einstein's Moon
Fig. 12.2: Picture Partners/Shutterstock
Fig. 12.3: Martin Valigursky/Shutterstock
Fig. 12.4: © Backcare UK
Fig. 12.5: itsjustme/Shutterstock
Fig. 12.6: Viorel Sima/Shutterstock
Fig. 12.7: Karramba Production/Shutterstock

CHAPTER 13: Unreliable Sensory Appreciation
Fig. 13.1: Blausen.com Staff Blausen Gallery 2014.
Wikiversity Journal of Medicine via Wikimedia Commons
Fig. 13.2: Henry Gray. *Anatomy of the Human Body.*
American 20th Edition, 1918.

CHAPTER 17: The Priority of Prevention over Cure
Fig. 17.1: Knumina Studios/Shutterstock

**CHAPTER 18: What Happens in an Alexander
Technique Lesson?**
Fig. 18.1: Isobel Knowles © Einstein's Moon
Fig. 18.2: TonyV3122/Shutterstock
Fig. 18.3: Mitch Gunn/Shutterstock

PART THREE

OPENING PAGE
Andes Huayhuash, Peru © David Moore

CHAPTER 19: Variability
Figs. 19.1A and 19.2F: Yin Yoga Teaching website
http://www.paulgrilley.com/bone-photo-gallery

CHAPTER 20: Flexibility
Fig. 20.1: iofoto/Shutterstock

CHAPTER 22: Breathing
Figs. 22.1 and 22.2:
Mannan Rao © Einstein's Moon
Fig. 22.3: From F. M. Alexander.
Man's Supreme Inheritance
Fig. 22.4: Mannan Rao © Einstein's Moon

CHAPTER 23: Autonomic Nervous System
Figs. 23.1 and 23.2: Alia Medical Media/Shutterstock

CHAPTER 24: Tensegrity
Fig. 24.1: tensegrity.wikispaces.com
Fig. 24.2: Orange-studio/Shutterstock
Fig. 24.3: BAR Photography
Fig. 24.4: T. Flemons, 2006,
http://www.intensiondesigns.com/
Fig. 24.5: Mike Degteariov/Shutterstock
Fig. 24.6: www.boundless.com/physiology
(Creative Commons)
Fig. 24.7: Henry Gray. *Anatomy of the Human Body.*
American 20th Edition, 1918
Figs. 24.8 to 24.10: © Einstein's Moon
Fig. 24.11: *Direction: A Journal of the Alexander Technique.*
ISSN 1039-3145 www.directionjournal.com
Fig. 24.12: Mannan Rao © Einstein's Moon
Fig. 24.13: ©2006 T. Flemons,
http://www.intensiondesigns.com/
Fig. 24.14: Shutterstock _43678258
Fig. 24.15: Sebastian Kaulitzki/Shutterstock

CHAPTER 29: Mindfulness and Meditation
Fig. 29.1: Worradirek/Shutterstock
Figs. 29.2 to 29.4: Michael Avery

CHAPTER 30: Pregnancy
Fig. 30.1: Mathom/Shutterstock
Fig. 30.2: Sergey Sukhorukov/Shutterstock

**CHAPTER 31: Constructive Rest:
Semisupine Position**
Figs. 31.1 to 31.3: Isobel Knowles © Einstein's Moon

PART FOUR

OPENING PAGE
Sakura in Nara, Japan © Curtis Martlew, 2012.

CHAPTER 32: *Tadasana*: **Mountain Pose and Good Posture**
Fig. 32.1: Shots Studio/Shutterstock
Figs. 32.2a, b, c: Loco Photo © Einstein's Moon
Fig. 32.3: John Wollwerth/Shutterstock

CHAPTER 33: **Floor Stretches**
Figs. 33.1 to 33.17: Isobel Knowles © Einstein's Moon

CHAPTER 34: **Monkey: Poses Based on the Position**
of Mechanical Advantage *(Utkatasana)*
Fig. 34.1: Photograph of F. M. Alexander ©2014,
     The Society of Teachers of the Alexander Technique, London
Fig. 34.2: Isobel Knowles © Einstein's Moon
Fig. 34.3: Grigoven/Shutterstock
Fig. 34.4: Praisaeng/Shutterstock
Figs. 34.5 and 34.6: Isobel Knowles © Einstein's Moon

CHAPTER 35: **Squatting**
Fig. 35.1: Photograph of F. M. Alexander ©2014,
     The Society of Teachers of the Alexander Technique, London
Fig. 35.2: Oleksii Natykach/Shutterstock
Fig. 35.3: Grei/Shutterstock
Fig. 35.4: Fiona Bryant © Einstein's Moon
Fig. 35.5: Marilyn Barbone/Shutterstock
Fig. 35.6: Piter HaSon/Shutterstock
Figs. 35.7 to 35.11: Isobel Knowles © Einstein's Moon

CHAPTER 36: **Standing Poses**
Figs. 36.1 to 36.17: Isobel Knowles © Einstein's Moon
Fig. 36.18: Michael Avery © Einstein's Moon

CHAPTER 37: **Twists**
Fig. 37.1: Loco Photo © Einstein's Moon
Fig. 37.2: decade3d - anatomy online/Shutterstock
Fig. 37.3: 3DDock/Shutterstock
Fig. 37.4: GunitaR/Shutterstock
Figs. 37.5 and 37.6: Mannan Rao © Einstein's Moon
Fig. 37.7: Winthrop Brookhouse/Shutterstock
Fig. 37.8: Pikoso.kz/Shutterstock
Fig. 37.9: Loco Photo © Einstein's Moon
Figs. 37.10 to 37.14: Isobel Knowles © Einstein's Moon

CHAPTER 38: **Forward Bends**
Fig. 38.1: Pavel L Photo and Video/Shutterstock
Figs. 38.2 and 38.3: Mannan Rao © Einstein's Moon
Figs. 38.4 and 38.5: © Einstein's Moon
Fig. 38.6: Isobel Knowles © Einstein's Moon
Figs. 38.7 and 38.8: Irit Rozenfeld © Einstein's Moon
Fig. 38.9: Henry Gray. *Anatomy of the Human Body.*
   American 20th Edition (1918)
Figs. 38.10 to 38.18: Isobel Knowles © Einstein's Moon
Fig. 38.19: wavebreakmedia/Shutterstock

CHAPTER 39: **Downward Facing Dog Pose:**
     Adho Mukha Svanasana
Fig. 39.1: nanka/Shutterstock
Fig. 39.2: S-F/Shutterstock
Fig. 39.3: Isobel Knowles © Einstein's Moon
Fig. 39.4: Irit Rozenfeld © Einstein's Moon
Fig. 39.5: Eugene Dudar/Shutterstock
Fig. 39.6: Irit Rozenfeld © Einstein's Moon

CHAPTER 40: **Back Bends**
Figs. 40.1 and 40.2: Mannan Rao © Einstein's Moon
Fig. 40.3: Yana Zastolskaya/Shutterstock
Fig. 40.4: CLIPAREA l Custom media/Shutterstock
Figs. 40.5 to 40.7: Isobel Knowles © Einstein's Moon
Fig. 40.8: Aspen Photo/Shutterstock
Figs. 40.9 to 40.18: Isobel Knowles © Einstein's Moon

CHAPTER 41: **Side Bends**
Figs. 41.1 to 41.8: Isobel Knowles © Einstein's Moon
Fig 41.9: Artur Bogacki/Shutterstock
Fig. 41.10: Isobel Knowles © Einstein's Moon

CHAPTER 42: **Poses from Kneeling**
Figs. 42.1 to 42.6: Isobel Knowles © Einstein's Moon
Fig. 42.7: Michael Avery

CHAPTER 43: More Hip Openers:
     Moving Toward Cross-Legged Sitting
Figs. 43.1 to 43.5: Isobel Knowles © Einstein's Moon

CHAPTER 44: **Inverted Poses**
Fig. 44.1: John Tenniel, from *Alice's Adventures in
     Wonderland* by Lewis Carroll
Fig. 44.2: Henry Gray. *Anatomy of the Human Body.*
     American 20th Edition (1918)
Fig. 44.3: Dr. Johannes Sobotta:
     Atlas and Text-book of Human Anatomy,
     Vol. III, *Vascular System, Lymphatic System,
     Nervous System and Sense Organs* (1909)
Figs. 44.4 to 44.9: Isobel Knowles © Einstein's Moon
Fig. 44.10: From Yoga Mimamsa 1926

CHAPTER 45: **Plank Variations**
Figs. 45.1 to 45.9: Isobel Knowles © Einstein's Moon

USEFUL CONTACTS

ORGANIZATIONS

The following national societies are jointly affiliated with one another and subscribe to similar training standards for Alexander Technique teachers. These societies cover nineteen countries. If your country does not have a national society, then refer to the UK society; STAT has quite a comprehensive listing of overseas teachers on their website.

Australia: AUSTAT www.austat.org.au/
Austria: GATOE www.alexander-technik.at
Belgium: AEFMAT www.fmalexandertech.be
Brazil: ABTA www.abtalexander.com.br
Canada: CanSTAT www.canstat.ca
Denmark: DFLAT www.dflat.dk
Finland: FINSTAT www.finstat.fi/
France: APTA www.techniquealexander.info
Germany: ATVD www.alexander-technik.org
Israel: www.alexander.org.il
Netherlands: NeVLAT www.nevlat.nl
New Zealand: ATTSNZ www.alexandertechnique.org.nz
Norway: NFLAT ww.alexanderteknikk.no
South Africa: SASTAT www.alexandertechnique.org.za
Spain: APTA www.aptae.net
Switzerland: SBAT www.alexandertechnik.ch
United States: AmSAT www.amsatonline.org
UK and Ireland: STAT www.stat.org.uk

WEBSITES

tensegrity.wikispaces.com This website is a wiki dedicated to exploring the field of tensegrity, a subset of energetic-synergetic geometry.

brainsciencepodcast.com This podcast site, hosted by Dr. Ginger Campbell, has more than one hundred podcasts and transcripts of interviews with a range of scientists.

alexandertechnique.com This site contains a great deal of information as well as links to most of the information on the Alexander Technique available on the web.

stat.org.uk Society of Teachers of the Alexander Technique. A good resource for latest research and news on the Alexander Technique.

alexanderschool.edu.au The School for F. M. Alexander Studies. Information on courses and workshops with David Moore, both in Melbourne and internationally, as well as training as an Alexander technique teacher or Alexander Yoga teacher in his school in Melbourne, Australia.

alexanderbabies.com Alexander Technique for babies and parents. Contains information about Jennifer Kellow, who is referenced in the Chapter 22 on breathing.

painscience.com Contains hundreds of articles about the science of pain and injury, manual therapies, sports and exercise, and much more. It's well researched, skeptical, opinionated, and written by Paul Ingraham in an engagingly accessible style.

Yogaforums.com Contains a range of articles and discussions.

yogajournal.com *Yoga Journal*. Has a great collection of articles from back issues of the journal.

intensiondesigns.com Contains many photos and in-depth articles by Tom Flemons, two of whose biotensegrity structures are pictured in Chapter 24, on tensegrity.

accesstoinsight.org Access to Insight: Readings in Therevada Buddhism. There are more than two thousand pages on this website containing hundreds of books, articles, and *sutta* translations. It contains a selection of good translations from the vast Pali Canon.

dhammatalks.org Dhamma Talks and writings of Thanissaro Bhikkhu.

BOOKS AND JOURNALS

There is a considerable literature on the Alexander technique and a vast literature on yoga. If you wish to read further in these subjects, here are just a few books and one journal that I recommend you begin with.

Alexander Technique

Alexander Technique: A Skill for Life, by Pedro de Alcantara
Body Learning, by Michael Gelb
Direction: A Journal on the Alexander Technique
Freedom to Change, by Frank Pierce Jones
F. Matthias Alexander: The Man and His Work, by Lulie Westfeldt
How to Learn the Alexander Technique, by Barbara Conable
Mind and Muscle, by Elizabeth Langford
Use of the Self, by F. M. Alexander

Yoga

Bhagavad Gita. This spiritual classic has many translations, each with its own strengths and
 weaknesses. The classic Penguin edition by Juan Mascaro is a good one to start with.
Yoga Sutras of Patanjali. There are numerous translations (or rather interpretations) of this text.
 Most do not accurately represent the work as they interpret it from Vendantic and/or Tantric
 viewpoint(s) which are foreign to the world-view of the original text. The translation by Barbara
 Stoller-Miller *Yoga: The Discipline of Freedom* is a good start with an excellent introduction.
*ExTension: The 20-Minute-a-Day, Yoga-Based Program to Relax, Release & Rejuvenate the Average
 Stressed-Out Over-35-Year-Old-Body*, by Sam Dworkis
Health Healing and Beyond: The Living Tradition of Krishnamacharya, by T.K.V. Desikachar
Yoga Body: The Origins of Modern Posture Practice, by Mark Singleton
Yoga Tradition, by Georg Feuerstein

Meditation and Spirituality

Buddhism Without Beliefs, by Stephen Batchelor
Way of Chuang Tzu by Thomas Merton
Essential Rumi, interpreted by Coleman Barks
Meditation 101, by Eric Harrison
Path with Heart, by Jack Kornfield
Zen Mind Beginners Mind, by Shunryu Suzuki

GLOSSARY OF TERMS

Asana: Posture, yoga pose; the Sanskrit term for each yoga pose ends with "asana," e.g., Paschimottanasana.

Chakra: A Sanskrit term referring to wheels of energy. There are seven main *chakras* starting from the perineum and ending at the top of the head (or in some systems above the top of the head). They are located along the central channel or *Sushumna*. (For more details, see *nadis* and *kundalini*.)

Direct, direction, Alexander directions: Chapter 10, "Direction," refers to the conscious or unconscious instructions sent through the nervous system to initiate activity. Conscious directions assist in improving primary control.

End gaining: Going directly for an end result rather than taking account of the means whereby an action is most effectively done. see Chapter 15, "End Gaining and Means Whereby."

Fascia: A sheet or band of fibrous connective tissue enveloping, separating, or binding together muscles, organs, and other soft structures of the body.

Hypocapnia: Carbon dioxide deficiency, which makes the blood overly alkaline.

Inhibition: Stopping or preventing habitual harmful reaction. See Chapter 9, "Inhibition."

Kumbakha: Suspension of breathing after an in breath or an out breath in *pranayama*.

Kundalini: The primal energy, located at the base of the spine, described as a goddess, *Shakti*, or coiled serpent waiting to be awakened by Hatha Yoga or other practices.

Limbic system: A set of structures in the brain primarily responsible for our emotional life. The hypothalamus, which is one of these structures, regulates the functioning of the autonomic nervous system.

Means whereby: How an action can be effectively carried out. See Chapter 15, "End Gaining and Means Whereby."

Mechanisms: Alexander sometimes refers metaphorically to the body as a machine, so when he uses this term it refers to the whole of the body in activity.

Nadis: Sanskrit term referring to channels through which the energies are said to flow. Three key *nadis* are the *Sushumna* (which goes directly from the perineum to the crown of the head) and the *Ida* and *Pingala*, which originate in the perineum and move in ellipses alternating to the right and left side of five *chakras* as they ascend to the left and right nostrils respectively. However, there is a network of many *nadis* distributing energy to all parts of the body.

Pali: The language of the earliest Buddhist scriptures.

Position of mechanical advantage: In *Man's Supreme Inheritance* Alexander describes this as a position " which may or may not be a normal position," which assists the teacher to use manual guidance to quickly create a co-ordinated condition in the student. The most common of these positions used in Alexander Technique lessons is the "monkey."

Prana: The Sanskrit term for the life force or cosmic energy.

Pranayama: Literally means extension of the *prana*. It involves conscious regulation of the breathing pattern, which can change the flow of pranic currents through the body. The fourth of Patanjali's eight limbs of yoga.

Primary Control: The relationship of the head to the neck, torso, and the rest of the body. See Chapter 12, "The Primary Control."

Psychophysical: The essential interrelationship of all aspects of being: mental, physical, emotional, cognitive, etc. See Chapter 6, "Psychophysical Unity."

Samskara: (Sankara in Buddhist Pali texts) Impression or imprint left in the mind by experience in this and previous lives; it conditions a person's personality, actions, and reactions.

Sanskrit: The classical North Indian language in which many of the Yogic classics are written.

Semisupine position: Lying on the back with head on books, and feet on floor with knees bent. See Chapter 31, "Constructive Rest: Semisupine Position."

Sutra: A collection of aphorisms or a Hindu, Buddhist, or Jain religious text.

Sutta: Pali version of Sanskrit Sutra.

Use: The manner in which a person carries out all the activities of living and the underlying conditions that help to shape the manner of use. See Chapter 4, "The Use of the Self."

Vasana: Yogic and Buddhist term referring to a behavioral tendency that influences the present behavior of a person. Often linked with the term samskara.

INDEX

A

active back bends, 197–9
airline pilots, 39
Alexander, Frederick Matthias, 4, 10, 11,
    14, 24, 31, 38, 46, 48, 52, 72, 117, 132,
    150, 156, 223
  breathing, 75
  kinesthetic sensing, 39
  voice
    diagnosis of problem, 20, 21, 22, 23
    directions, 26–7, 40
    inhibition, 24
    kinesthetic sense, 39
    reasoning processes, 40
Alexander Principle (W. Barlow), 2
Alexander Technique. *see also*
    discoordination; misuse; use of the self
  amalgamation with yoga, 9
  application work, 55
  author's journey, 3
  balancing autonomic nervous system
    (ANS), 86–7
  components, 10
  core, 103
  diagnosis, 52
  elasticity, 91, 97
  history, 10–11
  indirect procedure, 46–7
  meditation, 118
  mindfulness, 115, 116
  muscular work, 99–100
  pain, 113
  pregnancy, 121
  prevention principle, 49, 50, 51
  purpose, 10
  relaxation, 87
  sensory perception, faulty, 136
Alexander yoga
  coordination, 62, 69, 101, 106
  energy flows, 98
  headstand, 213
  safe practice, 177
  semisupine position, 125
anatomy, 4, 58
Anguttara Nikaya, 116
asanas (yoga poses), 7, 8, 9, 47, 50, 86, 104,
    107, 113, 132–3
assessment, 52
Association for the International Study of
    Pain, 110
asthma, 73, 75, 83, 225
asynchronous stimulation, 92
atlanto-occipital joint, 28, 34, 92, 184

Australian Institute of Sport, 67
autonomic nervous system (ANS). *see also*
    parasympathetic nervous system;
    sympathetic nervous system
  balancing, 86–7
  functions and components, 84
  mediation, 86
  overstimulation, 84
  yoga, 86

B

babies
  coordination, 35
  premature, breathing, 75
back bends, 194–201
balance, upright posture, 34
Barbarigos-Rhode, L., 88
Barlow, Marjory, 104
Barlow, Wilfred, 2
Barstow, Marjorie, 29, 134
Basavanna, 4
Batchelor, Stephen, 22
Bhagavad Gita, 44
Bikkhu, Thanissaro, 115
biotensegrity, 89
Bird Dog pose, 207
blood pressure, 217
Bow Pose *(Dhanurasana)*, 200
brain, 23
brain science, 108
The Brain That Changes Itself (Doidge), 108
breathing, 72
  Alexander's, 75
  disorders, 73
  dysfunctional pattern, 72–3
  education, 82–3
  exercises, 76
  mechanics, 76–9
  miconceptions and errors, 79–80
  physiology, 73
  pranayama, 74
  premature babies, 75
  stressed, 83
  ujjayi, 74
  yoga, 81
Bridge *(Setu Bandha Sarvangasana)*, 197
bringing the ego into the practice, 45
Broad, William J., 68, 69
Buddhism, 2, 6, 8
Buddhist meditation, 72, 117
  retreats (Bodh Gaya), 3
Buteyko breathing method, 73

C

Camel Pose *(Ustrasana)*, 201
carbon dioxide deficiency, 73
carpal tunnel syndrome, 58
Carrington, Walter, 29
Cat pose *(Bidalasana)*, 206
cats, 36, 37
central mechanism, 36
central sensitization, 109, 112, 113
Cervero, Fernando, 109, 110, 112
chair work, 53
The Chair (Cranz), 156
chakras (energy centers), 30
Chapman, Karyn, 4
chi (flow of life energy), 31
childbirth, 104. *see also* pregnancy
Chinese medicine, 31
chronic pain, 109, 111–12, 113, 116, 225
Cobra Pose *(Bhujangasana)*, 198
Coghill, George, 36
compression structures, 88
conditioning, 32–3
conducting the energy, 30
constructive rest. *see* semisupine position
contraction, 31, 50, 53, 55, 62, 76, 79, 86, 87,
    91, 96, 100
coordination (primary control), 25, 27, 30,
    34, 39, 42, 53, 54, 55, 62, 64, 65, 69,
  babies, 35
  common errors, 43
  endurance and strength, 106
  as neurological action, 139–41
  reeducation, 90
  remedies, 47
core muscles, 102, 104, 107
core strength, 102–7
Corpse Pose *(Savasana)*, 86, 123, 125
correct position, 29
Coulter, David, 137
Cranz, Galen, 156

D

de Beer, G. R., 40
Desikachar, T. K. V., 3
Dewey, John, 11, 22, 33, 108, 135, 136
dharana, 9
dhyana, 9
diaphragm, 36, 76, 77–8, 79, 80, 81, 82, 160
directing, 26, 29
direction, 23, 25, 26–9
  and primary control, 37
  types, 28
  yoga and meditation, 30

discoordination, 10, 26, 31, 87, 95, 103, 106
Dog Pose (Adho Mukha Svanasana), 190–3
Doidge, Norman, 108, 109
Downward Facing Dog Pose (Adho Mukha
    Svanasana), 190–3, 217

E

Eight Limbs of Patanjali Yoga, 9, 113
Eightfold Noble Path of the Buddha, 86,
    113, 119
elasticity
    ligaments, 183
    maintaining, 91–5
    muscle, 89
    restoring, 91, 97
end gaining, 44–5
endurance, 106, 107
energy
    life, 30, 31, 213
    stored, 97
    types, 7
    using mechanisms, 26
energy channels (nadis), 7, 30
energy flow, 7, 28, 30, 98, 99, 133, 186, 191
enlightenment (samadhi), 8, 9, 119
The Examined Life (M. Barlow), 104
eyes (inversions), 217

F

faulty sensory awareness, 136, 154, 183
Feuerstein, Georg, 6, 84
First Noble Truth (Buddhism), 48
Flemons, Tom, 89, 96
flexibility. see also stretching
    knee, 66
    nervous system, 64
    spine, 65
    sport, 67
    and strength, 66
    variability, 62–3
floor stretches, 142–9
flow sequences (vinyasa), 8
force of habit
    Alexander's voice-body movement, 23, 24
    dysfunctional, 22
    habit, association, 22
    types, 23
forward bends, 180–1, 184–9
    extension from wall (Padahastasana), 185
    habit, 183
Four Horses parable, 49–51
Four-legged Staff pose (Chaturanga
    Dandasana), 218–19

Freeman, Walter, 111
Frost, Robert, 140, 141
Fuller, Buckminster, 88

G

Gate pose (Parighasana), 205
Gerhida Samitha (Hatha Yoga text), 8
Gorman, David, 172

H

habit. see force of habit
half moon pose (Ardha Chandrasana), 170–1
handstand poses, 216
Harrison, Eric, 117
hatha, meaning, 7
Hatha Yoga, 4, 6
    characteristics, 7
    history, 8
    pain, 113
    remedies, 47
    texts, 8
    western practices, 8–9
Hatha Yoga Pradipika, 8, 47, 132
head
    animals holding, 40, 94, 95
    balance, 34–5, 36, 47, 90, 99, 133, 137
    carrying weight, 31, 96, 138–9
    mispositioned, 41, 95
    pull of gravity, 92
    relationship to body, 33, 36, 37, 107, 133, 137
headstand (Sirasana), 70, 213–14
Hinduism, 6
hip joints, 61, 150, 157, 158, 160, 161
horses, 49, 94, 95
Hulstyn, Wouter, 102
Huxley, Aldous, 222
hyperlordosis, 120, 162
hypermobility, 64–6
hypocapnia, 73

I

illusions, 31, 39
impulses, 22, 25, 26, 62, 109, 111, 115
incorrect conceptions, 42–3
indirect procedure, 46–7
inflammatory pain, 110
inhibition (neurological), 11, 23, 24–5, 26,
    35, 46, 50, 52, 113
insight meditation, 2, 6, 112–13
Intension Designs, 89
inversions, 217
inverted poses, 212–17
Iyengar, B.K.S., 137, 213, 215
Iyengar Yoga, 3, 215

J

Jackson, Martin, 3
Jainism, 6
James, William, 11, 22, 108
joint hypermobility syndrome (JHS), 64

K

Kabat-Zinn, Jon, 116
Kellow, Jennifer, 75, 76
kinesthetic sense, 38, 39, 65, 109, 117, 118,
    132, 133, 136, 192, 219, 222, 225
Krishnamacharya, 3, 8
Krishnamacharya Yoga Mandaram
    (Madras), 3, 58

L

Lederman, Eyal, 105
Legs up the Wall pose (Viparita Karani), 216
Levin, Stephen, 89, 96, 97
ligaments, 182–3
Light on Yoga (Iyengar), 137
lobotomy, 111
lumbar spine
    hyperlordosis, 120
    joints, 121
    overextension, 100
    pressure, 125, 195
    S-shape curvature, 195
lunge, 54
lying down twists (Jathara Parivartanasana), 178
Lying Side Bend pose (Supta Chandrasana), 205

M

Macdonald, Patrick, 10, 28, 29
Magnus, Rudolf, 36, 37
Malunkyaputta Sutta (The Buddha), 115
Man's Supreme Inheritance (Alexander), 80
Masi, J., 93, 94
McGill, Stuart, 100, 150, 155n, 200
McLanahan, Sandra Amrita, 217
mediation
    autonomic nervous system (ANS), 86
meditation, 30, 72, 87, 112, 116, 117
    insight, 2, 6, 112–13
    pain, 112
    postural considerations, 118
mental habits, 23
mind body duality, 18
mindfulness, 114–17
    Buddhist, 114, 115
Mindfulness Based Cognitive Therapy, 116
Mindfulness Based Stress Reduction, 116

misuse, 10, 20, 50, 52, 53, 60, 68, 93, 103,
    120, 122, 173, 195
    Alexander's voice diagnosis, 20, 21, 22, 23
monkey, 54, 55
Monkey Pose (Utkatasana), 87, 97, 150–5,
    158, 160, 183, 184, 185, 193
Mosely, Lorimer, 111
Mountain Pose (Tadasana), 34, 100, 133,
    134–41
movement, 16
movement muscles, 98, 99, 101, 141, 174
Mulder, Theo, 102
muscle elasticity, 89
muscles. see also movement muscles;
    postural muscles
    brain relationship, 23
    coordination, 16
    core, 102, 104, 107
    voluntary musculature, 98
muscular endurance, 106, 107
Myers, Thomas W., 89, 93, 96

N

nadis (energy channels), 7, 30
Needle Tower (Snelson), 89
nervous system. see also autonomic nervous
        system (ANS)
    core muscle strengthening, 104–5
    stability, 106
neural pathways, 22, 109
neurological action, 139–41
neuromatrix, 111
neuropathic pain, 110
neuroplasticity, 11, 53, 108–9
New Method of Respiratory Vocal Re-education (Alexander), 80
Nietzsche, Friedrich, 18
niyama (personal observances), 9
nociceptive pain, 110, 111, 113

O

overcontraction, 35, 63, 76, 81, 83, 90, 100,
    139, 161, 173, 183, 195, 197, 198

P

pain, 109
    chronic, 109, 111–12, 113, 116, 225
    components, 110–11
    definition, 110
    elements, 113
    management, 112–13
    semisupine position, 127
    types, 110

pain matrix, 111
Pali Buddhist suttas, 11, 115
Palmer, Parker, 21
parasympathetic nervous system, 84, 85, 87
passive back bends, 196–7
Patanjali, 8
Patanjali yoga, 50, 86, 113
Peacock Pose (Mayurasana), 47
pelvic pain syndrome, 112
perception and reality, 39
physical habits, 23
Pigeon pose (Eka Pada Rajakapotasana), 210
Plank pose (Phalakasana), 219
plank variations, 218–21
plasticity, 108
position, 28, 29, 36, 38, 40, 42, 87
position of mechanical advantage, 87, 150
postural muscles, 43, 92, 98, 99, 102, 104,
    105, 106, 122, 139, 141, 146, 174, 183,
    190, 207, 218
prana (life energy), 30, 213
pranayama (breathing exercises), 3, 6, 8, 9,
    72, 74, 76, 79, 86, 87
pranic force, 30
pratyahara, 9
Prayer Pose, 179, 184, 193
pregnancy. see also childbirth
    body changes, 120–1
    semisupine position, 128
    use of self, 104
    yoga, 120, 122–3
prevention principle, 48–51
Pride and a Daily Marathon, 38
Principles of Psychology (James), 108
Prone Back Stretches (Shalabhasana
    Variations), 200
proprioceptive senses, 38, 39, 95, 101, 117,
    136, 192
psychological habits, 23
psychophysical unity, 18
and yoga practice, 21
psychotherapy, 116, 117

Q

qi (flow of life energy), 31
qigong, 31
Quadriceps Stretch, 208–9

R

reasoning processes, 40
reconditioning, 23, 32, 109
relaxation, 86, 87, 125

resistance training, 60
respiratory acidosis, 73
Reverse Plank pose (Purvottanasana), 220
Roberts, T. D. M., 40
Rumbaugh, Desirée, 103
Rumi, 84

S

samskaras (unconscious ingrained patterns),
    32, 50, 51
sati, 115
Satipatthana Sutta—The Foundations of
    Mindfulness, 114, 115, 117
School for F. M. Alexander Studies
    (Melbourne), 11, 129
Schumacher, John, 137
The Science of Yoga (Broad), 68
Seated Forward Bend (Paschimottanasana),
    60, 69, 157, 184, 186–7
seated forward bends, 186–9
Seated Side Bend pose (Parivrtta Janu
    Sirsasana), 202–3
semisupine position
    alternative, 128
    back pain, 127
    benefits, 124, 125, 129
    instructions, 126–7
    knee and leg, 128
senses, 38. see also kinesthetic sense
sensory awareness, 26, 64, 101. see also faulty
    sensory awareness
Shaw, George Bernard, 1
Sherrington, Charles, 23, 24, 36
Shiva Samitha (Hatha Yoga text), 8
Shoulder Stand pose (Salamba
    Sarvangasana), 215
Side Angle pose: (Utthita Parsvakonasana), 168
Side Plank pose (Vasisthasana), 220
The Silken Tent (Frost), 140, 141
sitting forward bends (Paschimottanasana),
    186–7
sixth sense, 38–41
Snelson, Kenneth, 89
spatial relationships, 39
Sphinx Pose (Salamba Bhujangasana), 199
squatting, 156–61
stability, 106, 107
standing forward bend (Uttanasana), 184
Standing Pigeon, 211
standing poses, 120, 162–71
Standing Side Bend pose (Chandrasana), 204
sternocleidomastoid (SCM) muscles, 93
sthira-sukhamasanam, 45

stimulus-response model, 25
stretching, 63, 64, 66, 67, 86, 107, 122, 127, 137, 180, 182, 185, 189n, 190, 215
Swami Kuvalayananda, 8, 217
sympathetic nervous system, 72, 84, 85, 86–7

T

Teach Us to Sit Still (Parks), 112
tennis, 138
tensegrity structure. *see also* biotensegrity; elasticity
    balance, 90
    body as, 89, 94, 95, 96
    concept, 35, 88
    energy, 97
Tinbergen, Nikolass, 11, 20
Todd, Mabel Elsworth, 140
Triangle pose (*Utthita Trikonasana*), 168–9
twists, 172–6
    awareness points, 177
    lying down, 178
    prayer position, 179

U

unconscious muscular activity, 16
unduly excited fear reflexes (overstimulation), 84
unlocking, 28
upright posture, 34, 90, 93, 98, 100, 134, 135, 141, 182, 183, 204
    improving, 101
Upward Bow pose (*Urdhva Dhanurasana*), 201
Upward Facing Dog (*Urdhva Mukha Svanasana*), 199
use of the self
    elements, 15
    end gaining, 44–5
    focus, 16
    functioning, 17
    human being as unified whole, 46
    lower back pain, 103
    pattern, altering, 109
    structure, 17
    use, meaning, 15
Use of the Self (Alexander), 40, 75, 101

V

variability, 58–61
vasanas, 50
vestibular system, 38, 41
Viparita Karani (legs up wall), 216, 217

Vipassana meditation, 112
visual illusions, 39, 111
voluntary musculature
    types, 98

W

Wall Gluteal Stretch, 211
Warrior Poses (*Virabhadrasana*), 120, 162–7
Waterman, Mr, 38–9
Watts, James, 111
Wheel pose (*Urdhva Dhanurasana*), 201
whispered ah, 82
wide-legged standing forward bend (*Prasarita Padottanasana*), 185
Withers, Glenn, 106

Y

yama (universal morality), 9
Yin Yoga, 61
yoga. *see also* Alexander yoga; Hatha Yoga
    autonomic nervous system (ANS), 86
    breathing, 81
    end gaining, 44–5
    flexibility, 66
    hypermobility, 64–5
    and individuality, 21
    injuries, 68–71
    prevention principle, 49, 50, 51
    psychophysical unity, 18
    term, 6
    traditions, 6, 98
yoga poses, 7, 8, 9, 47, 50, 86, 104, 107, 113, 132–3
    back bends, 194–201
    Bird Dog, 207
    Bow, 200
    Bridge, 197
    Camel, 201
    Cat, 206
    Cobra, 198
    Corpse, 86, 123, 125
    Downward Facing Dog Pose, 190–3, 217
    floor stretches, 142–9
    forward bends, 180–1, 184–9
    Four-legged Staff, 218–19
    Half Moon, 170–1
    handstands, 216
    headstand (*Sirasana*), 70, 213–14
    inverted, 212–17
    Legs up the Wall (*Viparita Karani*), 216, 217
    Lying Side Bend, 205
    Monkey, 87, 97, 158, 160, 183, 184, 185, 193
    Mountain, 34, 100, 133, 134–41

Paschimottanasana (seated forward bend), 60, 69, 157, 184, 186–7
Peacock, 47
Pigeon, 210
Plank pose (*Phalakasana*), 219
Prayer, 179, 184, 193
Prone Back Stretches, 200
Quadriceps Stretch, 208–9
Reverse Plank pose (*Purvottanasana*), 220
Seated Side Bend, 202–3
Shoulder Stand (*Salamba Sarvangasana*), 215
Side Angle, 168
side bend poses, 202–5
Side Plank pose (*Vasisthasana*), 220
Sphinx, 199
Standing Pigeon, 211
Standing Side Bend (*Chandrasana*), 204
Triangle pose, 168–9
twists, 172–9
Upward Facing Dog (*Urdhva Mukha Svanasana*), 199
Wall Gluteal Stretch, 211
Warrior, 120, 162–7
Wheel or Upward Bow, 201
Yoga Shikha Upanishad, 7
Yoga Sutras of Patanjali, 3, 9, 11, 84
Yoga Sutras of Patanjali (texts), 8, 38, 45, 48, 51
The Yoga Tradition (Feuerstein), 6

To order a copy of this book go to:
www.einsteinsmoon.com

For more information about the professional training course*
in Melbourne, about attending workshops or courses in Melbourne
or in your area, or to add your name to the mailing list contact:

David Moore
School for F.M. Alexander Studies
330 St Georges Road
North Fitzroy, Victoria 3068
Australia
Tel: 61 3 9486 5900
Email: info@alexanderschool.edu.au

How did you find this book? David Moore would love to hear your feedback
or your own story. Please email at david@alexanderschool.edu.au

*Students enrolling for the Advanced Diploma of Alexander Technique
Teaching can apply for a three year student visa in Australia.

40222069R00140

Made in the USA
San Bernardino, CA
14 October 2016